Lesbian Desire
in the
Lyrics of Sappho

Jane McIntosh Snyder

COLUMBIA UNIVERSITY PRESS
New York

Columbia University Press
Publishers Since 1893
New York   Chichester, West Sussex

Library of Congress Cataloging-in-Publication Data
Snyder, Jane McIntosh.
Lesbian desire in the lyrics of Sappho / Jane McIntosh Snyder.
p.   cm.
Includes bibliographical references and index.
ISBN 0-231-09994-0 (cloth)
1. Sappho—Criticism and interpretation.   2. Love poetry, Greek—History
and criticism.   3. Women and literature—Greece.   4. Lesbians in literature.
5. Desire in literature.   I. Title.
PA4409.S64   1997
884'.01—dc20   96-31981
                                                                                      CIP

♾ Casebound editions of Columbia University Press books are printed on
permanent and durable acid-free paper.
Printed in the United States of America
Designed by Linda Secondari
c   10   9   8   7   6   5   4   3   2   1

FRONTISPIECE:
Red-figured kalathoid vase attributed to the Brygos Painter, c. 500–475 B.C.,
showing Sappho and Alkaios singing and playing the barbitos. Courtesy of the
Staatliche Antikensammlungen und Glyptothek, Munich.

CONTENTS

PREFACE

This book attempts to make the lyrics of Sappho of Lesbos, written in Greek some twenty-six centuries ago, come alive for the modern reader. Only one of Sappho's songs has survived in its entirety since then; the rest are bits and scraps of various lengths, some probably nearly complete poems, others only a word or two. Sappho is important not only because she was the most famous woman writer in the ancient Western world but also because she remains a persistent and effective voice for the expression of a woman's desire for a woman—out of all proportion to the actual number of her surviving words.

For the English-speaking reader who wishes to gain a quick impression of Sappho, I recommend the still unsurpassed translations of Sappho by Mary Barnard, reissued in 1994 in a tiny pocket-sized edition by Shambhala Press. The reader will find in the present volume, I hope, a detailed introduction to Sappho's poetry, with an emphasis not on the historical Sappho but rather on an interpretation of her poetry within the framework of homoerotic desire. As the result of nearly four decades of training and teaching in the field of ancient Greek and Latin, my approach is inevitably that of the classical philologist who pours over the meanings of obscure words in obscure languages. As one whose college and graduate school years fell during the 1960s, I find myself heavily influenced by the assumptions of New Criticism and the tradition of close textual analysis. As a feminist scholar, however, I trust that these habitual tendencies on my part have been significantly colored by the questions raised through the influence of women's studies, gay and lesbian studies, and postmodernism.

I want to emphasize that the reader need not have any familiarity with ancient languages in order to understand this book. I have tried, however, to entice my audience into the sound of Sappho's poetry (or at least an approximation of it) by including transliterations of her Greek into our Roman alphabet. If this volume inspires even one person to take up the study of classical Greek in order to read Sappho in the original, I will be delighted.

I am deeply indebted to a number of people for their assistance, support, and inspiration. In particular I want to thank the members of PMS (Post-Modern Studies, that is) at Ohio State University for profitable discussions of people—who run the gamut from Walter Benjamin to Hélène Cixous to Judith Butler and Eve Sedgwick—whose ideas I would otherwise have found far less intelligible. These colleagues include Suzanne Damarin, Gisela Hinkle, Nan Johnson, Marilyn Johnston, Patti Lather, Mary Leach, Linda Meadows, Laurel Richardson, Amy Shuman, Patricia Stuhr, and Amy Zaharlick.

I began writing this book during a sabbatical leave from Ohio State University in 1992–93, which was funded generously by the College of Humanities, to whose dean at the time, G. Micheal Riley, I am indebted for guidance and support over a number of years. I owe a debt of gratitude as well to my former students at Ohio State University in both Classics and Women's Studies, particularly Dianna Rhyan, Rod Boyer, Kai Heikkilä, Karen Wilson, Bridget Thomas, and Elaine Madwar. I am grateful as well to many colleagues and friends for their assistance and encouragement, including Judith Hallett, Marilyn Skinner, Eva Stehle, Helene Foley, Marilyn Arthur Katz, David Halperin, Anna Benjamin, Charles Babcock, Ann Cothran, Yung-Hee Kim, Nancy Kushigian, Timothy McNiven, Kay Slocum, Marjorie Anne Price, Lillian Faderman, Martin Duberman, Mary Search, Nan Sweet, Marion Garbo Todd, Kate Kitchen, Rhonda Rivera, and Leila Rupp. I would also like to thank Ann M. Miller of Columbia University Press for her patience and friendly advice, and Kerri Cox for her helpful copyediting. I am especially thankful for twenty-five years of stimulating conversation about ideas of all sorts with my late colleague at Ohio State University Carl C. Schlam.

I am indebted as well to the Department of Women's Studies at Ohio State University (including in particular Susan Hartmann, Sally Kitch, and Mary Margaret Fonow) for financial, intellectual, and moral support over many years.

In addition, I am thankful for the support of the members of my family, including my brother, John Jerome Snyder, and my sister, Mary Ann Nirdlinger.

Finally, I would like to express my gratitude to my teachers and guides in my early studies of Greek and Latin, several of whom now populate the Elysian

Fields: Helen Stevens (University High School, Urbana, Illinois); Mark Nauomides and Alexander Turyn (University of Illinois); Margaret Taylor, Barbara McCarthy, Mary Lefkowitz, and Katherine Geffcken (Wellesley College); and Henry Immerwahr and Kenneth Reckford (University of North Carolina, Chapel Hill). To all of them I am thankful for what they taught me. What I have written is no doubt not what they would have envisioned at the time they were my mentors. However, as a recent retiree, I have had the leisure to reflect that perhaps the greatest gift any teacher can give is the freedom to transcend the facts that he or she has insisted the student labor to learn.

Lesbian Desire ❀ in the ❀ Lyrics of Sappho

INTRODUCTION

A Woman-Centered Perspective on Sappho

When we look at the fragments of Sappho's songs at the close of the twentieth century, we cannot really hope to reconstruct in any detail from them what life was like among the aristocracy of the island of Lesbos in 600 B.C.[1] Nor do we have sufficient information to determine precisely for what sort of group Sappho composed her songs. Theories abound, but hard facts are in short supply. Indeed, the gaps in the available information about Sappho have sparked some lively and valuable debates among professional scholars in the field of classics in recent years concerning her role as a performer and the audience whom she addressed.[2] Had Sappho lived in fifth-century B.C. Athens, we would have a mass of detail from literary and archaeological sources to help us construct a context for her work. In fact, we know enough about the position of women in fifth-century Athens to realize that the mere idea of a woman poet becoming famous by writing songs that are mostly about other women is virtually unthinkable in that place and time. As for the Aegean island, Lesbos, that did produce such a woman, we know comparatively little about its inhabitants in the Archaic Age of the Greek lyric poets.[3]

My approach here, then, is not to probe any further the many recent and useful attempts to place Sappho in a historical framework but rather to read what is left of her songs for what they say to women (and men who are willing to abandon a masculinist frame of reference) who hear her words today. Until recently, Sappho's songs were for the most part read and interpreted against a "normalizing" matrix of presumptive heterosexuality; my aim here is instead to read them against a woman-centered framework in which emotional and/or erotic bonds between and among women take center stage.[4] If it is not tautological to speak of *lesbian* in connection with Sappho of Lesbos, I use that term as well to refer to such emotional and/or erotic bonds—*pace* the term's unfortunate medicalized overlay involving implications of abnormality, stunted growth, inversion, and perversion. Debates around the question "Was Sappho a lesbian?" strike me as idle; the important point is that her songs focus on women, on women's emotional lives with one another, and on female erotic desire directed toward other females. Sappho's poetic world, whatever its sources of inspiration or origin, was a female one—a world in which male figures, when they do appear, stand on the periphery. As to what her *actual* world was like, we can only make educated guesses, but her poetic world, as the fragments clearly show, was centered on women and on homoerotic desire.[5]

For the sake of clarity, let me add that when I speak of "female" desire or of a "woman-centered" perspective in Sappho, I do not mean to suggest that these are necessarily fixed entities determined by biological gender.[6] I refer primarily to the cultural construction of gendered existence. To Sappho, living on a Greek island during the Archaic Age, the concerns of postmodernism about the instability of gender categories would doubtless have seemed more foreign than her songs, in their broken state and obscure dialect, seem to us today. From what we can gather from information elsewhere in Greece and from what scanty knowledge we have of Archaic Lesbos, she lived in an aristocratic society in which the cultural distinctions between female and male were firmly demarcated. And whatever modern theories we may subscribe to about gender, the fact is that most women alive today have been raised in contexts where gender demarcation has been relatively firm. The male is the norm, the female the aberrant; the male is active, the female passive; the male is rational, the female emotional, and so on. As women we may resist these notions, but we are always operating in their presence nonetheless. Despite the passage of twenty-six centuries from Sappho's time to our own, the cultural construction of the female in Eurocentric societies has probably changed less over the course of two and a half millennia than we would like to think. That is one reason Sappho's words (besides their sheer beauty of expression) still speak so directly to us as women (or men of sympathetic imagination) at the close of the twentieth century; she may write in Greek, but she is really not speaking in a foreign tongue.

I hasten to add—in connection with the woman-centered perspective that I shall adopt in this book in interpreting the fragments of Sappho's songs—that my readings of Sappho are not derived from any modern vision of some sort of lesbian utopia. Although I am pleased if Sappho's poems have inspired idealistic visions among feminist critics, as a classicist with knowledge of the language and literature of the Greeks I hope to offer a point of view that will help bridge the gap between ancient singer and modern reader by making Sappho's words as intelligible as possible to a contemporary audience.[7] Since there are so many *literal* gaps in the tattered texts with which we are dealing, in effect all readings of Sappho are really fictions of Sappho; I can only hope that the fiction I have created is one that Sappho—were she to appear before us and converse with us as Amy Lowell once wished—would at least be somewhat likely to recognize as being about herself.[8]

In order to accommodate both readers of Greek and the Greekless, the latter of whom, after all, constitute by far the largest audience of people potentially interested in the lyrics of Sappho, for each text discussed I include (1) a translit-eration into our Roman alphabet so that those who wish may sound out some-thing resembling the original words of the song; (2) my own relatively literal translation; and (3) in an appendix, the Greek text for those who wish to con-sult it.[9] Although every translation is of course an interpretation, I have tried not to overinterpret, and have avoided filling in large holes in the songs with modern guesswork. Gaps in the original Greek text are indicated with ellipsis dots (. . .), and square brackets ([ ]) indicate an educated guess as to a missing word or short phrase.[10] In general, I have tried to stay as close as possible to the words of the original without creating awkward or unintelligible English. For those who are Greekless, I should point out that ancient Greek is a highly inflected language; that is to say, the meaning depends heavily on various different endings attached to words that indicate their function in a sentence, somewhat like the difference in English between *who* (subject case) and *whom* (object case). In the discussion of particular words in the transliterated Greek text, I always use the subject case of nouns, e.g., *thumos* ("heart"), whereas the word as it appears in context may be the object case, *thumon,* or some other case with yet a different ending. For verbs I generally cite the first person singular of the present tense, e.g., *philemmi,* "I love," whereas the verb in its context may well appear in some other person ("*you* love" or "*she* loves") and/or some other tense ("she *will* love," for example).

A friend recently said to me, "Reading Sappho in translation is like being offered a huge cup of chocolate mousse and then only getting to taste part of a spoonful." Still, I hope that this book will help the reader enjoy the flavor of that bite to the fullest, while at the same time appreciating what the rest of the cup might have tasted like.

The Fragments of Sappho's Poetry

Roughly two hundred fragments of Sappho's songs survive today, along with one complete poem, a hymn to Aphrodite in her capacity as goddess of love. Although several relatively long fragments have endured the passage of time, most of the fragments consist of at most two or three lines of poetry, and often of only a short phrase or even just a single word. Frustrating though this circumstance is, the one complete song and the longer fragments do give us at least some idea of Sappho's interests, techniques of composition, and poetic style.

Where do we find these bits and pieces that have managed to survive? Modern editions such as the one used here and the bilingual (Greek-English) version of David A. Campbell rely on two kinds of sources: (1) quotations of Sappho's works by ancient grammarians or literary critics (most of them of the first or second century A.D.) and (2) scraps of ancient papyri, usually torn or poorly preserved, found in the dry sands of Egypt (especially at a town named Oxyrhynchus) and laboriously deciphered for us by professional papyrologists.[11] These papyri, most of them written long after Sappho's time, show that her poems were still being copied and circulated as late as the third century A.D. Two substantial fragments (94 V. and 96 V.) were found in a sixth-century A.D. parchment first deciphered in 1902.[12] Another fragment turned up scratched onto a piece of broken pottery; this potsherd, dated to the third century B.C., was studied and published by Medea Norsa in 1937, and provided several more lines of a fragment (fragment 2 V.) that was already (albeit partially) known through two brief quotations in later writers.[13] New papyrus finds do continue to turn up from time to time, providing our best hope for a new poem of Sappho's or for another, more complete copy of a song already known to us.

What do we know about the extent of Sappho's "published" works? From various ancient sources we learn that at one time the Greek scholars at Alexandria, Egypt, collected all Sappho's songs and arranged them into nine "books" (more like our idea of sections or chapters). The arrangement was based on the meter of the songs; for example, Book 1 had a total of 1,320 lines of poetry composed in so-called Sapphic stanzas, or probably some sixty poems each consisting of several four-line stanzas. From a torn papyrus fragment (second century A.D.) that quotes the first line of several of Sappho's poems, we can tell that Book 8 had only about 130 lines.[14] If we use these two figures as extremes (which they may well not be, of course), we can conjecture that each book might have averaged some 700 lines for a total of a little over 6,000 lines of poetry. Using the four-line Sapphic stanza of Book 1 as a kind of benchmark, and assuming that most songs were the equivalent of about five stanzas in length, we can arrive at a very rough total of something on the order of three hundred songs for the entire collection known to the Alexandrian scholars who edited the poems.[15] An awareness of this figure (however approximate) certainly puts into perspective the tattered remains available to us today: one complete song left out of perhaps three hundred, along with substantial glimpses of a dozen others, and the merest hints of the rest.

CHAPTER ONE

Sappho and Aphrodite

Difficult though it is to extract many consistent themes from the fragments of Sappho's poems, one relationship emerges quite distinctly: the singer as the protégé of Aphrodite, goddess of love. If we had the complete collection of Sappho's songs, it is a reasonable guess that we would find Aphrodite to be the most prominent among the gods and goddesses whom Sappho addresses or describes. It is little wonder that the notion of Sappho as a "priestess" of Aphrodite (founded on no ancient evidence whatsoever) has gained currency in modern assessments of our poet, for the songs reveal an intimate connection between singer and goddess.[1]

Sappho's "Hymn to Aphrodite"

Aphrodite is the central figure in the one completely extant song left to us:

FRAGMENT I V.[2]

Poikilothron' athanat' Aphrodita
pai Dios doloploke, lissomai se,
me m' asaisi med' oniaisi damna,
4 *potnia, thumon.*

O immortal Aphrodite of the many-
    colored throne,
child of Zeus, weaver of wiles, I be-
    seech you,
do not overwhelm me in my heart
with anguish and pain, O Mistress,

Alla tuid' elth', ai pota katerota
tas emas audas aioisa peloi
eklues, patros de domon lipoisa
8   *chrusion elthes.*

But come hither, if ever at another time
hearing my cries from afar
you heeded them, and leaving the home of your father
came, yoking your golden

Arm' upasdeuxaisa; kaloi de s' agon
okees strouthoi peri gas melainas
pukna dinnentes pter' ap' oranoaithe-
12   *ros dia messo,*

Chariot: beautiful, swift sparrows
drew you above the black earth
whirling their wings thick and fast,
from heaven's ether through mid-air.

Aipsa d' exikonto; su d', o makaira,
meidiaisais' athanatoi prosopoi
ere' otti deute pepontha kotti
16   *deute kallemmi,*

Suddenly they had arrived; but you, O Blessed Lady,
with a smile on your immortal face,
asked what I had suffered again and
why I was calling again

kotti moi malista thelo genesthai
mainolai thumoi; tina deute peitho
. . . sagen es san philotata; tis s', o
20   *Psaph', adikesi?*

And what I was most wanting to happen for me
in my frenzied heart: "Whom again shall I persuade
to come back into friendship with you? Who,
O Sappho, does you injustice?

Kai gar ai pheugei, tacheos dioxei,
ai de dora me deket', alla dosei,
ai de me philei, tacheos philesei,
24   *kouk etheloisa.*

"For if indeed she flees, soon will she pursue,
and though she receives not your gifts, she will give them,
and if she loves not now, soon she will love,
even against her will."

Elthe moi kai nun, chalepan de luson
ek merimnan, ossa de moi telessai
thumos imerrei, teleson, su d' auta
28   *summachos esso.*

Come to me now also, release me from
harsh cares; accomplish as many things as my heart desires
to accomplish; and you yourself
be my fellow soldier.

Aphrodite dominates every single stanza of this remarkable hymn, and her presence, as evoked by the singer, fills both past and future; as she has aided the singer on many previous occasions, so will she come to the rescue anew. Sappho here employs one of her favorite metrical patterns to celebrate the goddess, the verse-form named for her frequent use of it—the Sapphic stanza, in which all of the songs collected together in the opening book of the Alexandrian edition of her poetry were composed. There are various ways of analyzing the patterns of long and short syllables that make up the four-line units, but simply put, the Sapphic stanza consists of three eleven-syllable lines followed by one five-syllable line that always falls into the pattern of -◡◡-x, that is, a long syllable followed by two short syllables, another long syllable, and a final syllable that may be either long or short. Every fourth line thus forms a rhythmic "shave-and-a-haircut" ending to each stanza. Each of the first three lines of the stanza follows the pattern -◡-x-◡◡-◡-x, essentially an expansion of a basic unit of Aeolic meter called the choriamb (-◡◡-, for which an easy mnemonic device is "mother-in-law").[3] The rhythm was such that a long syllable would be sustained for roughly twice the length of a short syllable: MOTHer-in-LAW, where the syllables in capital letters would be sustained for twice as much time as the others. (In modern Western musical notation, in other words, a choriamb would be a half-note, two quarter-notes, and a half-note.) We are probably correct in assuming that in performance, the tune of the song repeated itself with each successive stanza.

If we compare this hymn with similar petitions to a deity in ancient Greek literature (of which there are many in Homer's *Iliad* and *Odyssey*), we find a standard pattern of features shared in common: (1) the address to the god or goddess, along with identifying epithets or places; (2) a reminder of some past relationship or past help rendered to the petitioner; and (3) the present request for the deity's assistance.[4] While Sappho's hymn contains all of these standard features, and in that sense conforms to the expected formula for an appeal to a god or goddess, it simultaneously subverts the traditional assumptions of a masculinist frame of reference. Unlike the helpless ninny that Aphrodite is sometimes made out to be in Homer's *Iliad,* (e.g., 5.330–430, where she is wounded), this Aphrodite is a powerful goddess indeed, capable of uniting opposites into a whole: fleeing and pursuing, receiving and giving, not-loving and loving. The Sappho figure, as speaker of the poem, has derived power from the goddess in the past and expects to do so again in the future. The song presents us with a firm relationship between the two female figures—the goddess on the divine level and Sappho on the human level. Let us look more closely at how the poet portrays female erotic power and the desire of one woman for another through the medium of this hymn to Aphrodite.

The song's opening stanza contains the traditional identifying tags that en-sure contact with the appropriate deity—in this case Aphrodite as daughter of Zeus. Ignoring a rather more grotesque version of Aphrodite's origins ac-cording to which she arose from the foam surrounding the severed genitals of Uranus after he was castrated by his son Kronos, Sappho follows the Homeric story in identifying the goddess as the offspring of Zeus and his consort Dione. She further characterizes the goddess (not surprisingly) as immortal, as having a many-colored throne upon which she sits (*poikilothron'*), and as being a "weaver of wiles."[5] In this choice of epithets she differs from Homer, who usu-ally refers to Aphrodite as *philommedes* ("laughter-loving") or simply as "golden." Instead, she selects three qualities or characteristics that serve to portray the special powers of the goddess as the one who can help in matters of love. The epithet *poikilothron'*, occupying as it does the emphatic position at the opening of the first line of the song, calls attention to the value attached in Archaic-period aesthetics to *poikilia*, "variegation" (see chapter 5 below).[6] The Greek word suggests a texture that is shimmering and sparkling, along with a rainbow of colors, and is a favorite not only of Sappho but also of other poets of the same period. Perhaps in opening the song with the word *poikilothron'* Sappho is thinking of the goddess as sitting on an intricately wrought chair of various colors and textures. In any case, the appearance of the word *poikilia* in the epithet describing her identifies the goddess as representative of a whole set of aesthetic values to which we shall return in more detail in chapter 5.

In addition, Sappho's characterization of Aphrodite as a "weaver of wiles" (*doloploke*) connects the goddess both to an exclusively female occupation (at least in ancient Greek culture)—weaving—and to the much-admired ability to devise schemes, an ability usually associated with the male figures of Greek mythology like Odysseus.[7] In the space of just the opening two lines, then, Sappho has announced a different Aphrodite—not the helpless, girlish whiner of the *Iliad,* but an immortal goddess, seated on her rainbow-colored throne, the powerful daughter of Zeus who knows how to weave wiles on behalf of her suppliant.

Sappho's petition, phrased first in negative terms, fills the rest of the song's opening stanza: "Do not overwhelm me in my heart / with anguish and pain, O Mistress." The power of the goddess is thus contrasted with the helplessness of the suppliant in the face of erotic desire; only through the presence of Aphrodite can the suppliant hope to escape the overwhelming anguish and pain in her *thumos* (line 4), to the Greek way of thinking the center of all emo-tional response.

The remainder of the song proceeds to create that presence, almost as if by magical incantation.[8] By singing of Aphrodite's repeated appearances on past occasions and her descent from Olympus in her golden chariot drawn by sparrows, Sappho effectively brings the goddess before our eyes at the present moment, capping the scene before us with her request in the final stanza for help *now* in the erotic pursuits that are of immediate concern to her: how to change rejection into desire, or more specifically, how to transform a one-sided desire into mutual desire. In other words, even though the song deals primarily with events in the past, namely Sappho's earlier repeated contacts with the goddess, its focus is really on the power of Aphrodite to assist with the present.

Sappho's Method of Composition

Since this hymn is, after all, the one complete song left to us, it will be profitable to examine it in some detail in the hope of learning everything we can about Sappho's method of composition. How does the poet create the presence of Aphrodite for us? What details of description help to make the goddess so vivid as we listen to the song?

As the singer opens the second stanza with the direct request to the goddess to "come hither," she slips gracefully into the past relationship through the conditional phrase "if ever at another time." If ever you came before, so please may you come now. Yet clearly there is no real "if" here; Aphrodite *has* come in the past, as the singer goes on to describe, even including a kind of "transcript" of their previous dialogue. The reiteration in stanza two of Aphrodite's status as the daughter of Zeus ("leaving the home of your father") and the emphasis on the distance between goddess (resident of Olympus) and speaker (as mere mortal living on the earthly plane) call attention again to the powerful position of the deity. The epithet normally attached to the goddess herself, "golden," is here attached instead to her means of transport, a sparrow-drawn chariot (or to the "golden" home of Zeus—the position of the adjective *chrusion* in the Greek text allows either or both interpretations).[9] The idea of a sparrow-powered chariot might strike us as strange, but to the Greeks sparrows were thought to be excessively prolific, and were therefore closely associated with fertility and fecundity and hence with the goddess of love herself.[10] If Aphrodite were arriving in a BMW instead of a golden chariot, Sappho would make us hear the ticking of its engine; as it is, the poet suggests the whirring of the sparrows' wings in the plosive sound of line 11, especially the repeated consonant *p*.

By stanza four, we are suddenly no longer in any sort of conditional situation; the sparrows have brought the goddess from her (golden) house on her (golden) chariot to black earth, and immediately we see her engaging Sappho in a conversation of which we are given only the goddess's side; we are told only the questions she asks, not the answers. No fewer than three stanzas are devoted to this exchangeless exchange, made even more vivid by the inclusion in stanzas five and six of direct quotation of the goddess's words.

At first Aphrodite's questions are put into indirect discourse as the singer of the poem reports what the goddess asked. Addressing the goddess yet again ("O Blessed Lady"), the Sappho persona emphasizes the distinction in levels between goddess and mortal by calling attention to her "immortal face" and to the serene smile she bears—in contrast to the singer's patent distress. The singer reports three questions, saying that the goddess asked what she had suffered again (*deute*), why she was calling again (*deute*), and what she wanted to happen. The repetition of the adverb "again" stresses the fact that Aphrodite has assisted the singer on previous occasions. This is not a new relationship between goddess and petitioner; rather, the history of the connection between the two inspires our sense of confidence in the power of the goddess to effect change once more. The repeating of the repetitious questions adds to the incantatory effect of the lines, almost as if the answers will be created through a kind of magical spell brought on by the words themselves.

In the second line of stanza five, the singer then slips easily into direct quotation of Aphrodite's questions: "Whom again (*deute*) shall I persuade / to come back into friendship with you? Who, / O Sappho, does you injustice?" The direct quotation, coupled with the goddess's direct address to the singer as she calls her by name, brings us a sense of the presence of the deity and of the immediacy of the scene, almost obliterating the fact that the song is describing something that occurred in the past. The further repetition of *deute* perhaps suggests a mild bemusement on the part of the smiling goddess, who is having to come to the rescue yet one more time. Unfortunately, the poet's exact wording of the first question is not entirely certain, due to textual problems in the manuscripts of the author who quotes the song for us (an ancient rhetorician named Dionysius of Halicarnassus, who taught in Rome during the first century B.C.). Parts of the first twenty-one lines are also preserved in a papyrus (P. Oxy. 2288), but unfortunately it does not help much with the problematic text of line 19. Educated guesses as to what Sappho actually intended lead to a variety of possible translations, depending on what one reads for the words that I have translated rather loosely as "to come back"; alternative interpretations include "whom shall I persuade *to lead you back* to *her* friendship" or "*to be broken again* to *your* friendship" or "*to be ranked again* in *your* friendship."[11]

Whichever version we may prefer, the general sense of the line is clear, given the context that follows. A woman (on this past occasion that by now seems so present) who was once in the relationship of "friend" is no longer in that position; the Greek word here translated as "friendship," *philotas,* includes both the sense of nonsexual closeness (as in a familial relationship) and the notion of erotic desire.[12] In other words, it has a broader range of meaning than *eros* (the god Eros or simply "sexual desire") or *pothos* ("desire"), both of which refer primarily to physical passion. The context here, however—given the appeal to the goddess of love and the lines that follow about flight and pursuit, gift-giving, and the transformation of response from not-loving to loving (*philemmi,* line 23, the verbal form from the same root as *philotas*)—would leave no doubt that Sappho is speaking of erotic desire. The woman in question may be either the woman of the past encounter with the goddess or the woman who is presently on the singer's mind—the two become blended in this song. But she is clearly a lover or potential lover who has resisted the singer's overtures and with whom the singer now hopes to effect an erotic relationship.

The element of repetition in the reporting and quoting of Aphrodite's words becomes especially apparent in stanza six, which concludes the section of direct discourse. Here Aphrodite assures her petitioner that "if indeed she flees, *soon* will she pursue, / and though she receives not your gifts, she will give them, / and if she loves (*philei*) not now, *soon* she will love (*philesei*)." As K. J. Dover observes regarding this section of the poem, "a marked degree of mutual eros is assumed: the other person, who now refuses gifts and flees, will not merely yield and 'grant favours' but will pursue Sappho and will herself offer gifts."[13] In the Greek, each line of the verse ends with the action that the desired woman will perforce take as the result of Aphrodite's power: she will pursue, she will give, she will love. The structure of this verse closely resembles the formulae of ancient magical papyri that aim through the power of their words to bring about a reversal in some troubling situation.[14] The repetition of "soon" (*tacheos*) in two of the three predictions for the future adds further to the incantatory qualities of these magical lines.

The Power of Aphrodite

The power of the goddess in the "Hymn to Aphrodite" is not simply the power to bring about reversal of fortune. Besides sheer potency, the goddess's power seems to include potentiality as well; she can create the space in which the potential of erotic desire can be fulfilled. Her *Kraft* (to use the German word for "strength" or "power") is craft, as Sappho hints at by calling her a "weaver of wiles." It is important to note that the speaker of the poem—the Sappho figure—does not seem to desire to *possess* the desired woman, but rather to enter into a reciprocal relationship with her through the trading of roles; today Sappho is the pursuer and the would-be gift-giver, whereas tomorrow (Aphrodite willing) the lover will be the one who takes up those roles. Thus it is the creative power of the goddess on which Sappho calls when, in the last stanza of the song, she once again addresses Aphrodite: "Come to me now also." In a sense, the ongoing exchange between goddess and singer, repeated on many occasions, provides the model for the desired human relationship: one of reciprocity and exchange, not rejection or alienation.

Seen in this light, the military imagery of the last line of the song, when Sappho asks Aphrodite to be her fellow-fighter or fellow soldier (*summachos*), is ironic.[15] The earlier part of the poem has in fact not been about the power to conquer but about the power to transform—not about mundane soldiering but rather about divine magic. Indeed, given the usual associations of the Homeric Aphrodite with noncombat duty, so to speak, Sappho's use of the term *summachos* here seems even to offer the possibility of complete redefinition; what she means by *summachos,* despite its root *machomai* (to fight), is perhaps really more along the lines of "ally." Sappho desires a collaborator who has the power to bring about reversals, magically transforming unrequited love into a mutual exchange and thus soothing the heart of the petitioner. Just as the song opens with the singer's request that the goddess not cause her heart (*thumos*) anguish and pain, so it ends with the petition that Aphrodite bring to pass whatever the singer's heart (*thumos*) desires. Thus the direction of the hymn moves from negative to positive, from a request not to do something to a request to do something, and from suffering to the pleasant potential of mutual desire. Ironically, this sense in the final stanza of direction toward the future has been largely accomplished through the poet's vivid description of the encounter with Aphrodite that occurred at some indefinite time in the past.

Woman-Centered Desire and the "Hymn to Aphrodite"

The "Hymn to Aphrodite" has all the hallmarks of a well-crafted song: vividness of imagery, particularity of detail as well as a generalized appeal, and an enticing balance and structure. In addition to these qualities as well as the pleasing sound effects of the original (the majestic opening line, for example, consists of only three multisyllabic words in the Greek: *poikilothron' athanat' Aphrodita*), part of the appeal of the song over the twenty-six centuries since its composition has been the fact that it describes a specifically female erotic desire, the desire of one woman for another.

From the viewpoint of presumptive heterosexuality, the poem has a prurient, almost illicit, appeal, for it touches on desire that has generally been unspoken, unarticulated, and unsung. Without providing any sort of graphic detail, the song nevertheless asserts the primacy of female relationships (on both the divine and human levels) and the repeating of a pattern of desire of one woman for another. It cannot be dismissed as an aberrant, "one-time only" case, for the whole song treats lesbian desire as routine and normal, not to mention as something worthy of writing a song about. The only way "out" is to substitute masculine pronouns ("if indeed *he* flees," etc.), as some eighteenth- and nineteenth-century translators did.[16]

From the viewpoint of a homosexual identity, the "Hymn to Aphrodite" provides a positive construction of lesbian desire, articulating both its intensity and its disappointments within the framework of divine assistance. Far from being isolated or rebuked, the singer here is portrayed as the object of intense attention on the part of the goddess and the recipient of her help on many occasions. Unrequited love in such a supportive context is depicted as the common phenomenon that it in fact is in human relationships, not as the inevitable consequence of some kind of perverted behavior. Such a notion of "abnormal" desire lies not far below the surface of much twentieth-century Freudian-inspired criticism of the poem, which assumes that the song is about the continual frustrations of an inherently defective form of desire that is automatically doomed to failure. Here I propose that we instead view the song as the clearest statement that we have from Sappho's *oeuvre*—partly because of its completeness—of the primacy of the female bond in a woman-centered context. The "Hymn to Aphrodite," as we have seen, celebrates both the connection between goddess and singer, which is of a long-standing nature, and the longing for an emotional and sexual bond between the singer and the woman with whom she hopes to enter into a mutually desired relationship.

Another striking quality of the "Hymn to Aphrodite" is its sheer intensity. The movement in the song—the swift descent of the goddess, the fluttering of wings, the motion through the air—and the colors in its images reinforce the emotional intensity of the desire that Sappho describes. As we will see in other examples of Sappho's poetry, *eros* for her is both a powerful and an empowering force, a force that is capable both of weaving stories and of causing pain. In Sappho, *eros* is almost never represented as a playful boy (as he seems to be in some Greek male homosexual poetry such as that of Anakreon), nor as the cherubic Cupid of later writers. Rather, *eros* seems to represent a kind of dangerous energy that can be channeled and enjoyed provided that one has the help of Aphrodite.[17] The strongly emotional overtones of the words that the singer uses to describe her own condition—or potential condition should the goddess fail her—emphasize the fine line on which one stands between anguish and the peaceful state of fulfilled desire.

One of the ways in which Aphrodite seems to confer a feeling of power upon the woman in love is simply by giving her the voice with which to declare her desire and call upon the goddess for assistance. Although (as we will see below, chapter 2) one of the physical characteristics of overwhelming passion as Sappho describes it is the temporary loss of speech, the emphasis in the "Hymn to Aphrodite" is on the repeated ability of the petitioner to call out to the goddess, and then to articulate what the trouble is on each particular occasion. Despite the helplessness of the petitioner on one level (insofar as she has been unable to transform the disinterest on the part of the desired woman), voicelessness is hardly a part of her condition. She can not only summon the goddess each time she needs her, but she can also engage in a dialogue with her to express the nature of her suffering and to request whatever she wishes the goddess to do on her behalf. Indeed, part of the power of this song today derives from the fact that it gives voice to the desire of one woman for another in a way that few poets until the late twentieth century have been able to echo.

Sappho and the Subversion of Tradition

Another way in which Sappho's achievement in this song stands out as unique among women writers of the ancient world involves its subversion of the tradition from which it comes. I have already discussed the liberties that the poet takes with the traditional hymn form by prolonging the section dealing with the goddess's past services and at the same time reducing the present petition to the song's final stanza. Besides her appropriation in the last stanza of the military image (*summachos*) borrowed from the Homeric world of male combat in war, Sappho also subverts the traditional system of female subordination by creating a female authorial self that is of key importance in this song as well as others. If this song and one other poem (fragment 94 V., see chapter 3) are typical (along with the appearance of the name Sappho in fragment 65 V. and fragment 133 V., discussed below), Sappho seems to create herself as a named character as one among the several named characters who speak or are spoken of in her lyrics. Besides "Sappho" herself, we hear from or about Irana, Atthis, Dika, Gongula, Kleis, Andromeda, and several other female characters who populate the tattered lines remaining to us. I must emphasize that in speaking of these four examples in which Sappho employs her own named character, I do not mean to imply that we should read these or any other of her songs as literally autobiographical. But I think it is important to note the novelty in ancient literature of a female author creating a strong female persona who is totally independent of male authority.

Such a fictive persona is all the more striking when one recalls that in the most important works of earlier Greek literature, Homer's *Iliad* and *Odyssey,* the most desirable status that a mortal female can enjoy is connection by marriage to a male of high rank. In the world of the Homeric epics, there are no

No Image Satisfies

A Visual Interpretation of the Rule of St. Albert

artist
Arie Trum, Netherlands

translator
Paul Chandler, O. Carm, Australia

Carmelite Institute
1600 Webster St, NE • Washington, DC 20017

design/photography: Center for Educational Design and Communication, Washington, DC

Rule of Carmel

independent females, unless we count Cassandra—and she is presented as the victim of rape and lunacy. All the more striking, then, is the sudden emergence of this fictive "Sappho," a woman who sings of and to other women and who presents herself as enjoying a close relationship with a powerful Aphrodite.

The exact relationship between Sappho's lyrics and the Homeric epics of a century or so before her time has been a matter of intensive linguistic study and scholarly debate, and is an issue to which we will return in more detail in chapter 4. But it is safe to say that on some level Homer is always present as a kind of palimpsest in Sappho's songs, and that those who read Sappho's "Hymn to Aphrodite" (and other poems as well) against the Homeric background are right in seeking a multilayered text and subtext in Sappho's words. Here in the "Hymn to Aphrodite" Sappho has the powerful goddess as her patron saint, just as the heroes Odysseus or Diomedes, for example, enjoy a special relationship with their protector, Athena. In effect, Sappho creates her own self as a new hero in the battlefield—a lyric hero in the battlefield of love, that is, not an epic hero in the battlefield of war.[18]

Aphrodite and *Eros* in Other Fragments

Several related fragments bear on the question of Sappho's portrayal of desire and of her special relationship with Aphrodite and the forces of *eros*. The most important of these is a fragment of a lovely poem addressed to the goddess that has only been generally known (except for a couple of brief quotations from the song that were preserved in later ancient writers) since its publication in 1937 by an Italian scholar with the wonderfully classical name Medea Norsa.[19] Norsa published a corrected version of the song as it appeared scratched onto a third-century B.C. potsherd, the ancient equivalent of scrap paper. The text as it was found is so full of mistakes in the Greek that we must assume it was written down by a student or by someone not very well versed in the Greek language, or at least not in Sappho's dialect of Greek (Lesbian-Aeolic). Although the exact wording of the Greek text is still a matter of scholarly debate, the sense is relatively clear:

FRAGMENT 2 V.

1a . . . *anothen katiou[s]-*	Hither to me from Crete, to this holy
. . . *Deurummekretesip [ ]r. . . . nauon*	temple, where your lovely grove
agnon opp[ai] charien men alsos	of apple trees is, and the altars
mali[an], bomoi d' e<n>i thumiame-	smoke with frankincense.
4 *noi [li]banoto<i>.*	

En d' udor psuchron keladei di' usdon	Herein cold water rushes through
malinon, brodoisi de pais o choros	apple boughs, and the whole place is
eskiast', aithussomenon de phullon	shaded
8 *koma katairion.*	with roses, and sleep comes down
	from rustling leaves.
En de leimon ippobotos tethale	Herein a meadow where horses graze
tot . . . rinnois anthesin, ai d' aetai	blooms with spring flowers, and the
mellicha pn[eo]isin [	winds
12 [ ]￼	blow gently . . .
Entha de su su . . . an eloisa Kupri	Here, O Cyprian, taking [garlands],
chrusiaisin en kulikessin abros	in golden cups gently pour forth
<o>m<me>meichmenon thaliaisi	nectar mingled together with our fes-
nektar	tivities. . . .
16 *oinochoeisa.*	

Here Aphrodite (addressed as the "Cyprian" in honor of her birth on the island of Cyprus) is invited to join in some kind of ritual at a temple in the midst of a lovely grove of apple trees. Unlike the "Hymn to Aphrodite," this song does not seem to follow the conventional form of an ancient prayer at all. Indeed, here the entire emphasis of the extant portion of the song is on place— on the description of the enticing surroundings in which the (unspecified) ritual is occurring.[20] The singer here transports us to a magical space in which our senses of sight, smell, touch, and sound are wonderfully satisfied; we see the grove, we smell the frankincense, we feel the cold water and the cool of the shade, and we hear the rustling leaves and the gently blowing wind as we drift off for (perhaps) an afternoon nap.

One critic, in commenting on the numinous qualities of the song, notes the soothing sound effects of the Greek text (especially the preponderance of *m* and *n* sounds in the opening two stanzas) and compares the effect of Tennyson's *Princess* (section 7): "The moan of doves in immemorial elms, / And murmuring of innumerable bees."[21] Another scholar comments on the daydream qualities of the song and characterizes it as follows: "Almost the whole poem is a description of the pleasures Aphrodite will enjoy when she arrives, but the real audience for these pleasures is Sappho's circle, the girls who are to be convinced, as much as the goddess herself, that the place and moment are aphrodisiac."[22] Although this reading falls into the "social context" category of interpretation that I am choosing to avoid here as much as possible (given its assumptions regarding the existence of a "circle" of Sappho's "girls" and of Sappho's intention of "convincing" them of anything), I would like to pursue for a moment the notion that the song is directed less at its addressee than at its audience (any audience).

Unlike the "Hymn to Aphrodite," fragment 2 seems to focus not on the goddess herself so much as the space into which she is being invited. Without insisting on any necessary correlation between the symbolism of the song and any presumed function, we may note that meadows, apples, and roses, all of which figure in this lovely description, are closely associated in Greek literature with female sexuality.[23] The temple to which the goddess is invited seems to be encoded as female space, a peaceful space in which the (presumably female) participants in the ritual are enjoying the festivities without fear of intrusion or attack. Although female sexuality is suggested through the sensual details and the imagery of the song, no specific desire is described. Instead, Sappho here defines for the audience the kind of space in which desire is able to flourish. Indeed, Sappho's description in this song of the sacred grove to which Aphrodite is invited would seem to have much to offer the postmodern feminist who wishes to define spirituality as involving not a system of beliefs nor a hierarchy of deities but simply sacred space.[24]

If the opening line (line 1) of the fragment is correctly restored, the singer once again puts herself in a direct relationship with Aphrodite by summoning the goddess to come from Crete "to me." Although the rest of the extant portion of the text moves away from the personal in favor of the communal, this song nevertheless reiterates the close association of singer and goddess that seems to recur again and again in the fragments of Sappho's work. Far from springing forth in a vacuum, lesbian desire as Sappho envisions it blossoms in a nurturing space under the benevolent patronage of the Cyprian goddess herself. In this song, then, Sappho constructs not so much desire itself as the framework for desire. I will examine in further detail below (see chapter 5) the subtle implications contained in the description of Aphrodite's apple orchard as a *charien alsos,* literally, "a grove full of *charis,*" or "grace."[25] In the plural form, *Charites,* the word refers to the three Graces, who were symbols of erotic attraction and the attendants of the goddess.

Other, less substantial fragments of Sappho's songs also indicate the prominent role played by Aphrodite. In this badly mutilated fragment, Sappho calls on the goddess by another of her placenames, Cytherea (after the island of Cythera, connected—like Cyprus—with her birth story), and seems to ask the goddess for her help:

FRAGMENT 86 V.

] akala[	. . . peaceful(?)
] aigiocho la[	aegis-bearing [Zeus?]. . . .
] Kuthere euchom[	Cytherea, I(?) pray [to you],
]on echoisa thumo[n	having a [willing(?)] heart:
kl]uthi m' aras ai p[ota katerota	Heed my prayer, if [ever before]
]as prolipoisa k[	. . . leaving . . .
] ped' eman io[	. . . to my . . .
] n chalepai [	. . . difficult. . . .

Although the text is too fragmentary to be certain, it may be that this song, like the "Hymn to Aphrodite," was structured according to the traditional divisions of an ancient prayer; the fragment breaks off just as the deity is evidently being reminded of some past service that she rendered on the suppliant's behalf.

Another short fragment from a poem that was in Sapphic stanzas similarly calls upon the goddess for some sort of help:

FRAGMENT 33 V.

aith' ego, chrusostephan' Aphrodita,	O golden-crowned Aphrodite,
tonde ton palon . . . lachoien	would that I might obtain this lot . . .

Two very short fragments also allude to Sappho or the Sappho persona calling on Aphrodite, perhaps also in the context of a request for assistance in a love affair:

FRAGMENT 133 V.

Psaphoi, ti tan poluolbon	Sappho, why do you [call upon?]
Aphroditan. . . . ?	Aphrodite who is rich in happiness?

FRAGMENT 134 V.

Za<.> elexaman onar Kuprogenea	I addressed [you] in a dream, Cyprus-born

Lacking the context, we cannot tell whether fragment 133 is part of a dialogue represented within the song, or perhaps an instance of self-address. Another fragment, barely intelligible, seems to have Aphrodite addressing Sappho by name and apparently promising her fame even in Hades, that is, posthumous glory:

FRAGMENT 65 V.

] a [	[Andromeda?] . . .
]rome[	Sappho, I love(?) you . . .
]elas[	Cyprus . . . queen . . .
rotenneme[	yet great . . .
Psaphoi, sephil[	to all for whom the shining [sun?] . . .
Kuproi b[a]sil[	everywhere fame . . .
kaitoi mega d[	even in the house of Acheron you . . .
o]ssois phaethon[	
pantai kleos [	
kai s' enn Acher[ont	
. . . np[	

The device of having Aphrodite address Sappho is alluded to by an ancient commentator, who reports that in one of the songs the goddess, speaking to Sappho, refers to "you and my servant Eros" (fragment 159 V.). Another fragment preserves what seems to be a dialogue between Aphrodite (addressed as Cytherea) and a group of young girls who are engaged in the worship of Adonis, the goddess's young consort who was mortally wounded during a hunt:

FRAGMENT 140A V.

Katthnaskei, Kuthere', abros Adonis.	"Tender Adonis is dying, Cytherea.
Ti ke theimen?	What are we to we do?"
kattuptesthe, korai, kai katereikesthe	"Beat your breasts, maidens, and tear
chitonas.	your chitons."

Aphrodite is also mentioned in this badly mutilated fragment from a third-century A.D. papyrus:

FRAGMENT 73A V.

]nb . . . u	. . . Aphrodite . . .
]a	Loves(?) that speak sweet words . . .
]an Aphrodi[ta	. . . throws . . .
a]dulogoi d' er[	. . . having . . .
] balloi	. . . blooms(?) . . .
a]is echoisa	. . . dew. . . .
]ena thaas[s	
]allei	
]as eersas[	

The allusion to "sweet words" calls to mind the report of an ancient commentator who says that according to Sappho, "Peitho [Persuasion] was the daughter of Aphrodite" (fragment 200 V.). Perhaps the reference in fragment 73a is to the goddess's power of persuasive speech, particularly in assisting with a love relationship.

Besides these songs in which Aphrodite herself is mentioned, a few other short fragments are important for an appreciation of the ways in which Sappho speaks of erotic desire. Of these, the most famous are her descriptions of Eros as an irresistible force, a characterization certainly worthy of his status (according to the early poet and mythographer Hesiod) as one of the primeval powers of the universe:

FRAGMENT 130 V.[26]

Eros deute m' o lusimeles donei,
glukupikron amachanon orpeton.
* * *
Atthi, soi d' emethen men apechtheto
phrontisden, epi d' Andromedan
   pote<i>

Eros the loosener of limbs shakes me
   again—
Bittersweet, untamable, crawling
   creature.
* * *
Atthis, it has become hateful to you to
   think
of me; but you fly instead to Andromeda.

FRAGMENT 47 V.

Eros d' etinaxe <moi>
phrenas, os anemos kat oros drusin
   empeton.

Eros shook my heart, like the wind
assailing the oaks on a mountain.

The language and imagery of these two fragments are extremely strong, for Sappho depicts Eros as an overpowering force that resembles a wild animal or a hurricane-force wind capable of completely overwhelming one's body.[27] The emphasis in both is on the physical impact on the lover's body—the loosening of the limbs (the weak-kneed response, in modern terms) and the shaking of the heart. The adjective that I have translated as "untamable" in fragment 130 is a complex word that implies as well the notion of helplessness; to the Greek way of thinking, whatever is amachanon is something that one has no way of dealing with (the adjective means "without device," "without a mechane," the word from which the English "machine" is derived). Eros is irresistible, and at the same time glukupikron, literally "sweet-bitter," seeming to promise both pleasure and pain. Elsewhere, in fact, Sappho evidently described Eros in a less ambiguous way as *algesidoros* (fragment 172 V.), "giver of pain." Despite the forcefulness of Eros's effects, however, Sappho avoids portraying love as an annihilating cataclysm. After all, in fragment 130 Eros is shaking her *again,* with the implication that she withstood the blast the last time, and oak trees are strong. The lover, then, is no tender sapling that will be uprooted in one fell swoop. Given the power of Eros, however, it is no wonder that even the strong lover needs the assistance of Aphrodite to help cope with the gale-force winds.

Elsewhere Sappho speaks of Eros in gentler terms, on one occasion referring to him as *muthoplokos* (fragment 188 V., "weaver of stories") and another time describing him as "coming from heaven wearing a purple cloak" (fragment 54 V.). The application in fragment 188 of an adjective involving weaving to a male mythological figure is unusual, for in Greek society weaving was the exclusive province of females; perhaps the adjective calls special attention to the narrative power of Eros to provide the stuff of stories—the raw material out of which the poet weaves her songs. The image of Eros wearing a purple cloak is perhaps more conventional, reminding one of the descriptions of Eros in male lyric poets and in Plato as a handsome young man. No doubt if we had a more complete collection of Sappho's songs, we would find a range of epithets and descriptions. But on the basis of what is left, what sticks in the mind as the predominant image of Eros is the bittersweet crawling creature and the powerful blast of wind.

Sappho's construction of the erotic as a powerful force is reflected also in a short fragment in which she speaks of *pothos,* "desire." As in other fragments (e.g., fragment 94 V.), the word clearly indicates sexual desire:

FRAGMENT 48 V.

elthes, kai epoesas, ego de s' em-	You came, you did [well(?)], and I
aioman,	wanted you;
on d' epsuxas eman phrena kaiomenan	You made cool my heart, which was
pothoi.	burning with desire.

The word that I have translated as "heart," *phren* (as in "frenetic," also spelled "phrenetic"), literally means the "midriff," thought by the Greeks to be the seat of emotional and intellectual response. The problem of tone aside, the word might even be translated into English as "gut." As we will see particularly in connection with fragment 31 V. (see chapter 2), Sappho portrays the physical effects of desire in strong language, just as she does here through the image of the *phren* burning hotly with the flames of desire.

In the "Hymn to Aphrodite" we can see most clearly what becomes evident in other songs as well, namely, that Sappho creates herself as the darling of Aphrodite. This Sappho persona is not only a worshipper of the goddess, but also her protégé, her confidant, and her comrade-in-arms. A look beyond the "Hymn to Aphrodite" suggests an element of triangulation in the relationship, however, for Aphrodite is closely linked to her servant Eros, that primeval force which according to Greek cosmology came into existence at the very earliest stages of the universe. Schematically, we might represent the connections as an inverted triangle with "Sappho" stationed at the bottom point, while Aphrodite and Eros occupy the two upper corners:

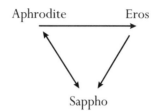

The Sappho figure, subject to both Aphrodite and Eros, is helpless to influence Eros directly, but because of her close relationship with Aphrodite, can enlist the goddess's aid in ameliorating or redirecting the force of Eros.

The "Hymn to Aphrodite" offers us a clear paradigm for a woman-centered perspective on the universe, one in which the goddess and the relationships between women take center stage. The emotional energy of the song concentrates only on the female—on Aphrodite, on the Sappho figure as desiring subject, and on the woman (whether past, present, or future) whom she has desired, does desire, or will desire. The primacy of Aphrodite here presents a striking departure from most of the rest of early Greek literature, particularly Homer, in which the weighty omnipotence of Zeus the Father forestalls all but the briefest moment in the spotlight on the part of other deities. In Sappho's hymn, Zeus is present (lines 2 and 7), but only briefly, and only as a (literal) point of departure.

Virginia Woolf, who studied classical Greek extensively in her youth, was a staunch admirer of the language. She praised its compactness of expression and asserted that "no language can move more quickly, dancing, shaking, all alive, but controlled." She goes on to state: "there are the words themselves which, in so many instances, we have made expressive to us of our emotions, *thalassa* [sea], *thanatos* [death], *anthos* [flower], *aster* [star]. . . . It is useless . . . to read Greek in translations. Translators can but offer us a vague equivalent."[28] As an advocate for the study of ancient Greek, I must agree with her that there is no substitute for reading the language in the original in order fully to appreciate its nuances. However, I hope that the method of analysis in this and subsequent chapters will help to bring the Greek text of Sappho's songs—or rather, of what is left of them—closer to the contemporary reader who has not studied the original language.

CHAPTER TWO
The Construction of Desire

Joan DeJean has trenchantly pinpointed the pervasive influence of nineteenth-century German scholarship in fostering an almost universal desexualization of Sappho's lyrics. Whereas male homosexual poetry (e.g., by Sappho's compatriot Alkaios) was hailed as defining a noble, vigorous manhood, Sappho's songs were superficially and rather lamely praised for their artlessness and chastity. As DeJean rightly asserts, according to the interpretation of the mid-nineteenth-century classicist Karl Müller, "because Sappho's poetry provides no instruction in the acquisition of virility it is unworthy of the official sanction of either the Greek state or the German philologists who are its modern interpreters. This means finally that Sappho's poems will essentially not be read or discussed, beyond perfunctory remarks about her candor and ingenuous frankness, by the philologists who claim to understand her essence."[1] She goes on to demonstrate how this view of the "chaste" Sappho held sway among classical scholars for the next one hundred years.

Sappho's Most Famous Love Poem: Fragment 31 v.

Here is the most famous and, from the viewpoint of presumptive heterosexuality, the most dangerous of the remaining fragments of Sappho's poetry—the song that caused the most difficulty for the proponents of the "chastity" line of interpretation:

FRAGMENT 31 V.

Phainetai moi kenos isos theoisin
emmen' oner, ottis enantios toi
isdanei kai plasion adu phonei
4   sas upakouei

He seems to me to be like the gods
—whatever man sits opposite you
and close by hears you
talking sweetly

kai gelaisas imeroen, to m' e man
kardian en stethesin eptoaisen.
os gar <es> s' ido broche' os me
   phone-
8   s' ouden et' eikei,

And laughing charmingly; which
makes the heart within my breast take
   flight;
for the instant I look upon you, I cannot anymore
speak one word,

alla kam men glossa eage, lepton
d' autika chroi pur upadedromaken,
oppatessi d' ouden oremm', epirrom-
12   beisi d' akouai,[2]

But in silence my tongue is broken, a
   fine
fire at once runs under my skin,
with my eyes I see not one thing, my
   ears
buzz,

ekade m' idros kakcheetai, tromos de
paisan agrei, chlorotera de poias
emmi, tethnaken d' oligo 'pideues
16   phainom' em' autai.

Cold sweat covers me, trembling
seizes my whole body, I am more
   moist than grass;
I seem to be little short
of dying. . . .

Alla pan tolmaton, epei kai
   peneta. . . .

But all must be ventured. . . .

Fragment 31 was greatly admired in ancient times. Greek and Roman writers subscribed to the theory that imitation was the sincerest form of flattery,
and they often adapted an earlier poem on the assumption that their readers
would both notice the allusion and admire the new version even more than the
original. In the case of fragment 31, the famous Roman poet Catullus (first
century B.C.) adapted it into a Latin version (his poem 51) that formed part of
a collection of love poems, many of which were addressed to a lover whom he
referred to by the code name of "Lesbia." (Later in this chapter I turn to intertextual questions of how Catullus's adaptation of Sappho has colored later interpretations of her poem.) In addition, a literary critic (pseudo-Longinus) of the

first century A.D. who wrote a treatise called *On the Sublime,* in which he at-tempts to define what constitutes great literature, includes this poem of Sappho's as an example of sublime selection and arrangement of detail in the description of the passion of love.[3] In fact, it is to this "Longinus" that we owe the preservation of the fragment, defective only at the end, in what seems to be the beginning of the poem's final stanza.

However we choose to interpret this intensely emotional song, we cannot escape one central fact: it is a description of a female narrator's passionate reac-tion upon seeing another woman with whom she is in love. The poet describes the reaction in terms that reveal a shocking—even to our present-day sensibili-ties—degree of raw physicality: a fluttering heart, speechlessness owing to a broken tongue, fire under the skin, blindness, a ringing in the ears, sweat, trembling, and moisture—in short, the sensation that death itself is imminent. We shall return in more detail to these physical reactions in order to see how they can be read as part of Sappho's construction of desire, rather than (as they so often have) as a list of pathological symptoms of perverted behavior; such pathological interpretations are, of course, based on what might be termed the disease model of lesbian sexuality.[4]

Despite the immediacy and vividness of the narrator's physical reactions, the song also takes on an almost dreamlike quality as the result of the opening two words: *phainetai moi*—"he/it seems to me" The same notion of seeming (rather than being) is echoed later in the song in the opening word of line 16, *phainomai* ("I seem to myself"). The verb here is the one from which the English "phenom-enon" is derived, that is, some thing or process that has been observed; what the song describes is not so much experience per se as the *perception* of experi-ence. As we shall see, despite the role played by the woman whom the speaker observes, the song focuses on self-reflexive perception; the speaker observes not so much an external object as her own self.

The Wedding Song Theory

Before we turn to a more detailed look at the song itself, I must first mention—in order to dismiss—the predominant reading of fragment 31 over the better part of the twentieth century. Absurd as it may seem to most of us at the close of the century, this piece has been taken by many prominent classical scholars over the last several decades to be a wedding song written for performance at the nuptial ceremonies of the "groom" supposedly mentioned in line one ("He seems to me to be like the gods") and the "bride" to whom he is sitting opposite.

This androcentric interpretation got its start in 1913 with a publication by a

famous German scholar of wide-ranging learning and considerable influence
on the whole field of classical studies, Ulrich von Wilamowitz-Moellendorff.[5]
Building on the earlier arguments of Müller and other compatriots, Wilamowitz vigorously promoted Sappho's honor and chastity—as defined by Victorian heterosexual mores. I will not rehearse the particulars of his argument
here except to point out that he was the first to identify the unnamed man of
line one as the "groom." Suffice it to say that the wrenching detail of Sappho's
description of a woman's passion for another woman was too much for his Victorian sensibilities. Engaging in a spectacular kind of circular reasoning, he ac-
knowledges that the song is about Sappho's burning love for the "bride," but
asserts that (contrary to the report in a mediaeval encyclopedia called the *Suda*
to the effect that she indulged in "shameful friendships"), she obviously must
be expressing an honorable kind of love, given that she speaks of it so openly
in the context of a wedding.[6] In this manner Wilamowitz co-opts Sappho's song
and its construction of lesbian desire back into the safe framework of presumptive heterosexuality. It is no longer a song about the desire of one woman for
another—or about the effects of that desire; rather, it becomes merely an odd
song about a wedding (lacking, of course, in any details about that presumed
event), at which the singer expresses her "honorable" love for the bride. Thus
the central "event" of the poem becomes the hypothetical wedding, and the
singer's emotions are reduced to a kind of sideline commentary of dubious
relevance, not to mention questionable taste.

The Triangulation of Desire

Much more could be said about the influence of the wedding song theory of
interpretation of fragment 31, but perhaps it is time to examine the text itself.
If we abandon the androcentric approach in favor of a gynocentric one, what
can the text reveal to us about Sappho's construction of lesbian desire?

However we may view the unnamed man of the opening stanza, it is clear
that as the song progresses, he becomes less and less significant in the singer's
description.[7] The man is godlike because of his lucky proximity to the woman,
but after the opening stanza we hear no more about him. Instead, he seems to
fade from our gaze, having fulfilled his function as a foil for the singer. While
the man (*oner ottis*, "whatever man," line 2) remains calmly godlike as he hears
the woman speaking and laughing, the singer, by contrast, experiences a parox-
ysm of bodily reactions whenever she sees the woman. In the Greek text as it
is printed in Voigt and in most other modern editions, the verb for "see" here
(*ido*) is in the subjunctive mood, indicating a general condition that is true over
time rather than a specific event that occurred at a particular moment.[8] I hasten

to add that the pronoun "you" (*s[e]*, line 7) is singular in the Greek. Many have ignored this fact and have tried to read the whole piece as a song about jealousy; such a misreading runs along the lines of "When I see the *two of you* having your little tête-à-tête, I turn green with envy." Such an interpretation is further bolstered by the assumption that the phrase *chlorotera de poias* in line 14 means "greener than grass," an error to which I shall return below, and by the further erroneous assumption that the Greeks subscribed to our metaphorical notion connecting the color green with envy.

Even though the man fades in importance as the song proceeds to describe the singer's intense physical reaction to the sight of the woman, his brief appearance in the opening stanza does set up a certain triangulation that recurs elsewhere in the fragments of Sappho's poems, as I shall argue at the end of this chapter in connection with the intriguing and little-discussed fragment 22 V. In this instance we may represent the relationships with another inverted triangle, as in our earlier discussion of "Sappho"-Eros-Aphrodite in chapter 1:

(man)   (woman)

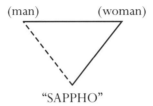

"SAPPHO"

The man is only of marginal connection to the Sappho figure, serving as he does as a point of contrast. In fact, the woman is not of particularly great importance in the song either, or at least she is not as central to the workings of the song as the opening stanza might suggest. Instead, the focus of attention turns to the speaker's awareness of her own body and how it changes in response to her feelings for the unnamed woman whenever she sees her.[9] As one scholar puts it, "the protagonist is Sappho, the deuteragonist the girl, the tritagonist the man."[10] It is almost as if in order for the Sappho figure to be the protagonist, there has to be a cast of other characters, in this case two; one recedes into the backdrop of the scene, and the other—the woman—retains her centrality only as one object of the singer's gaze, the other object being, of course, the singer herself.

Eros *and the Disruption of the Body*

The singer's location of her discourse within her own body becomes clear even before she catalogues the list of the various sites of passionate reaction. The woman's sweet talk and charming laughter (lines 3–5) cause the singer's heart (*kardian,* line 6) to flutter; Sappho arranges the word order in such a way that *kardian* occupies the emphatic opening position in the line, while the verb governing it (meaning "to cause something to flutter") falls at the very end of the line (*eptoaisen*). Thus even before we learn more specifically of the singer's experience of her bodily reactions (speechlessness, a burning sensation, etc.), we know that the site of response includes one of the central organs of the body— the heart, whose steady rhythm has been completely disrupted by what seems to have had only minimal effect on the man of the opening stanza.

The motif of the fluttering heart, while not original with Sappho, seems to be one that particularly appealed to her as a means of describing in concrete terms the disruptive power of the erotic gaze, for she uses the language of flight and fluttering elsewhere in her songs in connection with erotic desire (see below on fragment 22).[11] Homer had used the same verb (*ptoeo,* "to set aflutter") to describe Athena's power over the suitors to confound their wits (*phrenes, Odyssey* 22.298) so that they stampede about wildly as Odysseus and his allies slaughter them and retake the palace at Ithaka. It appears that Sappho's fellow poet Alkaios (fragment 283 V.) employs the same verb (although the text is so fragmentary as to prevent certainty) to describe the fluttering of Helen's *thumos* ("heart," "spirit") when she is stricken with love for Paris. In later Greek literature *ptoeo* becomes commonplace in descriptions of the effects of erotic desire. In a recent analysis, Ruth Padel reminds us that expressions like "my heart shook" were for the Greeks not merely quaint metaphors for cardiac arhythmia; the Greeks really did believe that their emotions were centered in organs like the heart and the liver.[12] Given this fact, along with the apparently parallel evidence from Alkaios about Helen's heart fluttering for the love of Paris, we can easily see that Sappho's words in stanza two, "which / makes the heart within my breast take flight," present the audience with an extremely forceful description of the singer's internal disruption. The man and the woman are doing simple, ordinary things—sitting, talking, laughing—while the narrator suffers a total fracture of the psyche, a fibrillation of the soul.

The singer goes on to describe in detail the bodily effects she experiences whenever she gazes upon the beloved woman. Ironically, given that the role of a singer is to articulate words and shape a melody, the most pronounced among these effects is total speechlessness. The moment the singer sees the woman, she cannot utter even one word (lines 7–8); indeed, she describes her tongue as literally broken or shattered (line 9). In view of some metrical peculiarities, the Greek text of line 9 is not entirely certain, and some scholars have proposed emendations for the verb *katagnumi* ("to break").[13] To some readers of the poem, the expression "my tongue is broken" seems excessively graphic or even ugly, perhaps partly because when Catullus later adapted this song, he used a much more subdued phrase in his Latin version: *lingua sed torpet,* "but my tongue is numb." However, in the absence of compelling reasons to alter Sappho's text, I think it can be argued that "my tongue is broken" fits perfectly into the list of intensely felt reactions experienced by the singer as she beholds the beloved woman. Besides enhancing the contrast between the sweet talk of the woman and the utterly speech*less* narrator-observer, the image of the broken tongue contributes to the ironic tone of self-awareness in this song; the singer claims to be undone to the point of being unable to utter a word, yet she goes on verbally at some length to catalogue the other bodily sensations that she experiences.

Equally as vivid as the broken tongue is the sensation of fire running under the singer's skin; she does not just feel uncomfortably warm—she is, in fact, burning up. Her eyes, only a moment ago operative organs of sight that enabled her to behold the object of her gaze, suddenly no longer function at all, for she sees nothing. Her ears perceive only the sound of a bull-roarer (the verb that Sappho evidently uses is *epirrombeo,* "to buzz like the sound of a *rhombos*"), sweat drenches her, and trembling seizes her all over. The final specific sensation is the feeling that she is *chlorotera de poias,* "more moist than grass"; to this reaction we must turn in more detail, for the phrase has often been misinterpreted.

Translators of Sappho have routinely taken *chlorotera de poias* to mean either "greener than grass" or "paler than grass," interpreting the word *chloros* in a visual sense. However, Eleanor Irwin demonstrates that in early Greek *chloros* means "liquid" or "moist," and only later comes to take on the visual connotation of "green," because of its application to plants.[14] Thus the singer seems not to be making a metaphorical statement about her emotions (as in our "green with envy") but rather a literal observation about her own physical condition. In what exact sense to take the expression "more moist than grass" is left to the hearer's imagination—whether Sappho means sweat, tears, or vaginal secretion. A strong argument in favor of the last is the next phrase in the song, where the singer claims to feel as if she were dying. In an erotic context such as the present one, "death" and orgasm often become one and the same in the Western literary imagination.[15] In any case, as Irwin remarks, *chlorotera de poias* "is taken not as a symptom of exhaustion, but of excitement."[16] Like tender, moist grass, the singer quickens with life in response to the passion she feels for the beloved woman—at the very same time she seems to herself to be dying of love.

How the song ended in anyone's guess. Catullus's adaptation is of little help, for his poem seems to take an altogether different turn, venturing off as it does to a miniature sermon on the dangers of *otium* (the opposite of *negotium,* "business," as in the English derivative "negotiation"). One recent suggestion is that the notion of "venturing all" as the fragment breaks off implies a kind of call to arms. The singer is like a Homeric warrior whose weapon has been broken (the "weapon" in this case being the singer's tongue); despite her near death on the battlefield of love, the singer will now fortify herself for a counterattack, and in so doing will find her weapon once again.[17] Lacking all but the opening line of what appears to have been the song's final stanza, we have no way of confirming such a theory. However, an implicit comparison with the masculine Homeric battlefield certainly informs the song, for its details of bodily transformations are no less vivid than Homeric descriptions of a body pierced by the slings and arrows of close combat. It is almost as if the poet is telling us that it was fine for Homer to have devoted his *Iliad* to the battles between Greeks and Trojans, but that she herself will write of a different kind of life-and-death struggle, the struggle of passion within a woman's body and soul.[18] As we will see below (chapter 4), Sappho elsewhere quite directly alludes to and explicitly rejects Homeric male values, so that it should not be surprising to us that consciousness of the Homeric epics pervades her songs, as indeed is the case for a large proportion of post-Homeric Greek literature.

Winkler has also made the intriguing suggestion that fragment 31 may profitably be read as a response to the famous scene in the *Odyssey* in which the bedraggled Odysseus, still recovering from shipwreck (or, more precisely, raft-wreck) and in need of help on the island of the Phaiakians, lavishly praises the king's daughter Nausikaa, whom he has accidentally encountered while she is doing a batch of laundry at the seashore.[19] Eventually he asks her for clothing (of which she happens to have a convenient supply) and directions. The basic formula of praise in Odysseus's speech is strikingly similar to what we later find in Sappho fragment 31:

> That man is blessed in heart beyond all others,
> whoever bestows upon you dowry gifts and takes you
>   home.

> Never have I seen such a one with my own eyes—
> neither man nor woman. Awe [*sebas*] takes hold of me
>   as I gaze upon you.   (*Odyssey* 6.158–61)

As Winkler notes, if Sappho is indeed addressing the beloved woman as if she were Odysseus addressing Nausikaa, there are only two key players in the scene, namely, the singer and the woman; the anonymous man "is a rhetorical cliché, not an actor in the imagined scene."[20]

Even more interesting than the similarities between the two passages, however, are the differences. Odysseus's whole speech (much longer than the excerpt quoted above) is a masterpiece of rhetorical strategy, designed to get what indeed it does: Nausikaa's sympathy and assistance. The bulk of the speech is devoted to expressions of wonderment over the beauty of Nausikaa, followed by a few lines on the suppliant's fate at sea, and concluding with a specific request for help from Nausikaa, along with felicitations for a happy marriage. Sappho's song, by contrast, seems (on the basis of the extant portion) to aim at no specific goal. The singer does not ask for anything. Rather, the entire focus of the song is inwardly directed, so that our attention is riveted almost solely on the effects of passion on the singer. Nothing else is of importance, for in Sappho's song we have no wandering hero who must flatter the marriageable Nausikaa yet avoid actual marriage with her so that he may return home to Ithaka and to the faithful Penelope. What is important is not so much the beauty of the woman but its effects on the body of the singer. Sappho stands as one among few writers in the Western world who have presented the female body as a landscape for desire in an active sense, not merely as the passive object of male lust.[21] From a modern perspective, it is ironic that in a song in which the speaker asserts her own blindness in the face of passion, Sappho has for the first time in Western literature articulated the female gaze.[22] Woman is simultaneously subject as well as object, and even the active subject— the narrator gazing upon her beloved—is looking as much at her self as at the woman; in her "blindness" she sees very clearly the nature of her own passion.

In many ways Sappho fragment 31, with its emphasis on the singer's bodily disruption, prefigures the expression of lesbian desire in a recent prose work of compelling emotional force, a novel tellingly entitled *Written on the Body:* "Articulacy of fingers, the language of the deaf and dumb, signing on the body body longing. Who taught you to write in blood on my back? Who taught you to use your hands as branding irons? You have scored your name into my shoulders, referenced me with your mark. The pads of your fingers have become printing blocks, you tap a message on to my skin, tap meaning into my body. Your morse code interferes with my heart beat. I had a steady heart before I met you."[23]

The Influence of Catullus's Adaptation of Fragment 31

By way of striking a contrast to what we might call the "somagrams" of lesbian desire represented by Sappho fragment 31 and by Winterson's poetic prose, I return now to the question of Catullus's influence on later perceptions of Sappho's song. Here is his adaptation of fragment 31, rendered into Latin in the first century B.C.:

Ille mi par esse deo videtur,	That man seems to me equal to a god,
ille, si fas est, superare divos,	that man—if it's permissible to say
qui sedens adversus identidem te	it—surpasses the gods,
spectat et audit	who, sitting opposite, gazes upon you
	again and again,
	and hears you sweetly laughing,
dulce ridentem, misero quod omnis	Which snatches away all my senses.
eripit sensus mihi: nam simul te,	For as soon as I see you, Lesbia,
Lesbia, aspexi, nihil est super me . . .	nothing is left for me . . .
. . .	. . .
lingua sed torpet, tenuis sub artus	But my tongue is numb, a fine flame
flamma demanat, sonitu suopte	creeps under my limbs, my ears
tintinant aures, gemina teguntur	ring with their own sound, my eyes
lumina nocte.	are covered over with twin night.
otium, Catulle, tibi molestum est:	Idleness, Catullus, is bad for you.
otio exsultas nimiumque gestis:	In idleness you take too much
otium et reges prius et beatas	pleasure.
perdidit urbes.	Idleness has in olden days destroyed
	both kings and blessed cities.

The imitation is close enough to be immediately recognizable as an echo of Sappho's song, and part of its effect on the Roman audience of the mid-first-century B.C. was surely owing to its allusion to the earlier poem.[24] Given that Catullus in many of his poems refers to the woman whom he loves as "Lesbia," the appropriation of the Sapphic model is particularly apt. Yet Catullus has most definitely heterosexualized the context of the poem. As a male persona (note the self-address in the concluding stanza), the speaker of the poem clearly identifies with the man of the opening stanza, whose prominence is enhanced by the repetition of the demonstrative pronoun *ille* ("that one"), and by the expansion into two lines what Sappho had dealt with in one: the man seems equal to a god—no, indeed, he *surpasses* the gods. The whole scenario is given particularity by the insertion of the name "Lesbia." One can easily imagine that the Catullus-speaker wishes he were in "that man's" place.

As I mentioned earlier, the physical reactions are considerably toned down, and indeed truncated, for *chlorotera de poias* and the sensation of near death are dropped altogether from Catullus's version. The broken tongue becomes merely a sluggish tongue, the ears "ring" with a nice onomatopoeic verb (*tintin-nant,* as in "tintinnabulation") instead of hearing a noise like a bull-roarer, and the eyes, rather than seeing nothing at all, are covered over with "twin night," the epithet "twin" being transferred artfully from the twin eyes to which it properly applies. It is a much tidier list of symptoms than we find in Sappho's catalogue. At the end, Catullus veers off onto a peculiarly Roman topic, the notion that *otium* is a destructive force; a good Roman citizen is really much better off engaged in its opposite, *negotium* ("business"). Enlarging his thoughts to epic proportions, Catullus's seems to be indulging himself in the idea that his passion for "Lesbia" might lead to the same sort of destruction that was wrought from the passion of Paris for Helen—the fall of Troy.

In Catullus's version, the underlying framework of the poem is heterosexual; the speaker is male (Catullus often creates himself as a persona in his own po-etry, addressing himself in the vocative case as *Catulle*), the man sitting next to "Lesbia" is a prominent part of the poem's opening scenario, and the implied analogue for the Catullus-Lesbia pairing is Paris-Helen. It is perhaps not sur-prising that so thoroughly a heterosexualized rendering (which I suspect Catul-lus, as sophisticated an artist as he was, thoroughly enjoyed creating) has col-ored the later interpretations of Sappho fragment 31. It has even been suggested that Catullus has not only done away with Sappho-as-subject in the song (by replacing her with himself as subject), but has also indeed transformed her into Sappho-as-object by using the name "Lesbia" to refer obliquely to his mistress, probably the historical figure Clodia.[25] The influence of Catullus's version is particularly noticeable in the case of modern readers who are uncomfortable with the bold expression of lesbian desire and of female sexual agency found in the original song. Even current analyses still sometimes seek to expunge the lesbianism from Sappho's lyrics. A reviewer of Joan DeJean's important book on Sappho in the French literary tradition, for example, has argued as recently as 1991 that only two of the songs (fragment 1 and fragment 31) in the extant corpus can serve as the basis for identifying Sappho as a "female homosexual"; regarding fragment 31, the reviewer claims that

> Sappho, who does not here include her name as she does in fragment 1, is presumably the speaker expressing jealousy of a man over his being in the immediate presence of a woman whose very being sends the speaker into throes of frustrated affection: heartache, speechlessness, hot flashes, fuzzy vision, ringing ears, cold sweat, trembling, and pallor. There can be no doubt about the speaker's love of the woman; but, if Sappho is inventing a speaker who is not in fact herself, there is no call to see the poet as homoerotic.[26]

This seems a peculiar logic, and one that I trust the weight of evidence from several of Sappho's songs (not only fragment 1 and fragment 31) will contravene. As the translator Willis Barnstone rightly points out, "until Denys Page's *Sappho and Alcaeus*, 1955, classical scholars uniformly denied Sappho's lesbianism, proposing that her poems to women were wedding songs."[27] Although we are approaching the close of the twentieth century, it will take probably several more decades for scholars to rid themselves of Victorian and Freudian overlays surrounding the subject of homosexuality in sufficient measure to address gay and lesbian literature on its own terms.

Fragment 22 v.: The Gongula Poem

I turn now to a much more fragmentary song of Sappho's, and certainly one that is much less remarked upon than the *phainetai moi* song (fragment 31) that we have just considered: fragment 22. This poem, insofar as can be determined given the broken state in which it survives, like fragment 31 also emphasizes the visual component of lesbian desire. In this instance, the texture and sweep of a woman's diaphanous dress are spoken of as inspiring her lover (whose name seems to be Abanthis) to take up her lyre and sing. Relying on several proposed supplements to fill in the missing letters in the papyrus (indicated in the transliteration with square brackets), I translate the most intact portion of the fragment as follows:[28]

FRAGMENT 22 V.

. . . k]elomai s' a[eiden	. . . I bid you to sing
Go]ngulan [Ab]anthi laboisan a . . .	of Gongula, Abanthis, taking up . . .
pa]ktin, as se deute pothos t . . .	[your] harp, while once again desire
12 amphipotatai	flutters about you,
tan kalan. a gar katagogis auta[s s'	[As you gaze upon?] the beautiful
eptoais' idoisan, ego de chairo.	woman. For the
kai gar auta de po[t'] ememph[et'	drapery of her clothing set your heart
agna	aflutter as you
16 K]uprogen[ea,	looked, and I take delight.
	For the holy Cyprus-born goddess
	herself
	once blamed me . . .

os arama[i . . .	As I pray . . .
touto to[pos . . .	this word . . .
bolloma[i	I wish . . .

Like the "Hymn to Aphrodite" and the *phainetai moi* song, fragment 22 is composed in four-line Sapphic stanzas. In what may be the opening stanza of the song, the speaker seems to be bidding the addressee, the woman called Abanthis (if the supplemented letters are correct), to take up her *pektis* (a small harp associated elsewhere with Sappho, see fragment 156 V.) and sing of the woman named Gongula; the speaker asserts that *pothos* ("desire") for Gongula once again "flits about" or "flutters about" the addressee. In the next stanza, someone is described as beautiful, presumably Gongula, although the adjective could refer instead to the addressee. Then follows the explanation for the speaker's exhortation: Gongula's flowing dress (*katagogis,* literally something "reaching downward") set Abanthis's heart aflutter when she saw it. The speaker adds her approval, saying "I take delight." A further explanation seems to follow, something about holy Aphrodite ("Cyprus-born") having blamed the speaker once. The fragment breaks off with the speaker evidently stating a prayer and a wish or desire.

The Configuration of Desire in Fragment 22 v.

Fragment 22, despite its poorly preserved text, reveals a configuration of erotic desire that parallels what we have already seen in the "Hymn to Aphrodite" (chapter 1) and in fragment 31 (discussed above). If we examine fragment 22 in the light of these two songs and some of the other fragments to which I shall turn in more detail in subsequent chapters, we find several general aspects of desire that recur as leitmotifs: song, repetition and renewal, fluttering and flight, rejoicing, and gazing.

We begin with song, for song is, of course, the chief mode through which Sapphic desire is articulated. The speaker's urging of Abanthis to take up her harp and sing of Gongula while desire flits about her is closely paralleled by a line in fragment 96 V. (see chapter 3) where the addressee of that poem is reminded of how her singing had once been especially pleasing to a now absent woman. Just as the absent woman (who had gone away from Lesbos to the mainland of Lydia) once took delight in the addressee's songs—presumably about desire—so now the poet consoles the addressee with a song describing the departed figure's desirability. She is like the moon outshining all the stars and shedding its light on the sea and the fields of flowers, and she continues from afar to feel desire for the addressee. Song, then, is the current through which the energy of Sapphic desire, so poignantly expressed in this particular poem of consolation, is transmitted.

A second aspect of desire revealed in fragment 22 and present elsewhere in Sappho's lyrics is that of repetition and renewal. The adverb *deute* ("again," line 11), referring to the fact that desire *once again* flies about the addressee, strikes a familiar note because of its repeated presence in the one complete song of Sappho's, the "Hymn to Aphrodite."[29] As we have already seen, the adverb there is spoken in the voice of Aphrodite herself, who asks the speaker what she has suffered *once again,* and why she is calling for help *once again.* The same notion of repetition and renewal is signaled by the adverb *deute* in one of Sappho's more vivid short fragments:

FRAGMENT 130 V.

Eros deute m' o lusimeles donei,   Eros the loosener of limbs shakes me
glukupikron amachanon orpeton.   again—
* * *   Bittersweet, untamable, crawling
Atthi, soi d' emethen men apechtheto   creature.
phrontisden, epi d' Andromedan   * * *
*   pote<i>*   Atthis, it has become hateful to you to
                                     think
                                     of me; but you fly instead to An-
                                     dromeda.

Desire, according to Sappho's construction, seems to be not so much a static force as a dynamic motion that finds continual renewal in a neverending process of regeneration. Abanthis has experienced the effects of *pothos* before, and the speaker urges her to recognize its return by expressing her desire through the medium of song.

Yet another aspect of Sapphic desire prominent in fragment 22 and shared in common with other fragments involves the idea of fluttering and flight. As we saw in chapter 1, in connection with the epithet *poikilothronos* applied to Aphrodite, the Archaic aesthetic emphasized *ta poikila,* "dappled things," and *poikilia,* "variegation." As Barbara Fowler has carefully shown, fluttering is one of the many facets of variegation that so appealed to the Archaic lyricists, along with shimmering, sparkling, and glittering. As she further points out, Sappho in particular frequently employs the notion of a fluttering wind in a metaphorical sense. Commenting on the fragment at hand, she notes that "Sappho (22.12–14) tells of how desire flutters about . . . the lovely one . . . and how the sight of the girl's drapery sets the beholder aflutter."[30] The verb for fluttering here, *ptoeo,* occurs in the same form as in fragment 31.6 (discussed above), where the sight of the beloved woman has set the speaker's heart aflutter. Similarly, in fragment 130.3–4, Atthis "flits off" (*potei*) to Andromeda, and in fragment 55.4, an uneducated woman is referred to as "flitting among" (*ekpepotamena*) the corpses, gone and forgotten by all. Finally, in fragment 21.8, someone (Eros?) "flies in pursuit of" someone (*petatai diokon*). The notion of fluttering and flight, then, need not be taken as a pathological symptom, as it so often has in connection with fragment 31, but rather as a major component of Sapphic aesthetic sensibilities, laden with overtones of other facets of *poikilia*.

In fragment 22, the double presence of the image of fluttering—both the personified *pothos* and the addressee herself are aflutter—reinforces the definition of desire here as a positive construction, as part of a larger design (to which I shall return in chapter 5) of what is thought to be beautiful and pleasing: the speaker of the poem says immediately following the images of fluttering: *ego de chairo,* "and I take delight."

The motif of delight and rejoicing is, in fact, also part of the configuration of desire elsewhere in Sappho's songs. I have already noted the reference in fragment 96.5 to the absent woman's rejoicing in Atthis's song, and a similar strain occurs in the exhortation in fragment 94.7, where the departing woman is bidden to go off rejoicing, remembering the speaker and the delights that they shared in the past (see chapter 3). Here in fragment 22, as far as one can tell without the full context, the speaker's statement of her own delight seems to be directly related to her awareness of the presence of desire. Not surprisingly, then, the speaker invokes Aphrodite (lines 15–16), recalling her role on some previous occasion as a direct participant, albeit as a critic. Perhaps the goddess, as in the "Hymn to Aphrodite" discussed in chapter 1, is called upon now to assist in some way, or at least to add her divine presence to the erotic triangle of lover, beloved, and rejoicing spectator. Perhaps, as in the "Hymn to Aphrodite," the repeated presence of the goddess lends divine sanction to the proceedings and empowers the lover in the pursuit of her desire.

Fragment 22 is also one among several fragments in which the gaze is an important part of the dynamics of desire as Sappho presents them. As we have already seen, fragment 31 (*phainetai moi*) provides an emphatic "yes" in answer to the question "Is there such a thing as the female gaze?" In the song at hand, in addition to the obvious presence of the verb "to see" (*idoisan,* participial form describing the addressee), we ought to notice that the fragment seems to emphasize the visual impression made by the beloved woman and her garments. The Greek word that Sappho uses to indicate those garments, *katagogis,* literally means something "reaching downward." Fowler suggests that Sappho is speaking of "both the elegance of the drapery and its relative transparency when she says that the [*katagogis*] of a certain girl excites the beholder."[31] Just as in fragment 16.18 (see chapter 4), where the speaker wishes to gaze upon the "lovely walk and the bright sparkle" of Anaktoria's face, so here it is the total affect of the beloved—the flow of the drapery of her garment, the way she wears it, the texture of the material, and the implied movement of the woman's body it-self—that inspires a sense of desire in the addressee and the consequent delight on the part of the observing speaker. This is a far cry from the flat interpretation put on this passage by M. L. West: "Abanthis (if that was the name) sees a dress that belonged to Gongula, and is reminded how she misses her."[32] Sappho is not speaking of a faint longing brought about by seeing someone's dress hanging passively in a closet. On the contrary, the flow of the woman's drapery, itself "reaching downward" and presumably most evident as the woman herself moves about, has actively set in motion the beholder's heart and brought about the fluttering of desire.[33]

Desire, then, as it is articulated in the Gongula fragment (fragment 22), is not a frustrated attempt to grasp an object, as later Platonic dialogues some-times suggest as a definition, but rather a heightened experience of what is beautiful, a fluttering excitement aroused by motion and by visual stimulus, an active sense of repeated engagement in which the desirer is moved to express desire through song. It is a desire based not on possession but on celebration: "and I take delight."

The Desire to Die: Another Gongula Fragment (Fragment 95 v.)

The restoration of the name Gongula in fragment 22 (of which the first three letters are missing in the papyrus) is confirmed as a likely supplement by the certain appearance of the same name in fragment 95 V.[34] This fragment, written in what appears to be a three-line glyconic stanza (see fragment 96, discussed in chapter 3), offers barely enough context for us to make a few guesses about what the song might have dealt with:

FRAGMENT 95 V.

ou[. . . Gongula . . .

er' a[
derat [
4   Gongula [

e ti sam' ethe[Surely some sign . . .
paisi malista [. . . especially . . .
7   mas g' eiselth' ep[[Hermes?] came . . .

eipon: o despot', ep[	I said, "O Master . . .
o]u ma gar makairan[	By the blessed [goddess],
10 *o]uden adom' eparth' aga[*	I have no pleasure in taking up(?) . . .

katthanen d' imeros tis [echei me kai	But a desire to die [seizes me],
lotinois drosoentas [o-	and to gaze upon the dewy
13 *ch[th]ois iden Acher[*	lotus-covered banks of Acheron. . . ."

Like the "Hymn to Aphrodite," the song seems to describe an encounter between the narrator and a deity, in this case possibly Hermes, who escorted the souls of the dead to the Underworld; the first three letters in line 7 (*-mas*) may represent the last syllable of his name. Although the context is very sketchy indeed, preventing us from knowing how Gongula fits into the song, several interesting parallels with other fragments do emerge. Besides the epiphany of the deity and the dialogue between deity and speaker (as in fragment 1), pleasure, desire, the gaze, and death recur configured together in this song.[35] The speaker no longer feels pleasure in something (the text is highly uncertain— perhaps in taking up her lyre to sing?) and is seized by the desire to die. This time the word for "desire" is *imeros,* which (like *pothos*) can include erotic desire. Is this desire to die perhaps analogous to the near-death experience of the *phainetai moi* song (fragment 31)? The expression "I want to die" occurs in a clearly erotic context in fragment 94 (see chapter 3), so that it is perhaps not farfetched to interpret the stanza in question as a metaphor for the transports of passion. The "dewy / lotus-covered banks of Acheron" upon which the speaker wishes to gaze sound curiously appealing; this Acheron is a river so flourishing in its fertility that it seems remote from the unpleasant aspects of Hades. Certainty is impossible, given the state of the text, as Denys Page points out when he surmises that it is "an obvious but unverifiable conjecture that it was unsatisfied love for Gongyla which was the cause of Sappho's despair."[36] Equally obvious, it seems to me, and of course equally unverifiable, is the conjecture that it was *satisfied* love (for Gongula? for some third party?) that has overwhelmed the speaker with ecstatic feelings; as we say in English, "God, I'm dying!"

While the readings of Sappho fragments 31, 22, and 95 offered in this chapter cannot be said to be any more "correct" than the interpretations of the nineteenth-century German classical philologists and their latter-day shadows, I certainly hope that they are much more interesting than Müller's or Wilamowitz's theories are likely to be to those modern readers who celebrate the female body as the locus of erotic agency. Reading Sappho's poetry as homoerotic, rather than as desexualized, grants enormous power to her songs. Read in this way, even in their broken state, Sappho's songs proclaim women as complete beings both emotionally and physically, beings who occupy the center of their own existence. The Sappho-narrator of fragment 31 is no bystander at a conventional wedding of a man and a woman; she is, rather, the focal point of the song. Just as the addressee of fragment 22 is urged to take up her harp and sing while desire for Gongula flutters about her, so the narrator of the *phainetai moi* song conquers her broken tongue and speaks of the speechlessness of her passion for the woman she loves.

CHAPTER THREE

Eros *and Reminiscence*

It seems appropriate to examine fragments 96 V. and 94 V. together in the same chapter, not only because these two substantial pieces (both written in three-line stanzas) were discovered together in the same parchment dating from the sixth century A.D. but also because they both point to the function of memory and reminiscence in Sappho's construction of desire.[1] Through the absence of the lover, and thereby the heightened memory of her presence, desire comes sharply into focus. In a sense—to return to the triangulation model of desire (see chapters 1 and 2)—memory becomes a kind of third party in the triangle that connects lover and absent beloved:

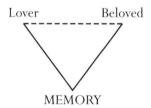

Whether the absence is impending (future separation), permanent (death or dissolution of the relationship), or temporary (an argument, a short separation), lack of the beloved is an inevitable component of desire. Recollection, constructed in the present moment of lack, makes acute the awareness of what is gone, thereby heightening the sense of desire for the absent beloved. It may seem an oxymoron, but the presence of the beloved's absence is a central feature of lesbian desire as Sappho configures it in her songs, particularly in the two fragments at hand. The creation of that presence through memory as expressed in song is one of the primary functions of Sappho's lyrics. Indeed, to the Greek way of thinking, the goddess Mnemosyne ("Memory") was the mother of the nine Muses and thus the ultimate source of all artistic creativity.[2]

The Rosy-Fingered Moon (Fragment 96 v.)

FRAGMENT 96 V.

sard. . . .

2   *pol]laki tuide [.]on echoisa*

. . . [Sardis?]
Often turning her mind here . . .

osp . . . oomen . . . . ch. . . .
   se theasikelan ari-
5   *gnota, sai de malist' echaire molpai.*

[She honored you]
like an easily recognized goddess,
she rejoiced especially in your song.

nun de Ludaisin emprepetai gunai-
   kessin os pot' aelio
8   *duntos a brododaktulos <selanna>*

But now she stands out among the
   Lydian women
as after sunset
the rosy-fingered moon

panta per<r>echois' astra; phaos d'
   epi-
   schei thalassan ep' almuran
11   *isos kai poluanthemois arourais.*

Surpasses all the stars; the light
spreads over the salty sea
equally as over the many-flowered
   fields.

a d' <e>ersa kala kechutai, tetha-
   laisi de broda kapal' an-
14   *thruska kai melilotos anthemodes.*

And the dew grows beautifully liquid
and roses and tender chervil
flourish, and flowery honey-lotus.

polla de zaphoitais' aganas epi-
   mnastheis' Atthidos imeroi
17   *leptan poi phrena k[.]r. . . boretai.*

But she, roaming about far and wide,
remembers gentle Atthis with desire;
her tender heart is surely heavy [be-
   cause of your fate].

kethi d' elthen amm . . . isa tod' ou
   nonta . . . ustonum . . . polus
20   *garuei . . . alon . . . to messon.*

. . . to come . . .

eumar[es m]en ou . a. mi theaisi mor-
phan epe[rat]on exiso-
23   sthai su[. .]ros eche<i>stha[
. . .] . nideon

[   ] . . .to . . . . rati-
mal[   ] eros
26   kai d[.]m[   ]os Aphrodita

kam [   ] nektar echeu' apu
chrusias [   ]nan
29   . . . apour [ ] chersi Peitho

[   ]th [ ]e sene
[   ]akis
32   [   ] . . . . ai

[   ]es to Geraistion
[   ]n philai
35   [   ]uston oudeno[

[   ] eron ixo[m

It is not easy [for us] to equal
goddesses in loveliness of form. . . .

. . . eros . . .
. . . Aphrodite . . .

. . . pouring nectar from
golden . . .
. . . with her hands . . . Persuasion . . .

. . . into the Geraistion . . .
. . . dear . . .

   This lovely song has perhaps been most remarked upon in connection with
the simile that occupies the bulk of the surviving lines. Even without all of the
surrounding context, we can safely assume that the comparison of the absent
woman to the rosy-fingered moon, shedding its light over dew-covered fields
of flowers, must have comprised a substantial portion of the complete song.
Denys Page, revealing his disappointment with the relatively recent finds of
Sappho's fragments (the parchment on which this piece and fragment 94 V.
were discovered was published first in 1902 and then again in 1907), remarks
on this piece in dismissive fashion: "The dew and the flowers have nothing to
do with the grief of Atthis for a lover lost; but they impart to the poem such
colour and charm as it possesses."[3] I hope to show that, on the contrary, the
imagery of the simile is integral to the construction of desire as Sappho presents
it here. Homer can indulge in extended similes for their own sake—expansions
on and digressions from the epic subject matter at hand; a lyric poet like Sappho
cannot, for in a short song, every word is crucial to the meaning. While this
simile may indeed impart charm to the song, it also conveys its essence, or at
least the essence of what remains of the poem.[4]

Unlike the longer fragments presented so far, which were all in four-line Sapphic stanzas, fragment 96 is composed in a three-line stanza form. Each line has as its base the metrical pattern of short and long syllables called a glyconic (xx-ᴗᴗ-ᴗ-), but the opening line is preceded by a pattern of long-short-long (-ᴗ-), and the closing line adds on a coda in the form of short-long-long (ᴗ--). We do not know how the song began, for on the basis of the metrical patterns of the syllables, we can tell that the beginning of the extant portion must have formed parts of the second and third lines of this three-line stanza; we are missing the opening line (if indeed it was the opening line of the whole song and not just the beginning of a stanza *in medias res*).

Sardis and Lydia

The first four letters of the extant portion (*sard-*) almost certainly represent the name of the capital of the Lydian kingdom on the mainland of western Asia Minor. Famous for its wealth and for its invention of coinage, the kingdom of Lydia lay opposite the island of Lesbos (just slightly to the south), and its capital Sardis enjoyed a strategic location for commerce and trade en route from major coastal cities like Ephesus and Smyrna into the interior of Asia Minor. The Lydians, whose language was of the Indo-European family, had a great deal of exchange on both cultural and economic levels with the coastal Greek cities (sometimes, to be sure, in the form of the Lydians' plundering of Greek crops), with the off-coast islands, and even with the Greek mainland. The Greek historian Herodotus (1.8–12) provides us with vivid descriptions of the wealth given to the oracle at Delphi by Gyges, king of Lydia in the generation just before Sappho (c. 685–57 B.C.). Several of Sappho's songs reflect the contact between Greeks and Lydians through mention of Lydian goods or of personal names that can be connected with the area of Lydia. In the generations that followed Sappho, King Croesus of Lydia was defeated at the hands of Cyrus the Great, King of Persia, and Lydia was reduced to a satrapy of the powerful Persian Empire.

While we cannot say with any certainty what fragment 96 might have suggested (if anything) as the reason for the absent woman's departure to Sardis (if that is indeed the city alluded to in the first extant line), the third stanza does confirm the notion that the absent figure is now among the women of Lydia. What we have left of the song centers around the narrator's description of the absent woman (through the elaborate simile of the moon) and of her desire for Atthis, the song's addressee. The song's very framework, involving narrator, addressee, and the departed woman—who becomes a presence in the poem through the simile of the moon—reflects the triangular complexities of desire as Sappho constructs it here and elsewhere in her poetry.

The opening of fragment 96 is interesting for its comparison (evidently in the imagined mind of the absent woman) of the addressee to a goddess. Just as the speaker of fragment 31 likens the unnamed man of that song's opening stanza to a god, so here the woman who has gone away to Lydia casts her mind back to Lesbos and thinks of her friend, who had seemed to her like a goddess in human form. The narrator, in imagining for us the absent woman's westward gaze toward Lesbos, points out that not only did the woman think of Atthis as goddesslike, but she also took special delight in the *molpe*—the song—of Atthis. Thus the song at hand becomes one about the power of song—in particular, the power of Atthis's songs to charm even just through the memory of them; although the exact relationship of ideas between the opening two (partial) stanzas in unclear, there is the implication that the woman in Lydia is remembering in her mind's eye both Atthis's physical appearance and the effect that her poems had on her.

The song at hand then turns from past to present, the transition clearly marked by the introductory words of the third stanza, *nun de* ("but now," with the temporal adverb coming first in the Greek). *Now* the absent woman is preeminent among the women of Lydia; the verb that Sappho uses to define this preeminence (*emprepetai*) is employed by Homer, for example, to describe the Trojan hero Sarpedon as standing out above others of the best warriors in Troy (*Iliad* 12.104). Like Sarpedon, the nameless woman is the best of the best.

Scholars have sometimes made much of the fact that Sappho describes the woman's Lydian peer group as *gunaikes* ("women"), as opposed to *parthenoi* ("girls," "maidens").[5] The assumption is that the reference to the Lydian *women* indicates the absent woman's new status as a wife, and that her marriage was the cause of the separation from Atthis. However, the certainty of such a claim breaks down when we realize that Homer, for example, uses *gune* ("woman") to refer to an apparently unmarried woman named Diomede, one of Achilles' concubines who is described as a captive from Lesbos and as the daughter of Phorbas, without reference to any husband (*Iliad* 9.664–65). In any case, I prefer to let Sappho's text explain itself, rather than to impose on it a dubious conclusion about the reason for the separation that forms the poem's major fictive framework. To assume that the absent figure is now an "outstanding wife" is to attempt to place the song in a heterosexual context that may or may not be relevant at all to Sappho's portrayal of desire.

The Simile of the Moon

When we turn to the actual simile that Sappho employs to concretize the superior quality of the absent woman, we are struck immediately by a remarkable twist on one of the traditional Homeric epithets: rosy-fingered (line 8, *brodo-daktulos,* the Lesbian-Aeolic form of *rhododaktulos*). As Sappho's audience would have known well, "rosy-fingered" is always used by Homer to describe Eos, or Dawn. The standard way in the Homeric epics to describe sunrise, for example, runs along the lines of "But when beautiful rosy-fingered Dawn appeared," with the words *rhododaktulos Eos* always occurring as a formula at line's end. Here Sappho applies it instead to the moon as it appears after sunset, glowing more brightly than the stars.[6] In stealing the Homeric epithet away from its proper referent, Sappho creates a startling image of night transformed into day, for the moonlight in the unfolding simile is so bright and so potent that it appears to function like the sun in nurturing the flowers. Indeed, the rosy-fingered (*brodo-daktulos*) moon seems to nourish fields of the flowers that it resembles, roses (*broda,* line 13).

I will return to the significance of the floral imagery in this simile shortly, but first it is important to note that the moon itself functions as a symbol of the absent woman's surpassing loveliness. Elsewhere, in a fragment from a song in Sapphic stanzas, Sappho refers to the superior beauty of the moon as compared to the stars:

FRAGMENT 34 V.

asteres men amphi kalan selannan	The stars around the beautiful moon
aps apukruptoisi phaennon eidos	keep hidden their glittering radiance,
oppota plethoisa malista lampe	whenever in its fullness it shines
gan. . . .	[upon] the earth.

Given the use of Sappho's other references to nature (including in fragment 96) to reflect on female beauty, it would not be surprising if this fragmentary description was also once part of a comparison between a woman and the moon. In any case, it certainly provides a parallel for the use in fragment 96 of the moon as an example of superior brightness as compared to the stars.

In view of the context at hand in fragment 96, in which Atthis is likened to a goddess in her desirability, we may not go astray in seeing in the phrase "rosy-fingered moon" an allusion as well to "rosy-fingered Selene," the moon-goddess who (like her sister Eos, Dawn) was called by the same name as the cosmologi-cal phenomenon with which she is associated.[7] Although the text of the line is disputed, the most likely reading is in fact *selanna,* the Lesbian-Aeolic form of the word *selene.* The apparent allusion to the goddess Selene, although it is most closely connected with the woman in Lydia, also reinforces the notion of the divine loveliness of Atthis.

"Rosy-fingered Selene"—to the Greek ear—would also have called to mind the stories in Greek mythology about the moon-goddess bathing in the waters of Oceanus before yoking her chariot and setting forth on her nightly course.[8] It was thought that in dry summer months Selene drew up the moisture from Oceanus and sprinkled it over the earth in the form of dew, thus nurturing the crops. Although Sappho's use of the definite article ("*the* rosy-fingered *selanna*") suggests that the primary image in the song is of the moon itself, surely the myths surrounding the goddess Selene inform the simile as it unfolds, describing the beneficent effect of the moonlight on the fields of flowers.

The simile itself, which occupies lines 7–14, or the better part of three stanzas, stresses the preeminence of the moon as it outshines all the stars and sheds its light over both sea and land. Sappho describes the moisture of the dew and—paratactically—the flourishing of the roses, chervil, and honey-lotus. Even if she is not thinking specifically of the story of Selene dipping into the waters of Oceanus before her journey across the sky, the connection seems to be one of implied cause and effect: the moon causes the liquid dew to form, and the dew causes the flowers to blossom.[9]

The poet chooses these particular details partly for their association in the Greek mind with the female and with female sexuality. In Homer (*Odyssey* 5.467) the dew (*eerse*), for example, is described as "female" (*thelus*), perhaps because women were associated with fluids and moisture (blood, amniotic fluid, vaginal secretions, etc.). Furthermore, roses are (along with other flowers like the hyacinth) clearly connected in Sappho's songs with the female and with female sensuality, as we will see particularly in the case of fragment 94 V. (below); it is not surprising that a later Greek follower of Sappho, Nossis of Locri (c. 300 B.C.), refers to the "roses" of Aphrodite in a programmatic poem in which she declares that her theme is Eros.[10] The roses in fragment 96 are described as "tender," *apalos,* a favorite adjective of Sappho's that is applied elsewhere to a woman named Gurinno (fragment 82a V.) whose beauty is surpassed by Mnasidika, to the bosom of a (female) companion (fragment 126 V.), and to the neck of the addressee in fragment 94 V. (see below).

Sappho was of course not the first Greek author to associate female sexuality with dew and flowers, for in the so-called Deception of Zeus episode in Homer's *Iliad* (14. 153–351), Hera employs the assistance of Aphrodite to distract her husband from helping the Trojans by making love with him in a field of fresh grass, dew-covered clover, crocus, and hyacinths.[11] Although the song at hand is perhaps not intended to recall this Homeric passage directly, Sappho seems to be capitalizing on an already established pattern of symbolism whereby dew-covered flowers represent the female body. As others have noticed, the lovely description here in fragment 96 is also reminiscent of the close association in fragment 2 (see chapter 1) between the apple blossoms, roses, and blossoming fields of Aphrodite's precinct and the hoped-for presence of the goddddess herself.[12] We should also recall the highly fragmentary fragment 73a V. (chapter 1), in which the words *Aphrodite, blooms(?),* and *dew* suggest a similar collocation of ideas.

The moon itself, traditionally connected in many cultures with the female's monthly reproductive cycle, appears elsewhere in Sappho's songs in contexts that suggest its strongly female associations for her. Besides fragment 34 V. about the surpassing radiance of the moon in the probable context of a description of female beauty (discussed above), fragment 154 V. opens with the image of a full moon shining down on a group of women:

FRAGMENT 154 V.

Pleres men ephaint' a selan<n>a,	The moon gleamed in its fullness,
ai d' os peri bomon estathesan	and as the women stood around the altar . . .

Tantalizing in its incompleteness, the fragment is almost certainly the beginning of a song, for the lines are quoted by Hephaestion, the author of a second-century A.D. handbook on meter; he would likely have chosen the introductory words of a piece to use as an example of the rhythms under discussion. Whatever it was that the women do at the altar, it is the full moon that sets the stage for the action of the song.

When we realize how closely the imagery of the moon simile in fragment 96 connects with the song's theme of surpassing loveliness, the function of the simile becomes obvious. Sappho is not merely rambling on without purpose, as some commentators have implied.[13] The description of the moonlight is neither a fanciful digression nor a one-to-one correspondence to anything or anyone. Rather, the picture of the moon, sea, and dew-covered flowers perfectly evokes the extraordinary sensual beauty of both the goddesslike Atthis and the absent woman in Lydia who desires her.

At the conclusion of the simile, the song returns easily to the actions of the woman in Lydia, whose longing is conveyed in her restless movements (as we would say, she is "pacing the floor"), and in the explicit description of her mental state: she "remembers gentle Atthis with desire." The word that Sappho uses for "desire," *imeros,* is used (in its verbal form, *imerro*) in a clearly erotic context at the end of her "Hymn to Aphrodite" (1.27 V.).[14]

The Ending of Fragment 96

How fragment 96 may have ended is a matter for scholarly debate. The parchment contains bits and pieces of at least seven further stanzas beyond where most translators cease to attempt an intelligible rendition of the lines, ending their versions at line 17. Some have even assumed that a new song began in line 21, which is certainly a possibility, given the tendency of ancient copyists to run pieces together in order to economize on the use of writing surfaces.[15] Lines 18–20 are virtually unintelligible, but the stanza beginning at line 21 seems to declare that "it is not easy [for us] to equal goddesses in loveliness of form," where the phrase *theaisin . . . exisosthai* is remarkably similar to the words *isos theoisin* used to describe the anonymous man of fragment 31 (see chapter 2), who is "like the gods"; in both cases, the key idea is *isos*, "equal" (the root of the verb *exisosthai*, "to become equal to"). The only other words that can be made out toward the end of the fragment are the name of Aphrodite, something about her pouring nectar from a golden object with her hands (as in fragment 2, see chapter 1), the name of Peitho ("Persuasion"), and the name of a shrine called the Geraistion, probably the one in Euboea dedicated to Poseidon.

Although the very fragmentary state of the parchment at this point prevents certainty, I suggest that these references to deities and to the difficulty of mere mortals equaling the goddesses in beauty should perhaps be tied in with line 4 of the fragment rather than considered as the opening of a new piece. The song may have made the point that even though the woman in Lydia *imagines* Atthis as "like an easily recognized goddess," such an equation can in fact really only be approximated, and only with the help of Aphrodite and Peitho, "Persuasion," whom Sappho evidently considers a daughter of Aphrodite (see chapter 1). The absent woman may have thought Atthis was goddesslike in beauty and in the charm of her songs, but Atthis (and all other mortal women) can achieve such near-divine status only through divine assistance. Just as the ritual of the apple-grove fragment (fragment 2 V., see chapter 1) requires the presence of Aphrodite pouring nectar into golden cups, so perhaps here the lines suggest the necessity of Aphrodite's presence in order to instill mortal women with her divine grace and beauty. The particle *men* ("on the one hand") in the statement in line 21 about the difficulty of equaling the goddesses in beauty implies a subsequent statement with the complementary particle *de* ("on the other hand"); such particles, often difficult to translate into English, are integral to the system of logical relationships that can be expressed in the Greek language. Although the subsequent statement is missing amidst the ruins of the remaining bits and pieces of the song, it might well have been something along the lines of "But on the other hand, when Aphrodite and her daughter Persuasion graced us with their presence, we were like unto goddesses ourselves."

If these suppositions about lines 21 ff. are at all correct, we have one more thread that can be tied in with the simile of the moon in the earlier part of the fragment. Just as the absent woman in Lydia is likened to the moon and thereby to the moon-goddess Selene, so others on whom Aphrodite smiles may achieve such goddesslike qualities. If Aphrodite graces us with her presence, we, too, may become "like an easily recognized goddess."

The Question of Genre

A question that has puzzled readers of fragment 96 concerns its genre.[16] In what context are we to think of the moon simile? Is this a lament? a poem of consolation? or, as one scholar would have it, an "inverted" wedding song in which Sappho is deliberately playing with the conventions of the traditional epithalamium in honor of the bride and groom?[17] Much depends, of course, on how one interprets the highly fragmentary ending of the text (if indeed it is even part of the same song). If the tentative reconstruction that I have offered above is in fact correct, then we might be dealing with an altogether different kind of song—neither lament nor consolation, nor peculiar wedding song. We might find instead that the piece is simply descriptive of divine beauty in mortal form. Like the "Hymn to Aphrodite," the piece in its entirety might have focused as much on the transforming powers of Aphrodite as on the lovers themselves. It is possible that the separated lovers—in their divinelike grace—are examples intended to prove the point of the song, much as Helen and Anaktoria are illustrations of the "thesis" of fragment 16 (see chapter 4). Lacking the surrounding context and being certain neither of the song's beginning nor its ending, we cannot know exactly how the theme of separation fit into the song as a whole, and perhaps the safest course is not to make *any* assumption about the genre of the piece. Absence, memory, beauty, and desire are all elements of the song, but which were predominant in the text as a whole we cannot tell.

One last important feature of fragment 96 concerns its self-referential qualities as a poem about poetry. The unnamed narrator, in speaking of the special joy that the woman in Lydia feels in recalling Atthis's songs, is also making an implicit statement about her own song. Whether or not we understand the fragment as a formal consolation, certainly the narrator wishes for a similar effect of the song at hand—one of pleasure in calling it to mind. As we have seen earlier (chapter 2), the motif of rejoicing is an important component in the Sapphic construction of desire. In the case of fragment 22, it is the speaker herself who "rejoices" in the presence of desire, and she urges Abanthis (if that was the name) to take up her instrument and sing of Gongula while desire for Gongula flutters around her. In the extant portions of fragment 96, the narrator is less involved in the action of the poem, and it is only by indirection that we note the parallel between the songs within the song (that is, Atthis's songs, which produce rejoicing and desire) and the song at hand. If we had the complete text of both fragment 22 and fragment 96, it is possible that we would find a number of such motifs shared in common between the two poems, including not only the relationship between desire and song, but also the role of Aphrodite in fostering the pursuit of desire.

Separation and Memory: Fragment 94 v.

FRAGMENT 94 V.

	tethnaken d' adolos thelo.	. . .
2	*a me psisdomena katelimpanen*	"Honestly, I wish I were dead!"
		Weeping many tears she left me,
	polla kai tod' eeipe [moi	Saying this as well:
	oim' os deina pep[onth]amen,	"Oh, what dreadful things have hap-
5	*Psaph', e man s' aekois' apulimpano.*	pened to us,
		Sappho! I don't want to leave you!"
	tan d' ego tad' ameiboman.	I answered her:
	chairois' ercheo kamethen	"Go with my blessings, and remember
8	*memnais', oistha gar os se pedepomen.*	me,
		for you know how we cherished you.
	ai de me, alla s' ego thelo	"But if you have [forgotten], I want
	omnaisai . . . eai	to remind you . . .
11	*os . . . kai kal' epaschomen.*	of the beautiful things that happened
		to us:
	po[llois gar stephan]ois ion	"Close by my side you put around
	kai br[odon . . .]kion t' umoi	yourself
14	*ka . . . par emoi perethekao*	[many wreaths] of violets and roses and
		saffron. . . .
	kai pollais upathumidas	"And many woven garlands
	plektais amph' apalai derai	made from flowers . . .
17	*antheon e . . . pepoemenais.*	around your tender neck,
	kai p . . . muroi	"And . . . with costly royal
	brentheioi . . . ru . . . n	myrrh . . .
20	*exal<e>ipsao ka[i bas]ileioi*	you anointed . . .,

kai stromn[an e]pi molthakan	"And on a soft bed
apalan par[ ]onon	. . . tender . . .
23 *exies potho[n] nidon*	you satisfied your desire . . . .
koute tis[ou]te ti	"Nor was there any . . .
iron oud' u . . .	nor any holy . . .
26 *eplet' opp[othen am]mes apeskomen,*	from which we were away,
ouk alsos [ ] ros	. . . nor grove. . . ."
*] psophos*	
29] . . . *oidiai*	

Like fragment 96, fragment 94 is composed in three-line stanzas, but this time the first two lines of each stanza are simple glyconics (xx–⏑⏑–⏑–), and only the final line displays an expanded version of this meter that was so characteristic of the verse of both Sappho and Alkaios. Based on these metrical patterns, we can tell that we are missing the opening line of the first extant stanza (and, of course, quite possibly earlier stanzas as well). This gap has caused some difficulty in interpreting the dialogue of the song, for we cannot be sure to whom to assign the opening line—to the narrator or to the woman who is departing. Is the Sappho-narrator of the song crying out on a note of utter despair, "Honestly, I wish I were dead!," or is the line the narrator's report of what the departing woman said as she prepared to leave?

There is no easy solution to this dilemma, but Anne Pippin Burnett has argued persuasively that the song seems to contrast two personae—the more calm, reflective narrator on the one hand, and the more emotional, impulsive addressee on the other.[18] On this interpretation, it would certainly make more sense to assign the death-wish line to the departing figure rather than to the contemplative speaker of the poem. In any case, the next two extant stanzas (lines 3–8) make clear that the song is cast in the form of a recalled dialogue between the two speakers. Like 96, which represents indirectly at least three points of view (Atthis, the woman in Lydia, and the singer-narrator), this song, too, is polyvocal, conveying as it does the words of the narrator as the singer of the song, of the narrator as interlocutor within the song, and of the addressee in response to the narrator.[19] The narrator takes on particular importance here since (as in the "Hymn to Aphrodite") she is named by the interlocutor as "Sappho." The song thus requires its hearers to deal with Sappho's construction of her own poetic persona. The Sappho persona is further stressed by the repetition of the personal pronoun "I" (*ego*, lines 6 and 9)—a form used primarily for emphasis in a language like Greek that already contains the personal endings within the verb forms.

Remembered Experience

As in fragment 96, remembered experience seems to be a major theme in this song. Just as the woman in Lydia is pictured as remembering Atthis through her songs, so here the departing woman is bidden to remember "Sappho" through this song. The interlocutor's statement of her terrible experience and unwilling departure (lines 4–5) is emended considerably by the Sappho figure, who through her willful act of memory (lines 9–10, "I want / to remind you") constructs their shared past experience as one of sensual beauty that should be cause for joy rather than despair. The departing figure's wish to die is replaced by the Sappho figure's wish to remember.[20] The emphasis on remembering is stressed by the appearance of two different forms from the verb *mimnesko* in the initial position in two nearby lines: line 8, *memnais[o]*, an imperative form commanding the interlocutor to remember, and line 10, *omnaisai*, an infinitive from an expanded form of the same verb (*ana-mimnesko*), meaning "to remind."

The remembered experience as constructed by the singer-narrator is set in direct contrast to the interlocutor's statement of it through a similar kind of verbal echo. Whereas the departing woman asserts at the end of line 4 *deina pep[onth]amen* (literally, "we experienced dreadful things"), the Sappho figure counters with *kal' epaschomen* at the end of line 11 ("we experienced beautiful things"); in both clauses, the verb is from *pascho*, "to experience" or "to suffer."

The fifth surviving stanza (lines 12 ff.) begins the list of the remembered experience as the narrator presents it. If we accept the supplements to the text here, we seem to have a highly sensual description of intimacy between the two women in which one or both of them are wreathed in violets, roses, and saffron, and are anointed with sweet-smelling myrrh. The "bedroom scene" breaks off with the allusion to the interlocutor satisfying her desire (*pothos,* line 23, an unequivocally erotic term). Although the gaps in the text leave room for differing reconstructions of the exact details, there seems little doubt that the singer is remembering—and asking the interlocutor to remember—an erotic encounter that evidently brought pleasure to both participants.

Denys Page, in attempting to understand the song's description of the past intimacy between the two female figures, asserted that "the ulterior purpose of the long list of girlish pleasures which Sappho and her friend enjoyed together, and which the hour of parting provokes her to recall, is surely impossible for us to determine."[21] While his formulation of the problem is somewhat more useful than Wilamowitz' earlier claims that the description represented naptime at Sappho's finishing school for young ladies (who amused themselves in flower-picking and dancing, and therefore had to "still the need for rest," to translate into English his version of line 23), the notion of "girlish pleasures" seems to diminish the significance of the erotic encounter evoked in the song. Surely the detailed (though now fragmentary) description of the sensual surroundings (violets, roses, saffron, garlands, bodies anointed with myrrh, and a soft bed) is in some way central to the song, for it occupies four of the extant nine stanzas.[22] Curiously, a similar, though much more fragmentary, list appears in another piece (fragment 92 V.) preserved in the same parchment in which fragment 94 was found. Successive lines begin with the words *robe, saffron, purple robe, cloak, garlands,* and *purple,* but nothing other than these few words is visible.

A Space of One's Own

As Eva Stehle has noted, just as Sappho fragment 2 (chapter 1) creates a private "female" space in the description of the sanctuary to which Aphrodite is invited, so this song constructs a private world of intimate physical sensuality that can be recalled—again and again—through song.[23] The physical separation between the Sappho persona and the interlocutor becomes virtually irrelevant through the act of singing the song, which each time it is sung recreates the private world of the two women. The listener who understands the female-centered framework of the song is able to enter this private space and to find its encoded manifestations intelligible, whereas to the outsider (like Wilamowitz) the space is impenetrable, and, indeed, utterly unintelligible in its own context.

Thus the "ulterior purpose" of Sappho's description of pleasure in fragment 94 is hardly as mysterious as Page thought. Sappho's purpose is to celebrate female erotic desire for the female; what better way to celebrate it than to construct a Sappho-singer who recalls a dialogue in which she reminds the interlocutor of the details of their mutually shared intimacy. The shared pleasure—*or rather the recollection of the recollection of it*—brings pleasure to the hearer of the song; memory is layered upon memory, for each performance of the song recalls anew the Sappho figure's recollection of the past intimacy.

The Polyvocalism of Fragment 94

Like the pseudo-dialogue of poem 1 (in which Aphrodite addresses the Sappho figure, but the responses of the Sappho figure are never actually quoted), the dialogue format of fragment 94 encourages an open reading of this poem. As hearers we can align ourselves with any one of the several "voices" of the piece—with whoever the singer of the song at the present moment might be, with the Sappho persona, or with the departing woman—or with all of these simultaneously. Indeed, the poem's polyvocalism invites such a multiple response. Without the text of the poem's opening, we cannot be sure how extended the reported dialogue was, but it is tempting to speculate on the basis of what is left (especially line 3, "saying this *as well*") that it included at least two or three earlier stanzas. If this was indeed the case, then the characterization of the departing woman may have been delineated vividly and fully enough to encourage the listener's identification with her—not just with the more controlling voice of the Sappho persona.

The openness of such a reading becomes especially apparent when we consider the alternative interpretation of the first extant line (the "death wish"), according to which it is the speaker of the poem—the Sappho figure—who wishes to die. On that reading, the whole framework of the poem changes, for the speaker is then seen as uttering a cry of despair, the reasons for which are then supplied by the description of the tragic separation and desertion.[24] The "I" of the song thus becomes the voice of misery and hysterical grief. As Burnett has demonstrated, "It is hard to avoid the conclusion that the scholarly determination to discover a miserable woman behind Sappho's poems is connected with the scholarly recognition of the nature of the love she refers to. The unexpressed reasoning seems to be: unnatural, therefore unhappy."[25] On this "death wish" reading, the memory of past delights is viewed as painful and guilt-ridden—more a confession of sins of the past than a pleasurable reminiscence that has the power to connect through memory those who are separated at the present moment.

Symbols of Female Sexuality

The reminiscence portion of this song, when viewed as a positive gesture on the part of the Sappho-narrator (and of whoever is singing the song), forms a powerful description of female intimacy, particularly through the references to flowers and unguents. Indeed, in the classic seduction scene in the *Iliad* mentioned above (see discussion of fragment 96), Hera's first step of preparation after bathing is to anoint herself with sweet oil in order to make herself irresistible to Zeus. In the *Homeric Hymn to Aphrodite* (5.61–63), Aphrodite herself is prepared for her visit with Anchises by the Graces (*Charites*), who anoint her with perfumed oil. Myrrh in particular is the perfume of choice in the teasing seduction scene in the middle of Aristophanes' comedy (*Lysistrata,* 946) about the sex-strike organized by the women of Athens and Sparta to protest the war conducted by their husbands. As we have already noted, of the sweet-smelling flowers mentioned in fragment 94, roses are particularly suggestive of female sexuality in a way that makes Sappho's use of the phrase "rosy-fingered moon" in fragment 96 seem less strange than it might otherwise: both roses and Selene are highly evocative symbols of the female. To miss the implications of the floral and olfactory symbolism in this song, then, is to trivialize the effect of Sappho's list—not of "girlish pleasures" (à la Page), but of powerful, female-centered erotic images.

Memory and Desire in the Shorter Fragments

The appearance of words associated with reminiscence in a few of the shorter surviving fragments suggests that if we had a fuller collection of Sappho's songs preserved for us today, the interwoven themes of memory and desire would recur with some frequency. In the following short fragment from a song in Sapphic stanzas, the poet seems to allude to memories of youthful experience:

FRAGMENT 24A V.

]anaga[	. . .
]emnasesth' a[	you will remember . . .
k]ai gar ammes en neo[tati	for we also in our youth
taut' [e]poemmen.	did these things.
polla [m]en gar kai ka[la	For many lovely things . . .
. . . e [ ] men, poli[	. . . the city
.mme[ ]o[ ] eiais d[	we . . . with sharp . . .
. . .	. . .

Another short fragment seems, like fragment 96 discussed above, to be addressed to a woman named Atthis. Cited as an example of a particular type of Aeolic dactylic meter by Hephaestion (*Ench.* 7.7), in which he says that all of Book 2 of Sappho's lyrics were in this same fourteen-syllable line, the fragment (evidently the opening of the song) describes the narrator's recollection of how she felt toward Atthis in the distant past:

FRAGMENT 49 V.

eraman men ego sethen, Atthi, palai	I loved you, Atthis, once long ago. . . .
pota	You seemed to me a small and grace-
* * *	less child.
smikra moi pais emmen' ephaineo ka-	
charis. . . .	

Lacking any further context for these lines, it is impossible to speculate how the narrator's recollection functioned in the song as a whole. The erotic import of the lines is clear from the verb that Sappho uses, *eramai* (from the same root as *eros*). Apparently the most dominant feature of the remembered Atthis was her lack of grace, or *charis,* an essential component of the Sapphic aesthetic and one to which we shall return in chapter 5.

Finally, Sappho as poet seems to speak of memory in connection with her own future reputation, evidently asserting that her songs will not be forgotten in times to come. In a six-word quotation preserved for us by Dio Chrysostom (second century A.D.), she declares:

FRAGMENT 147 V.

mnasesthai tina pha<i>mi kai eteron   I say that even later someone will
ammeon. . .   remember us . . .

Mnemosyne, or "Memory," is indeed a goddess in Sappho's poetic world, for without memory there would be little for the singer to sing about. Like a painting, her lyric voice captures a moment of the past and makes it alive in the present. In this respect, Sappho stands in marked contrast to her compatriot and fellow-poet Alkaios, for while her lyrics foster remembrance of things past, his songs often urge the forgetfulness and blissful oblivion to be found in wine and drunkenness. For Sappho, the pleasures of the past ought not to be forgotten, but rather cherished and made present through the act of singing about them.

CHAPTER FOUR

Sappho's Challenge to the Homeric Inheritance

Despite obvious differences in scope, purpose, and tone, scholars have frequently noted the similarities between Homer's epics and Sappho's lyrics. Remarking on echoes in diction, phraseology, and themes, one critic inquires, "Why does [Sappho] use a pseudo-Homeric 'mode of writing'?"[1] He goes on to explain the parallels on the basis of social history, claiming that Sappho must have turned to the language of Homer's epics in an attempt to recover the lost heroic world of the old aristocracy, which was rapidly crumbling away during the period of political chaos in which she lived.

Here I would like to pose the question differently. Rather than viewing Sappho as a "pseudo-Homer," I ask instead, "In what ways can Sappho's allusions to and echoes of Homer be seen as a challenge to the epic tradition?" In other words, to what extent does Sappho present herself as a *new* Homer? Can she not be read as modifying and supplanting the old epics rather than as clinging to them? May Sappho perhaps be presenting herself as a "consciously 'anti-heroic' persona"?[2] These seem particularly important questions in view of the poet's explicit statement in a programmatic song, fragment 16 V., where she emphatically declares—using Helen of Troy as an example to prove her point—that contrary to what "some" say, the most beautiful thing on earth is "what one loves."

Sappho refashions the legendary Helen, the bane of all Greeks, as a positive figure in pursuit of her own erotic fulfillment, and in so doing transforms the Homeric material to suit her own purposes. In fragment 44 V., as we will see, she writes her own mini-epic, focusing on the vignette of the wedding reception at Troy for Hektor and his bride, Andromache. Although the subject matter of the piece is based on part of the overall narrative of the *Iliad,* it is really more reminiscent of the *Odyssey* in its attention to domestic detail and to a female-oriented world. Although the traditional cast of Trojan characters is present in the narrative—Hektor, Andromache, and Priam—and although the language of the poem is more heavily laden with Homeric epithets ("far-shooting" Apollo, and the like) than is usually the case, the piece is completely removed from the battle context that so constantly informs its Iliadic model. In fact the festive occasion described, in which the various roles of younger and older women are detailed, could perhaps almost be said to reflect Sappho's own society (if we knew what that was) as much as Homeric society. In other words, Sappho is producing her own new version of Homer—minus the warriors carrying on warfare—rather than merely reproducing epic themes in a lyric mode.

Seen in this light, Sappho's songs may be read as challenges to the patriarchal and heterosexually focused stories of earlier epic, particularly the *Iliad.* They reflect a strong female authorial self who offers the audience a new way of seeing the world, through a female-centered perspective. In challenging the old Homeric tradition in both subtle and obvious ways, Sappho presents a fresh alternative to Homer, not merely recycled epic. At the same time, she does not really reject Homer material so much as make use of it for her own purposes. Ironically, her ties with Homer have most typically interested (male) critics of her work and have in effect contributed to the view of her (especially in the nineteenth century) as a "mainstream" poet. The Homeric garb she chooses to wear from time to time has no doubt protected her from the fate of other women poets whose iconoclastic language has contributed to their marginal status.

Helen and *Eros*

FRAGMENT 16 V.

O]i men ippeon stroton, oi de pesdon,	Some say that the most beautiful thing
oi de naon phais' ep[i] gan melai[n]an	upon the black earth is an army of
e]mmenai kalliston, ego de ken' ot-	horsemen;
4 to tis eratai.	others, of infantry, still others, of
	ships;
	but I say it is what one loves.

pa]gchu d' eumares suneton poesai
p]anti t[o]ut', a gar polu perskethoisa
kallos [anth]ropon Elena [to]n andra
8 ton [ar]iston

It is completely easy to make this
intelligible to everyone; for the woman
who far surpassed all mortals in
    beauty,
Helen, left her most brave husband

kall[ipoi]s' eba 's Troian pleoi[sa
koud[e pa]idos oude philon to[k]eon
pa[mpan] emnasth[e], alla paragag'
    autan
12]san

And sailed off to Troy, nor did she
remember at all her child
or her dear parents; but [the Cyprian]
led her away. . . .

]ampton gar[
] . . . kouphost [   ]oe . [.]n
. .]me nun Anaktori[as o]nemnai-
16 s' ou] pareoisas.

[All of which] has now reminded me
of Anaktoria, who is not here.

ta]s <k>e bolloiman eraton te bama
k'amaruchma lampron iden prosopo
e ta Ludon armata kan oploisi
20 pesdom]achentas.
    [Largely unintelligible fragments of a
        few more lines follow.]

Her lovely walk and the bright sparkle
    of her face
I would rather look upon than
all the Lydian chariots
and full-armed infantry.
    [This may be the end of the poem.]

This song about beauty and desire is a striking example of Sappho's power to articulate a uniquely female, woman-centered definition of eros. Sappho's answer to the question "What is the most beautiful thing on earth?" is "what one *loves*," *eratai* (line 4), the verbal form of the noun *eros*. Although many have tried to deny that gender is a factor in this poem, arguing that Sappho is presenting her audience with universal truth, the appearance of the distinctly female Sappho figure in many of the songs that have already been discussed suggests that the "I" of this song must also be read as gendered.[3] The military focus of the opening and closing of the fragment, so obviously male-centered in terms of the Homeric background, may then be seen as contrasted with the female singer's point of view, as I argue further below.

The Priamel

Scholars in recent years have devoted an extraordinary amount of energy to an analysis of the poem's logic and of the exact import of its chief rhetorical device—the so-called priamel. Derived from a mediaeval Latin word, the term *priamel* refers to a catalogue or list in which several items are presented in succession, followed by a concluding statement that usually asserts the primacy of one item or otherwise ties the list together in some kind of concluding assertion.[4] An early example may be found in the Spartan poet Tyrtaios's definition of *arete* ("excellence," literally, "manliness"). Writing probably during about the same period as Sappho (second half of the seventh century B.C.), Tyrtaios claims (fragment 9 Diehl) that he would not consider a man truly worthy of account just on the basis of fleet-footedness, or of his wrestling skills, or strength, or good looks, or wealth, or persuasive powers; rather, he says, true "excellence" consists of steadfastness in the front lines of battle. Tyrtaios's catalogue of virtues is thus capped by his own statement of what is of the greatest value as far as he is concerned.

Turning to Sappho's priamel, which occupies the opening stanza of fragment 16, we see that she lists three groups of unspecified people (*oi men,* "some," *oi de,* "others," and *oi de,* "still others") who have certain preferences involving, in turn, cavalry, infantry, and naval forces. The *oi* here is simply the definite article ("the," as in the expression *[h]oi polloi*), and the particles *men . . . de . . . de* are used to mark a series of contrasting ideas. In the Greek, the first-person statement beginning *ego de,* "But I [say]," follows immediately after the statement of what these unspecified groups of persons are attempting to define, namely, "the most beautiful thing upon the black earth." The use of the personal pronoun, *ego* ("I"), which carries emphatic force in a language such as Greek in which the personal endings are already contained within the verb forms themselves, marks a particularly strong contrast that is reinforced by the third occurrence of the particle *de:* some people say the cavalry is the most beautiful (*kalliston*) thing on the earth, others the infantry, others ships, *but I* [say] it is that which one loves/desires. (In the Greek, the verb going with "I" must be supplied on the basis of the earlier third-person form in line 2, *phais'* ["they say"].)

In what is clearly the opening stanza of the song (as both the papyrus source and the internal rhetorical structure of the fragment indicate), Sappho has boldly set forth a definition of beauty that is linked directly to *eros* and that prides itself on its alterity. The Sappho figure, or the female singer of the song, declares a different point of view, and not one that poses simply as an alternative to *one* other point of view; no—this point of view, like Tyrtaios', follows a *list* of views against which it is counterpoised. The single figure of the poet-singer stands against the numberless unnamed persons who make up the three unspecified groups of "somes" and "others."

Perhaps because the form of this song is controlled—at least initially—by the rhetorical strategies of the priamel, critics have often sought in fragment 16 some kind of formal—even Aristotelian—logic.[5] Scholars argue, for example, over whether the final alternative ("but *I* say") is inclusive or exclusive; when the poet says that "whatever one loves" is the most beautiful thing on earth, does she mean that if you love ships or armies the most, then they are *kalliston* for you? Or does she posit her fourth definition of beauty as excluding mere things, like armies and ships? Does she mean to say, in using the verb *eratai* (line 4), normally applied to people rather than objects, that only human relationships qualify for the prize of "fairest"?

Sappho's Definition of Beauty

Perhaps the answers to such questions are not really very important to someone listening to this song, for the hearer's attention is immediately diverted in the next stanza to the singer's "proofs" of her generalization. I will examine these proofs (one mythological, one not) in detail below, but first it may be useful to look closely at exactly how the Sappho figure formulates her definition of beauty.

Although some translators render the fourth definition of the most beautiful thing on earth as "she whom one loves," the Greek word is actually a pronoun (*ken'*, or in Attic dialect, *ekeino*) that is neither masculine nor feminine in gender, but neuter, "that *thing* which one loves."[6] The fact that Sappho chooses a grammatically "neutral" expression does, of course, render the definition she offers more generalized, and certainly more open to multiple readings than if she had referred to "that man" or "that woman" whom one loves. There is a curious analogue here to modern gay discourse within a heterosexual context, in which a lesbian or gay speaker may render her or his language ungendered through the omission of all personal pronouns; in this way a man might recount events without overtly tipping off the audience that the trip last week to Bermuda, for example, was spent with another man. In the case of fragment 16, Sappho seems to be taking some pains to cast her generalization about desire in broadly applicable terms. In the phrasing she uses, not only the subject (the one loving) but also the object (the thing loved) are left indefinite—"*what one loves*" rather than, for example, "she whom I-as-woman love."

With stunning economy, the song lays forth its bold assertion in the time it takes to sing the opening stanza. The claim of the Sappho figure is immediately reasserted in the first line and a half of the next stanza by the further claim that "it is completely easy to make this intelligible to everyone." This adjunct claim is marked by the assonance and verbal play in the opening words of lines 5 and 6, *pagchu* ("completely") and *panti* ("everyone"), both from the root *pan-* ("all," as in "pan-Hellenic"). Sappho could have gone directly from the priamel to its "proofs," the examples of Helen and Anaktoria that follow, simply through the use of the particle *gar* ("for," line 6), which marks an explanation of what has preceded. The presence of the additional claim further emphasizes the authority of the Sappho figure, the *ego* of the priamel. Not only can the poet assert her own iconoclastic definition of beauty, but she can also prove it—with ease—to any and all! This is not a poem of self-doubt.

A pair of proofs now follows the pair of claims. In a song about beauty and desire, what could be a more appropriate first example than the archetypal fairest of all women, Helen of Troy? The theme of the song—what is "most beautiful" (*kalliston,* line 3)—is echoed in the allusion to Helen's own beauty (*kallos,* line 7). Yet as the example unfolds we begin to see that this Helen is cast in the role of neither helpless victim nor evil betrayer. Rather than being portrayed as the face that launched a thousand ships, this Helen (albeit under the influence of Aphrodite) seems to be captain of her own ship. She leaves behind her noble husband (Menelaus, evidently not named in the song) and sails off—remembering neither child nor parents—in pursuit of what she loves, that is, the (unnamed) Paris. As Page duBois was the first to point out, in this version of Helen's story she is a *subject* of desire, not merely its object.[7] Although she herself is beautiful, the emphasis in these lines is on her active seeking after what she regards as beautiful, that is, Paris. Sappho's Helen is not a passive victim but an active pursuer. Nor does Sappho's Helen seem to display the self-reproach evident in the *Iliad,* where even in the face of King Priam's kindly words toward her, as she recalls her own abandonment of home and child, she calls herself *kunopis,* "dog-faced" (*Iliad* 3.180).[8] Although the gap in the fourth stanza prevents certainty, it appears that this Helen simply forgets her past and goes off to Troy, "led" by someone or something, perhaps Aphrodite, or perhaps the ship in which she sailed.[9]

Those critics who have sought a kind of linear logic in this example of the story of Helen have of course been disappointed, and they complain that Sappho's account of Helen—as the most beautiful woman on earth—seems unclear in its focus. If the myth is cited to show how Helen found her own *kalliston* ("most beautiful thing") in her lover Paris, they say, why does Sappho begin the account with the allusion to Helen's own surpassing *kallos* ("beauty")?[10] In response we might argue that Helen provides the quintessential proof of the poet's thesis: even one who already possesses *kallos* within herself is still going to pursue what is *kalliston* to her—that which she loves. As in fragment 22 V. (discussed in chapter 2), desire in Sappho has little to do with possession of anything.

Because of the gap at the beginning of stanza four, we cannot tell exactly how Sappho makes the transition from the mythological proof to the personal proof—that is, to a narrative that is part of the poet's own fictive world of the present rather than Homer's fictive world of the past. In any case, in line 15 the temporal adverb *nun* ("now") seems to bring us firmly into the present moment as the poet begins to sing of Anaktoria, who is for some unspecified reason absent.

Anaktoria and the Sapphic Gaze

In contrast to Helen, who no longer remembers (*oude . . . emnasthe*) those once dear to her, the poet-singer does recall (*onemnais'*, lines 15–16) her beloved, Anaktoria—and as a result of the telling of the myth of Helen. Given the connections between memory and desire that Sappho frequently makes (see chapter 3), it is not surprising that the recollection of Anaktoria brings with it the desire, expressed in the first person, to behold her more than anything else in the world. The verb of desiring, *boulomai,* is here put into the optative mood of the Greek verb system, a mood that is itself often used to express a wish or some other conditional (as opposed to actual) form of action; along with the particle *ke,* the form *bolloiman* in line 17 (or in Attic Greek, *bouloimen*) conveys the notion "I would wish" rather than simply "I wish." In effect, the mood of the verb here (impossible to render in English except through vague equivalents involving auxiliary verbs like "would") renders the singer's statement a timeless one; she is not merely saying "I want to see Anaktoria now," but rather "I *would rather* see Anaktoria" even if I could look instead upon every war-chariot in Lydia. It is a statement of preference that is true without regard to time, despite the setting of the example within the fictive present.

Before we look more closely at how the desire to gaze upon Anaktoria is articulated, what about her name itself? Commentators note that it is an aristocratic name, but this fact is not surprising given Sappho's own evidently aristocratic status.[11] The name is related to the word *anax* (stem *anakt-*), meaning "lord" or "master." In Homer's *Iliad* the word is frequently used to describe Agamemnon as the chief general of the Greeks, the *anax andron* ("lord of men," as in *Iliad* 1.442). Curiously, then, the name that Sappho chooses for the "real-world" example to prove the thesis of the song has a kind of Homeric echo to it. The Homeric overtones of this most beautiful thing on earth, this "Maestra," as it were (to render "Anaktoria" in Italian), link this example to the mythical exemplum of Helen with which the proofs began. The "real-world" example, both through its timeless reference and through its epic associations, takes on some of the same larger-than-life qualities as the story of Helen. Both stories, that of Helen's desire for Paris and that of the Sappho persona's desire for Anaktoria, prove the same point: whatever one loves is the most beautiful thing on earth.

A closer look at the language of desire in the song's fifth (and possibly final) stanza reveals several links both to the opening of the song and to the construction of desire elsewhere in Sappho's poetry. In the Greek for line 17, the verb of wanting, *bolloiman,* is immediately followed by the adjective *eraton* ("lovely"), which is from the same root as the verb *eratai* in the song's opening stanza. As we have already noted in connection with fragments 31 and 22 (see chapter 2), desire in Sappho's songs is often configured in connection with gazing upon the beloved woman. Here the speaker would wish to gaze upon—in particular—Anaktoria's "lovely walk" (*eraton . . . bama*) and the "bright sparkle of her face" (*amaruchma lampron . . . prosopo*). The emphasis is on the dynamic—rather than static—qualities of Anaktoria, on the effect she creates as she moves and on the sparkling aura that surrounds her face.[12] As I argued in connection with fragment 22 (chapter 2), it is not the dress itself but the *flow* of the dress as it is worn by the beloved woman that elicits desire from the beholder.

Ironically, the language that Sappho chooses here to describe Anaktoria's face also suggests the military imagery with which the song opens and (probably) closes.[13] Sappho's compatriot Alkaios describes weapons and armor as "bright" (*lampron,* fragments 383 V. and 357 V.), and in the *Iliad* (4.432) weapons "glitter" (*elampe*) on the Greek soldiers as they march toward battle against the Trojans. (The Greek words here are derived from the same Indo-European root that gives us "lamp" in English.) The way that Sappho describes the narrator's desire further strengthens the song's claim in revising the old Homeric values: it is not the flash of weaponry that the narrator would wish to behold. Sappho seems almost to say, "War and weapons may be beautiful to some, but not to me; for I am the new Homer, and I sing not of war but of *eros* and desire."

As is the case with most of Sappho's more sensual songs, critics have sometimes tried to set fragment 16 within a strictly heterosexual context. The most amusing attempt has involved the explanation that Anaktoria is "not present" because she has gone off to marry a Lydian soldier—hence the military frame of reference in stanzas 1 and 5.[14] Although this kind of approach cannot completely remove the element of desire on the part of the narrator, it certainly neutralizes it by adding the implication of rejection. We note that the song itself—at least what survives of it—makes no mention as to the reason for Anaktoria's absence, any more than fragments 94 and 96 offer an explanation as to the reason for the separation between lovers. It seems more to the point to concentrate on what is in the song than what is not; just as in fragment 31, the focus is on the narrator's gaze (in this case, would-be gaze) upon the beloved woman. Here the image of the beloved woman, just as in fragment 96, must be called to mind through memory, for she is not in fact present at the moment of the song. The military images surely have more significance than as mere props for some alleged biographical underpinning of the song. Rather, they provide the framework within which Sappho argues for a new set of values: the primacy of *eros* as the determining factor in defining the most beautiful thing on earth.

By concentrating all the alternative definitions in the realm of the military in stanza 1 (whether cavalry or infantry or naval forces) and by setting the example of Anaktoria in opposition to the Lydian forces in stanza 5, Sappho in effect creates an opposition between war and *eros*. The Sappho persona, although not identified by name as in the "Hymn to Aphrodite" and elsewhere, comes through clearly in the "I" of the narrator's voice, which is set against the anonymous "some" and "others" of the priamel. The "I" of the song confidently asserts that *everyone* can see the validity of the new values set forth here. The example of Helen appears at first to be traditional in its subject matter and in the technique of drawing on myth to prove a point, but in fact it offers a radical treatment of Helen's story in focusing on her subjectivity and her agency. Even more radically, the narrator of the poem jumps from myth into the narrative of the present—into the story of Anaktoria and the narrator's desire to gaze upon her. In this way, the narrator's desire, her *eros,* supplants the "masculine" way of seeing the world as a struggle for control through military might; the splendor that the Sappho figure celebrates is not of swords but of the beauty of a woman.

Another Song About *Eros* and Helen

FRAGMENT 23 V.

erotos elp[	. . . of *eros* (hoped?)
2 *]*	
an]tion eisidos[	For when I look upon you face to face,
] Ermiona teau[ta	[not even] Hermione [seems] such as
] xanthai d' Elenai s' eis[k]en	you,
6 *]kes*	[nor is it unfitting] to liken you
	to fair-haired Helen.
] is thnatais, tode d' is[thi] tai sai	. . . for mortal women, but know this,
]paisan ke me tan merimnan	that by your . . . [you would free me]
]lais' antid[ ]athois de	of all my cares. . . .
10 *]*	
]tas ochthois	. . . river banks . . .
]tain	. . . all night long. . . .
pan]nuchis[d]en	
14 *][*	

Like fragment 22 (see chapter 2), found in the same Oxyrhynchus papyrus as this song, fragment 23 is composed in the four-line Sapphic stanza. The fragment opens with a reference to *eros* and proceeds in the next stanza to portray the narrator as being in much the same position as the man of the opening of fragment 31 (see chapter 2)—who sits opposite (*enantios*) a woman and hears her sweet laughter. Here the narrator is standing or sitting opposite (*antion*, line 3) the woman whose beauty she compares first to that of Hermione, the only child of Helen of Troy, and then to that of Helen herself.

The mention of *eros* in the first extant line of the fragment and the resemblance to the intimate proximity described in fragment 31 suggest an erotic context for this piece as well, but we cannot be sure exactly what shape the song took. However, the allusion to Helen is likely to have functioned less as a digression into old heroic tales of war and abduction and more as a way of illustrating the present moment of the lyric—the desire of the narrator for the woman who is at first compared to the daughter of the most beautiful woman in the world, and then to the most beautiful woman herself.

The reference to riverbanks (*dewy* riverbanks, according to the commonly accepted restoration of the partially missing adjective) is reminiscent of another short fragment (95 V.) in which the lotus-covered dewy banks of the river Acheron in Hades are mentioned in connection with the narrator's desire (*imeros*, 95.11) to die (see chapter 2). If this fragment about the likeness of a woman to Hermione and Helen is indeed erotic in nature, then the possible allusion to dying toward the end of the piece should perhaps be compared to the narrator's self-description in fragment 31 V., where the sensation of almost dying caps the list of the physical responses experienced by the singer as she gazes upon the woman whom she desires. Particularly in view of the apparent resemblance between the description of the narrator's proximity to the woman here and the opening scenario of fragment 31 V., we may not be too far wrong in imagining that the Hermione-Helen fragment began by mentioning the narrator's feelings inspired by *eros,* praised the beloved woman through the mythical comparisons, and went on to describe the narrator's own sensations resulting from the effects of the goddesslike woman on her.

The Wedding Reception of Hektor and Andromache

FRAGMENT 44 V.

Kupro [ ] as.	Cyprus . . .
karux elthe the[ ] ele [ ] theis	The herald came,

Idaos tadeka . . . ph [. .].is tachus an-
    gelos
"tas t' allas Asias .[.]de. an kleos aph-
    thiton.
5   Ektor kai sunetair[o]i agois' elikopida
Thebas ex ieras Plakias t' ap'
    [aï]n<n>ao
abran Andromachan eni nausin ep'
    almuron
ponton. Polla d' [eli]gmata chrusia
    kammata
porphur[a] kataüt[me]na, poikil' ath-
    urmata,
10   argura t' anarithma poteria kalephais."
os eip.' otraleos d' anorouse pat[e]r
    philos.
phama d' elthe kata ptolin euruchoron
    philois.
autik' Iliadai satinai[s] up' eutrochois
agon aimionois, ep[e]baine de pais
    ochlos
15   gunaikon t' ama parthenika[n] t
    . . .[. .]. sphuron,
choris d' au Peramoio thug[a]tres [
ipp[ois] d' andres upagon up' ar[mata
p [ ] es eitheoi, megalo[s]ti d[
d [ ] aniochoi ph[ ]
20   p [ ]xa o[
    [Several verses are missing here.]

        i]keloi theoi[s
        ] agnon aol[le
ormatai [   ]non es Ilio[n
aulos d' adu[m]eles [   ]t' onem-
    ignu[to
25   kai ps[o]pho[s k]rotal[on]os d' ara
    par[thenoi
aeidon melos agn[on, ika]ne d' es
    aith[era
acho thespesia gel[

Idaeus . . . swift messenger
[who said]:
" . . . and of the rest of Asia . . . the
    fame is undying.
Hektor and his companions are bring-
    ing a quick-glancing girl
from holy Thebes and the river
    Plakia—
tender Andromache—in ships upon
    the salty
sea; many golden bracelets and purple
    garments
. . . many-colored adornments,
countless silver cups and ivory."
So he spoke. Quickly [Hektor's] dear
    father leaped up;
the word went out over the broad-
    plained city to his friends.
At once the sons of Ilos yoked mules
to the well-wheeled chariots. The
    whole throng
of women and . . . of maidens . . .
But apart, the daughters of Priam . . .
and unmarried men yoked horses to
    the chariots,
and greatly . . .
. . . charioteers . . .

. . . like to the gods . . .
. . . holy . . .
set forth . . . to Ilium
and the sweet-melodied aulos [and
    kitharis] were mingled,
and the noise of castanets. . . . Then
    the maidens
sang a holy song; the divine echo
    reached the sky . . .

pantai d' es kat' odo[is	and everywhere along the road . . .
krateres phialai t' o [. . .] uede [. .] .	libation vessels . . .,
. eak[.].[	
30 *murra kai kasia libanos t' onem-*	myrrh and cassia and frankincense
eichnuto	were mingled.
gunaikes d' elelusdon osai progen-	
estera[i	But the women, as many as were older,
pantes d' andres eperaton iachon or-	cried out,
thion	and all the men shouted a high-pitched
paon' onkaleontes Ekabolon euluran	lovely song,
umnen d' Ektora k' Andromachan	calling upon Paean, the far-shooting
theo<e>ikelo[is.	and well-lyred;
[The evidence in the papyrus indicates	they sang of Hektor and Andromache,
that this is the point at which the	like to the gods.
song ended.]	

Fragment 44, of which all or parts of thirty-four lines have been preserved in another Oxyrhynchus papyrus, describes the return of Hektor to Troy together with his new bride, Andromache, as well as the preparations of the Trojans to celebrate the arrival of the newlyweds. Leaving aside the complete "Hymn to Aphrodite," this is the longest fragment of Sappho's poetry that we have. From the evidence in the papyrus in which the piece is preserved, we know that it was the last poem in Book 2 of the Alexandrian collection of Sappho's songs. Several writers of late antiquity (including Athenaeus, second century A.D.) also cite the song as they comment on particular details, thus doubly confirming Sappho's authorship.[15]

In form fragment 44 is unusual in that it was not written in stanzas but rather in a line-by-line arrangement, each line being in virtually identical rhythms. The meter is usually described as glyconic but with a dactylic expansion: xx/ –∪∪–∪∪–∪∪–/∪–. The dactylic element, a long syllable followed by two short syllables (–∪∪), is so named from the Greek word for finger, *daktulos,* representing one long element from the first to the second finger joint, followed by two short elements on either side of the joint nearest the fingertip. The long-short-short dactylic rhythms in this poem clearly echo, although they do not precisely duplicate, the dactylic hexameter in which both the *Iliad* and the *Odyssey* were composed. Thus even without the Trojan subject matter, the hearers of the song would most likely have been expecting something relating to epic.

The epic context would have been suggested as well by the several Homeric epithets and by the number of dialect forms in this song that are peculiar to the

Homeric form of the Greek language, as opposed to the dialect spoken on Lesbos (Lesbian-Aeolic dialect). To give just one example, the word for "city" in line 12 takes the Homeric form *ptolin,* whereas in Sappho's usual dialect the word would have been pronounced *polin* (or, in the subject case, *polis,* from which the English word "political" derives).

Although it is hard to say how much of the song is missing, we may have the essential narrative elements more or less intact: the herald Idaeus's announcement of the impending arrival of Hektor and Andromache along with his description of the bridal trousseau; the reaction of Hektor's father, King Priam; the spread of the news throughout Troy and the consequent preparations on the part of the women, girls, and young men; and, finally, the scene of celebration at the end involving musical instruments, incense, and everyone singing the praises of the bride and groom.

We note that in the course of the narrative as we have it Hektor and Andromache still do not seem actually to have arrived in Troy. It is their *impending* arrival, and the busy preparations of everyone expecting it, that gives this fragment a certain breathless excitement. The Iliadic context of the war fought over Helen's abduction to Troy seems far from the scene. No weapons are mentioned, nor war-chariots, but only the *satine* of line 13, a special kind of woman's carriage not mentioned in Homer.

The self-referential quality of fragment 44 becomes obvious when we realize that in the absence of the actual narration of the arrival of the bride and groom (at least in the extant portion), the piece is essentially a song about singing.[16] In fact the scene of singing at the end is so vividly presented that we almost sense the arrival of the subjects even though the extant narrative never actually says, "And then Hektor and Andromache disembarked and proceeded through Troy." Even if the actual arrival was narrated in the gap following line 20, as seems probable, the piece may still have focused more on the reaction of the townspeople and on their celebratory preparations than on the heroic couple themselves.

As I suggested earlier, the attention in this song to domestic details is really more reminiscent of the *Odyssey* than of the *Iliad,* except perhaps for the scene of domestic tranquillity that is part of the description of the decoration on Achilles' new shield (*Iliad* 18.561–72). The herald's report of Andromache's gold bracelets and purple garments and many-colored (*poikila,* see chapter 5) adornments, the music of the *aulos* (a double-reed instrument of the oboe family), lyre (if the supplement *kitharis* is accepted in line 24), and castanets, and the myrrh, cassia, and frankincense: all these details appeal to our senses of sight, sound, and smell, and evoke a world of beauty and harmony. The setting may be superficially Homeric, but Homer, or at least the Iliadic Homer, seems to have exited the scene. Instead of war and strife, we hear of finery and music, of joyful sounds to celebrate the union of the happy couple.

Troy Recast: An Old Myth in a New Context

Scholars have wondered whether this song about an epic bride and groom might not have been composed to be sung at an actual wedding on Lesbos.[17] While we have no way of knowing the answer to such a question for sure, it does seem relevant to point out that the Homeric subtext of fragment 44 suggests that such a function would have been unlikely.[18] After all, once the war begins (after the narrative time frame of Sappho's lyric piece), Hektor is eventually killed by Achilles (*Iliad* Book 22), young Astyanax (son of Hektor and Andromache) is thrown from the walls of Troy, and Andromache herself is taken captive and subjected to the life of a slave, as she herself foretells at the close of the *Iliad* (24.725–45). These tragic outcomes, although not directly alluded to in Sappho's song about the beginning of their relationship, cannot help but color the listener's perception of the joyful celebrations in honor of the two epic figures. Even though Sappho chooses to focus her song on celebration and joyful beginnings and a sense of eager anticipation, thus creating a mini-epic that provides a respite from the usual Iliadic themes of war and suffering and death, the vignette she creates represents only an initial moment of the story that is all too familiar in its unhappy outcome. In fact it is the inevitability of misfortune that gives Sappho's lyric version a special poignancy, for we know that the sounds of joy echoing among the people of Troy will one day be replaced by sounds of lamentation after Hektor meets his doom at the hands of Achilles. For the moment of the song itself, however, Hektor and Andromache are *ikeloi theois* (line 21, "like to the gods"), a theme echoed in the final word of the song describing them as *theoeikelois* (literally, "godlike").

If we consider this song without regard to its intended function (if any), we can turn our attention to the exquisitely colorful detail and the emphasis on women's roles that are characteristics of Sappho's other songs. The bride's dowry, for example, includes golden bracelets, purple robes, many-colored (*poikila*) adornments, and silver cups. The women and girls ride in mule-drawn carriages, whereas the young men are in horse-drawn chariots. The girls sing a holy song, while the older women (line 31) cry out and the men sing a song to Apollo, and everyone sings the praises of the bride and groom. Page is probably right in his conclusion that Sappho "is not at all concerned to portray a Homeric scene."[19] In addition to the lack of epic models for the type of scene she describes, the particular details such as the women's carriages (line 13), the castanets (line 25), and the myrrh, cassia, and frankincense (line 30) are not found anywhere in the *Iliad* or the *Odyssey.*

What are we to make of this un-Homeric scene drawn from the world of the Homeric heroes? Like fragment 16, fragment 44 offers us an old myth in a new context. Just as the Sapphic Helen of fragment 16 provides a positive example of erotic self-fulfillment, so here the celebratory scene of joyful anticipation suggests what the union of Hektor and Andromache might have been: a long and happy marriage unmarred by the scars of death and destruction. The sensual details of color, sound, and scent describe a delightful scene that is a far cry from the battlefields of Troy.[20] As I will suggest in the following chapter, the details in this song accord perfectly with the aesthetic ideal described elsewhere in Sappho's verses—a world in which delicate variegation (*poikilia*) is the hallmark of a beautiful and orderly microcosm. Here there is no need for heroic exploits, contests of strength, or battles of will, for none of these is critical to Sapphic *eros.*

It would be tempting to wonder—if we had more of Sappho's poetry on which to form a judgment—whether or not she tended to use Homeric and other traditional myths in the same way that the great choral lyric poets of the early fifth century did.[21] Writers like Pindar of Thebes or Bacchylides of Keos routinely include allusions to or retellings of the old myths in their odes in order to illustrate some maxim or suggest a connection between the old story and the subject of the song at hand, usually with a moralizing slant. Sappho's contemporary Alkaios—although it is hard to be certain in view of the fragmentary nature of his songs—also seems to have used the old tales to make moral statements, as in the contrast he draws between the destruction wrought by Helen and the heroic offspring produced by Thetis, mother of Achilles (fragment 42 V.).[22] I venture to hazard a guess that Sappho used the old myths as she saw fit to enhance her descriptions of her female-oriented world. The fragments of her songs suggest little concern with moral pronouncements. Instead, she freely adapts traditional material to suit her own purposes, whether to suggest an epic precedent for the primacy of *eros* as experienced by the archetypal woman, Helen, to compare female beauty to the legendary pulchritude of Hermione and Helen, or to narrate a scene of splendid nuptial celebration seemingly far removed from the epic context of the Trojan War.

CHAPTER FIVE

The Aesthetics of Sapphic Eros

The preceding four chapters have focused on specific Sapphic fragments (and the one complete song), in an attempt to show how a woman-centered reading of Sappho's poetry can offer to the modern audience a productive "fiction" of her that differs significantly from those readings that try primarily to place her in a historically determined social framework. Valiant and useful as those efforts are, they need to be tempered by an awareness of the paucity of our evidence for Archaic Lesbos and of the tendency of scholars to posit one or another social custom or ritual (often on the basis of analogy from other, better-known parts of Greece) and then to explain a fragment of a poem primarily in terms of that custom or ritual.[1] In many cases, such studies may of course deepen our understanding of ancient performance practices, and certainly they keep us from blithely assuming that ancient lyric poetry can be easily understood by analogy with modern lyric poetry. Here I offer instead another approach, one that assumes that Sappho's text—even in its battered state—has the power to stand alone, with the benefit of very little ancient social context to help explain the author's purpose or intention.

Now that we have looked in detail at most of the longer fragments of what is left, the question arises as to whether it is possible, with the aid of some of the shorter fragments as well, to reconstruct a model that describes the overall aesthetic framework of lesbian desire as it is articulated in Sappho's poetry. Can we determine a cluster of broad concepts that seem to serve as the basis for Sappho's construction of desire? We have already seen the importance of *poikilia*

("variegation") in connection with the "Hymn to Aphrodite" and with fragment
22 V. (see chapters 1 and 2). Both that notion and the ideals of *charis* (roughly
translated, "grace" or "favor") and *habrosune* ("delicacy," "lushness") occur frequently in Sappho's text and, as I will argue, offer a coherent framework for
interpreting many descriptive details in the fragments as significant symbols of
a Sapphic aesthetic, not merely as trivial minutiae. What might be seen as a
trifling bit of frippery in a reference to a woman's sandal that is *poikilos* (fragment 39 V.), for instance, may in fact carry an expressive power that is not at
all unrelated to the description of Aphrodite as *poikilothronos* in the grand opening line of the "Hymn to Aphrodite" (see chapter 1).

The present chapter, then, will attempt to explore the essential aesthetic
underpinnings of Sapphic desire, a desire that is closely associated with the
Archaic Greek notion of the *Charites* (the "Graces," thought of as three in number). It is clear from the fragments discussed so far that Sapphic *eros* is grounded
in physical beauty. In fragment 31 V., for example (see chapter 2), the narrator
reacts to the beloved woman not so much on any sort of spiritual or emotional
level as on a direct, physical one, and *eros* affects the narrator's body in a remarkably direct way. What is the source of this kind of physical beauty and the *eros*
that it inspires? It is not a question of symmetry and proportion, often said in
modern analyses to be the overriding factors in accounting for physical attrac-
tiveness.[2] Rather, to the Archaic mind-set physical beauty is attributable to the
three *Charites,* the daughters of Zeus and the otherwise obscure Eurynome:
Aglaia ("Radiance"), Euphrosyne ("Joy"), and Thalia ("Bloom").[3]

Although elsewhere in Archaic literature (in Hesiod's poems, for example)
the *Charites* may represent the double-edged sword of beguiling allurement, in
Sappho they are always viewed as a positive force.[4] The quality of *charis* associated with these deities is of prime importance, and only a child can be said to
be appropriately *acharis* (roughly speaking, "without grace"). The positive light
in which Sappho views the *Charites* and the special prominence that she grants
to the quality of *charis* (and related qualities) throughout her poetry give the
Sapphic corpus its unique stamp. If we can grasp the notion of erotic *charis*—
with its rich range of meanings, including "grace," "favor," "exchange," and
"pleasure"—we will go a long way toward understanding the frame of reference within which Sappho depicts erotic desire. It is a frame of reference that
emphasizes reciprocity and grace over qualities usually more apparent in male
homosexual contexts among some Greek writers, including, for example, hierarchy and subordination.[5] We will begin with the various aspects of *charis* in
Sappho's poetry and then proceed to examine the other aesthetic qualities that
seem to have erotic significance.

My task here is made much easier by the recent book by Bonnie MacLachlan,

The Age of Grace: Charis in Early Greek Poetry, to which I am much indebted.[6] She presents a detailed analysis of the word *charis* and its linguistic relatives, showing how the term developed in different genres and time periods. Those who want to explore the concept of *charis* (the parent of the English word "charisma") further should consult her excellent study, which is both readily accessible to the novice and helpful to the experienced reader of classical literature.

The family of words under investigation for the moment includes the following: *Charites* (the "Graces"); *charis* (the singular of the preceding, "grace," "favor," etc.); *charieis* ("full of grace," "elegant"); *chara* ("joy"); *charisdomai* ("I show favor to someone"); and *chairo* ("I rejoice," see discussion of fragment 22 V. in chapter 2). All these Greek words are derived from a common Indo-European root, namely **gher-*, meaning "pleasure."[7]

The Charites

The erotic connotations of the various words in the *charis* group may perhaps be most clearly seen in the Archaic poet Hesiod's description of the origins of the three Graces, or *Charites.* Hesiod (eighth century B.C.) relates that among Zeus's many mates was Eurynome, the daughter of Oceanus, who gave birth to the three "beautiful-cheeked" *Charites.* He goes on to explain that

> *Eros,* limb-loosening, drips from their eyes as they glance about;
> beautifully do they glance from beneath their brows.
>
> (Hesiod, *Theogony* 910–11)

Hesiod thus makes a direct link between *eros* and the *Charites,* who seem to radiate beams of erotic desire from their eyes.[8] A slightly later lyric poet, Alkman of Sparta (seventh century B.C.), similarly describes the *Charites* as *eroglepharoi,* "glancing *eros*" from their eyelids.[9]

It is not surprising, then, to find the *Charites* as a presence in several of the fragments of Sappho's songs. Two fragments in which they are mentioned in the context of an invitation sound like the opening lines of poems:

FRAGMENT 53 V.

Brodopachees agnai Charites, deute *Dios korai*	Rosy-armed divine Graces, daughters of Zeus, come hither[10]

FRAGMENT 128 V.

Deute nun abrai Charites kallikomoi te *Moisai*	Come hither now, tender Graces and beautiful-haired Muses

The likely initial position of these lines is confirmed by another similar fragment preserved in a list of various songs' opening lines:

FRAGMENT 103 V., LINE 5

] . . . *agnai Charites Pieride[s te]*	[Hither] divine Graces and Pierian
Moi[sai	Muses

These summonses to the Graces were most likely in the context of a song on erotic themes, whether a wedding song or a woman-centered song like fragment 31. A fourth-century A.D. Greek rhetorician named Himerius (Sappho fragment 194 V.) paraphrases what was evidently a wedding song, reporting that Sappho has Aphrodite herself come into the bridal chamber riding on the chariot of the *Charites,* accompanied by a chorus of *erotes* ("Loves," the plural of *eros*). Elsewhere the same rhetorician appears to allude to the lesbian aspect of Sappho's poetry, noting the prominent role of the *Charites* in her songs (fragment 221 V.): "Since Sappho alone was in love with women in her lyric, and for this reason offered up all her poetry to Aphrodite and to the Erotes, she made girls and the *Charites* the occasion for her songs."[11]

In another fragment assigned by most scholars to Sappho (fragment 44A V.) the *Charites* seem to be linked to the Muses as in fragment 128 and fragment 103 above, but the lines are too broken to offer much intelligibility. In fragment 81 V., however, the *Charites* are clearly associated with the pleasing effect of garlands of flowers:

FRAGMENT 81 V.

]aputhes [	O Dika, put lovely garlands on your
]chistal[	tresses,
] emp[	binding together shoots of dill in your
su de stephanois, o Dika, perthesth' era-	tender hands.
tois phobaisin	For the blessed Graces favor(?) more
orpakas aneto sun<a>errais' apalaisi	the well-flowered,
chersin.	but turn away the ungarlanded.
euanthea gar peletai kai Charites ma-	
kaira<i>	
mallon proteren, astephanotoisi d'	
apustrephontai.	

We have already seen the erotic connotations of garlands and flowers in Sappho's lyrics (most particularly in fragment 2 and fragment 94, see chapters 1 and 3), a connection that is confirmed here by the implication that the *Charites* are more likely to shed their grace on Dika if she is adorned with garlands of the delicate yellow flowers of dill. Although the Greek text of this fragment is corrupt and the larger context uncertain, the description suggests the prominent role that the Graces played in Sappho's songs, both as the inspirers of desire and (along with the Muses) of poetry itself.

Charis *and Related Words*

Once we have understood the erotic associations of the Archaic *Charites*—certainly much more potent deities than, say, the "Three Graces" of Renaissance poetry—then we can begin to have some appreciation of the resonance that attaches to related words like *charis* ("pleasure," "favor"), *chairo* ("I take pleasure," "I rejoice"), and *charieis* ("full of favor") in Sappho's songs. In fragment 2 V., for example, when the narrator summons Aphrodite to come to the "lovely grove of apple trees," the adjective describing the grove (*charien,* 2.3) means, literally, "full of *charis.*" The sacred space of the apple grove to which Aphrodite is being invited in fragment 2 is, in addition to being filled with the sound of rustling leaves and the smell of frankincense burning on the altars, permeated with *charis.*

Before we look at other occurrences of the *charis* family of words in Sappho's songs, a few general observations about the concept involved will prove useful. Although *charis* is somewhat more abstract than the personified *Charites* we discussed above, the word nevertheless basically indicates a physical property that can attach to things like the especially attractive earrings that Hera dons in preparation for the famous "seduction of Zeus" scene in *Iliad* 14. Relying on various forms of aid from Aphrodite and Sleep, she concocts her plan to distract Zeus long enough for Poseidon to grant the upper hand (for a while) to the Greeks in their struggle against the Trojans. In *Iliad* 14.183 Homer describes in detail the earrings that she selects to go along with the rest of her elaborate garb, concluding that "much *charis* shone from them." Like the *eros* dripping from the eyes of the *Charites* in Hesiod's description, *charis* is a quality that radiates visibly from the enticingly beautiful earrings.[12]

MacLachlan has clearly demonstrated the inherently reciprocal nature of *charis,* which to the Archaic Greek way of thinking implies not just "grace" or "pleasure" or "favor" but also an *exchange* of favors. The word suggests a symmetrical relationship between the giver and receiver of pleasure. As MacLachlan points out, the reciprocal quality of *charis* "was founded upon a very general psychological phenomenon, the disposition to return pleasure to someone who has given it."[13] Perhaps by now it will be apparent why it is so difficult to find a single word in English to translate what in essence describes both a physical *property* (e.g., the "grace" that emanates from Hera's earrings) and a *phenomenon* of pleasurable exchange (e.g., the pleasure given to Zeus in seeing Hera's attractive appearance, and the consequent pleasure that he returns to her in the course of their lovemaking).

The verbal form of *charis,* namely *chairo,* which I discuss in more detail below, shares all the same multiple layers of meanings as the noun. *Chairo* means "I feel pleasure" or "I rejoice," and at the same time at least hints at the notion of reciprocity—"I feel *charis* and will therefore return *charis* to you." The verb in fact comes to be used in Classical Greek as a term of farewell; "Go and rejoice" is a way of wishing someone well upon his or her departure, and this form of salutation survives to the present day in modern Greek *chaire!* (plural *chairete!*), a form of greeting used on either arrival or departure that carries simultaneously the meanings of hello, hail, and farewell.

The *charis* that permeates the apple grove surrounding Aphrodite's temple in Sappho fragment 2, then, is both a tangible property of the lovely grove and an expression of the reciprocity that binds together the inviters and the invitee, who is asked to join in the festivities at her temple. Just as the goddess is asked to pour nectar gently (*abros,* 2.14), so she herself will be honored by those present at the altars, and *charis* will be exchanged so that giver and recipient become one.

Aphrodite's close association with *charis* is evident in several other short fragments that appear to be from wedding songs. Here Sappho begins the song with an address to the groom and then turns in the third line to praise of the bride:

FRAGMENT 112 V.

Olbie gambre, soi men de gamos os arao	Fortunate bridegroom, your marriage
ektetelest', echeis de parthenon, an	that you prayed for
arao,	has been brought to pass, and you have
soi charien men eidos, oppata d' . . .	the girl for whom you prayed.
mellich', eros d' ep' imertoi kechutai	And you—your appearance is full of
prosopoi	grace, your eyes . . .
. . . tetimak' exocha s' Aphrodita.	gentle, and *eros* flows from your lovely
	face . . .
	Aphrodite has given you extraordinary
	honor.

Like the apple grove, the bride's face is *charien,* full of *charis.* Indeed, she is so lovely that she is practically like one of the *Charites* herself, for *eros* flows from her face just as it drips from the eyes of Hesiod's Graces.

A similar reflection of the notion that *charis* emanates from a person's eyes may be found in one of Sappho's short fragments whose specific context is unknown:

FRAGMENT 1 3 8 V.

stathi kanta(?) philos	. . . stand firm if you are a friend(?)
kai tan ep' ossois' ompetason charin	and spread around the grace that is on your eyes

Athenaeus, the second-century A.D. commentator who preserves the quota-tion, claims that the reference was to a man who was inordinately admired for his handsome appearance. In any case, Sappho's words suggest that the source of his appeal, like that of the bride in fragment 1 1 2, was in his eyes and face.

From what we can surmise from Himerius, who preserves the following snippet, this fragment, too, is from a wedding song and is addressed to the bride, who is described as full of *charis:*

FRAGMENT 1 0 8 V.

o kala, o chariessa kora	O beautiful woman, O one full of grace . . .

The same adjective appears to occur in a heavily mutilated fragment (fragment 90d. 1 3 V.) from a second-century A.D. papyrus that provides a commentary on several of Sappho's songs, but about all that can be deciphered from the surrounding context is a mention of the name Atthis, whose name also occurs as the addressee of fragment 96 (see chapter 3).

The verbal from of *charis, chairo* ("I rejoice," "I feel pleasure," etc.), must, to the Greek ear, have resonated with at least some of the same overtones of erotic reciprocity that is suggested in the various references to the *charis* that flows from a desired face. When the woman who has gone away to Lydia is described as having "taken pleasure" or "rejoiced" in Atthis's songs (fragment 96.5), there is an implication (however subtle) of pleasure received and pleasure given. In fragment 2 2.1 4 (see chapter 2), the flitting of desire around the song's ad-dressee (Abanthis) causes the singer to feel pleasure (*ego de chairo*) as she ob-serves how the flow of Gongula's dress stirs Abanthis. And in fragment 94.7, in a similar context of desire, the narrator bids the departing woman to go off rejoicing (*chairois'*) and to remember her. In two fragments that are both evi-dently from wedding songs (fragment 1 1 6 V. and fragment 1 1 7 V.), the bride and groom are likewise bidden to "rejoice" in a kind of "hail and farewell" greet-ing addressed to each.[14] In all of these contexts, the spirit of Aglaia, Euphro-syne, and Thalia is not far to seek. The three *Charites* shed their charms and work together with *eros* and the Muses to bring about both desire and song.

Now that we have seen the erotic associations of *charis* and related words, we are in a better position to understand one of Sappho's fragments in which a girl is described as *acharis*, literally, "without *charis*."

FRAGMENT 49 V.

Eraman men ego sethen, Atthis, palai pota . . .	I loved you, Atthis, once long ago. . . .
* * *	* * *
smikra moi pais emmen' ephaineo ka-charis	You seemed to me to be a small and graceless child.

It is not certain whether these two lines are consecutive, for the first line is quoted by Hephaestion as an example of the type of fourteen-syllable meter in which all the songs of Book 2 were composed (and is thus likely to be the opening line of a song), while the second line comes from a different source altogether (Plutarch). A Latin paraphrase by a grammarian named Terentianus Maurus suggests to some scholars that the two lines may have been part of the same song. In any case, allowing for considerable uncertainty owing to the textual problems, we may hypothesize that the narrator is declaring her love for Atthis at a time when Atthis herself was not yet old enough to respond to the reciprocal nature of *charis*. The literal English translation "graceless" hardly does justice to the layers of meaning here; it is not so much that the girl (*pais*, used to refer to a child, cf. English paedagogy) is described as "clumsy," for example, but rather that she is most likely prepubescent and therefore not yet subject—in Sappho's way of thinking—to the charms of Aphrodite and the Graces.[15] Desire (*pothos*) is not going to be flitting around a mere *pais*.

An awareness of the erotic and poetic associations of *charis* in Sappho's poetry can help us better understand even fragments in which the word *charis* is itself not actually present. We can assume, for example, that in the following prediction of a woman's shadowy existence in the afterlife, the unremembered and unmourned ghost never enjoyed the presence of the *Charites*. This fragment is written in the meter in which all of Book 3 of the Alexandrian collection of Sappho's lyrics were composed, a sixteen-syllable line (xx–◡◡––◡◡––◡◡–◡x) that is an expansion of the pattern known as the glyconic (xx–◡◡–◡–):

FRAGMENT 55 V.

katthanoisa de keisei oude pota mnamo-suna sethen	You will lie dead, nor will there be anyone
esset' oude pok' usteron; ou gar ped-echeis brodon	remembering or desiring you later; for you have

ton ek Pierias, all' aphanes kan aida domoi	no share in the roses of Pieria, but will roam unseen
phoitaseis ped' amauron nekuon ekpepotamena.	in the house of Hades, having flown off among dim corpses.

Without actually mentioning the word *charis,* Sappho seems to be implying that this woman, who has no share in poetry and song (the roses of Pieria, the birthplace of the nine Muses), stands far outside the charmed circle of those blessed by the *Charites.* As a result, after her death there will be neither any recollection of her nor any longing for her. The song condemns her to an eternal amorphous, anonymous existence among the shades of the dead.

Given what appears to have been a prominent *leitmotif* in Sappho's songs in the recurring presence of *charis* and the *Charites,* we find a fitting tribute to the great poet of Lesbos in a short epigram written by a later Greek woman poet, Nossis of Locri, in southern Italy. Writing in the Hellenistic period, perhaps about 300 B.C., or some three centuries after Sappho, the speaker addresses a passerby who is en route to Lesbos (or Mytilene, its chief city):

NOSSIS *A.P.* 7.718

> Stranger, if you sail toward Mytilene of the beautiful dances
> to be inspired by the flower of Sappho's charms [*charites*],
> Say that the land of Locri gave birth to one dear to the Muses,
> and when you have learned that my name is Nossis, go your way.

In this little epigram, modeled after tombstone addresses to the passerby, Nossis claims for herself a direct link to the earlier poet. The few remaining samples of Nossis's poetry suggest that she herself was indeed much inspired by the "flower of Sappho's *charites,*" whether we are to take the word simply as the plural of *charis* ("graces," or "charms") or as the three *Charites.* In either case, Nossis seems to be encapsulating a fundamental aspect of Sapphic song, which lends inspiration to and fosters the flowering of desire through the all-important presence of the *Charites.*[16]

Habrosune ("Lushness")

Another important quality repeatedly alluded to in Sapphic song is what the Greeks called *habrosune,* which translates roughly as "tenderness" or "lushness" or "delicacy." (This word and its related forms like *habros,* "tender," were all pronounced in the Lesbian-Aeolic dialect without the initial "h" sound.) Although in later Greek, even as early as the fifth century, the word takes on the connotation of excessive self-absorption and Oriental effeteness, in the Archaic period among the authors identified with the eastern Greek islands like Lesbos and Samos, it appears that *habrosune* represented an aesthetic ideal that was associated favorably with the charms of Eros and Aphrodite. The earliest occurrence of the adjective *habros* (which is not found in Homer) is in Hesiod fragment 218 (Rzach), who describes a young girl as "tender" or "lush."[17] It is primarily in the hands of later western Greek writers like the fifth-century historian Thucydides that "lushness" turns into something more pejorative, like "luxuriousness."[18]

The link between *charis,* Aphrodite, and the concept of *habrosune* can be seen clearly in Sappho's invitation to the goddess to join in the festivities at her temple in fragment 2 (see chapter 1).[19] Aphrodite is invited to come to the *charis*-filled apple grove and to pour nectar "tenderly" or "gently" (*[h]abros*). As we have already observed in connection with fragment 128 above, the *Charites* themselves are described as *[h]abrai,* "tender," "delicate," in what seems to be a joint invocation to the Graces and the Muses. In both of these cases, the context indicates that the underlying notion of *habrosune* (literally, the quality of being *habros*) is a positive, desirable one. Aphrodite and the *Charites* are identifed with a kind of tender, delicate lushness that is something to be emulated rather than avoided.

The notion of lushness can also be seen in the following fragment, in which the vegetation deity Adonis, who spends part of the year in the Underworld (like Persephone) and part as the consort of Aphrodite, is described as *[h]abros:*

FRAGMENT 140 V.

Katthanaskei, Kuthere', abros Adonis.	"Tender Adonis is dying, Cytherea.
ti ke theimen?	What are we to do?"
kattuptesthe, korai, kai katereikesthe	"Beat your breasts, maidens, and rend
chitonas.	your chitons."

Cast in dialogue form, the fragment apparently refers to the festival of the Adonia, in which Adonis's yearly death was mourned and his subsequent annual rebirth celebrated. In this instance it is not Aphrodite herself (Cytherea) but her consort, the young vegetation deity, who is described as *habros*. The adjective reminds us that it is only through Adonis's annual rebirth that the lushness of the crops returns to the world.

Besides its three occurrences mentioned above, the adjective *habros* is also found in four other passages from Sappho's fragments. In fragment 44 V. (see chapter 4), the bride Andromache is described as *habros,* certainly an appropriate epithet in view of the marriage context. In fragment 25 V. (line 4) the word appears, but in a totally unintelligible context, and in fragment 84 V. (line 5), the word *habros* can be deciphered in close proximity to the mention of the goddess Artemis (herself also connected with plants and animals). Finally, fragment 100 V., cited by the compiler who preserves the fragment as being from Book 5 of Sappho's lyrics, seems to mention some kind of soft clothing which is described as *[h]abros:*

FRAGMENT 100 V.

amphi d' abrois' . . . lasiois' eu	(She?) covered her well with delicate
<w'> epukassen	shag

The ancient compiler who quotes the passage claims that *lasion* here refers to pieces of finely woven linen. Whatever the exact nature of the clothing is, it is clear that the quality of *habrosune* can attach not only to brides like Andromache and to Aphrodite and the Graces and other deities, but also to *things* like fine clothing.

We come now to a badly shredded but relatively lengthy papyrus fragment in which the narrator of the song boldly proclaims at the very end of the song— in what seems to be a programmatic statement—that she loves *[h]abrosune.*[20] Although working with a text that is missing the first several words of most of its lines of verse is certainly frustrating, we can at least get some idea of what such a statement might imply, particularly in the light of the other contexts (discussed above) in which *habros* occurs. Enough of the text survives so that the meter in this song may be identified as a sixteen-syllable line that is a varia- tion on a pattern called the hipponactean; the pattern of long and short syllables in this case is x–∪∪––∪∪––∪∪–∪–x:

FRAGMENT 58 V.

	] . [		
	] . da[		
	]		
	] . a		
5	*] ugoisa[ ]*	5	. . . fleeing(?)
	] idachthen		. . . was bitten(?)
	]chu th [ ] oi [ ] all [ ] utan		. . .
	] chtho [ ] ati [ ] eisa		. . .
	] mena tan [o]numon se		name . . . you
10	*]ni thetai st[u]ma[ti] prokopsin*	10	. . . places success upon the
	]pon kala dora paides		mouth . . .

]philaoidon liguran chel-
    unnan
        pa]nta chroa geras ede
    leukai t' egeno]nto triches ek melainan
15   ]ai gona d' [o]u pheroisi
        ]esth' isa nebrioisin
        a]lla ti ken poeien?
            ] ou dunaton genesthai
            ] brodopachun Auon
20   es]chata gas pheroisa[
            ]on umos emarpse[
            ]atan akoitin
            ]imenan nomisdei
            ]ais opasdoi
25 ego de philemm' abrosunan,]touto kai
        moi
    to lampron eros aelio kai to kalon lel-
        ogche.

beautiful gifts [of the deep-
bosomed Muses?] . . . youths
. . . the song-loving, clear-
voiced tortoise-lyre
. . . old age already [dried up?]
all (my? his?) skin
and (my?) hair has all turned from
black to white
15 . . . and (my?) knees do not
support (me?)
    (to dance?) like fawns
        . . . but what am I to do?
        . . . not possible to become
        . . . rosy-armed Dawn [Eos]
20 . . . carrying [Tithonus?] to the
ends of the earth
        . . . but [old age?] seized
(him?)
            . . . immortal wife . . .
            . . . [he/she] thinks
            . . . would give . . .
25 But I love lushness. Eros has ob-
tained this(?) for me,
and the brightness and beauty of
the sun.

What we seem to have here is the right-hand side of this third-century A.D. papyrus (P. Oxy. 1787), along with the more-or-less intact final two lines of the song. Although certainty is impossible given the missing left side for most of the piece, it seems reasonably clear that the mythological material of the song concerns the story of Eos (Dawn) and Tithonus.[21] As the *Homeric Hymn to Aphrodite* (218–38) explains, when the goddess Eos fell in love with the handsome young mortal Tithonus and snatched him away to her home at the ends of the earth, she begged Zeus to grant him eternal life but forgot to request eternal youth as well. As a consequence, Tithonus eventually withered away into older and older age, shut up in a room and abandoned by his divine lover. Eva Stehle has shown that the pattern represented here (a goddess's desire for a young mortal man) is one that recurs in Sappho's poetry in various incarnations, including not only Eos and Tithonus but also Selene and Endymion, Aphrodite and Adonis, and Aphrodite and Phaon.[22] Whatever the exact significance of the pattern may have been, we may resonably assume that the Eos and Tithonus myth in this particular context was meant to illustrate the evils of old age.

In his discussion of fragment 58, Page compares Sappho's use of the story of Helen in fragment 16 (see chapter 4) as an example of a mythological reference used to illustrate what he calls a "personal theme," in that case the desire of the speaker for Anaktoria.[23] In fragment 58, because it is so fragmentary, it is difficult to know how the myth ties in with the first-person statement at the end of the song regarding the speaker's love for *habrosune*. But I offer the hypothesis that the song described various joys from which one is generally thought to be excluded by extreme old age: song, dance, the music of the lyre, *eros,* and beauty—things that might in fact be summed up in one word, namely, *habrosune*. The gifts of the Muses, the light of day, the rosy-armed Dawn, the delights of *eros*—these are all denied to the perpetually aging Tithonus, who withers away in impotent isolation. The singer of the song, however, distances herself from his experience, declaring emphatically *ego de philemm' abrosunan,* "But I love lushness." Just as in fragment 22.14 (see chapter 2), where the statement *ego de chairo* asserts the singer's sense of *charis* in relation to what has been described earlier in the song, so here the singer makes a programmatic declaration of values. Whether these values are political or poetic (or both) in nature is perhaps of less significance than the essential aesthetic quality encoded in the word *habrosune:* the delicate lushness denied to Tithonus but possessed in full measure by the *Charites* and by Aphrodite herself.

One final point must be made about fragment 58. Like fragments 22, 44, and 96, this song, too, seems in some way to be a song about singing. Whether the speaker is referring to herself at the outset of the fragment is uncertain, but in any case the reference to a tortoise-shell lyre (an instrument normally used to accompany lyric poetry) in line 12 is clear. The adjective "song-loving" in the same line could describe some missing noun, but it may well be an epithet of the lyre itself. (Elsewhere it is used to describe a shuttle, which makes singing sounds as it passes through the strands of the warp on the loom.[24]) Unless the context is a general description of the power of music and song, it may be that the singer is referring to her own poetic gifts and to the power of her lyre in providing the accompaniment to her song.

Poikilia

The third and final major component of the Sapphic aesthetic—in addition to *charis* and *habrosune*—is the quality of *poikilia* that we have already discussed in connection with the epithet *poikilothronos* in the "Hymn to Aphrodite" and also as a concept helpful for the interpretation of the theme of variegation in fragment 22 V. The adjective *poikilos* ("variegated," "intricate," "subtle") and its compounds or verbal forms occur a total of seven times in the fragments of Sappho's verse, and there are also several passages (like fragment 22) in which the underlying notion of variegation (if not the actual word) can be detected.[25]

The idea of variegation and texture contained in the word *poikilos* can be seen in an early occurrence of the word in *Iliad* Book 22, at the point in the narrative where Hektor has just been killed in combat with Achilles. Homer describes the robe woven by Andromache (who is still unaware of her husband's death) as follows:

all' e g' iston huphaine mucho domou hupseloio,	But she [Andromache] was weaving a web in the inner recesses of the lofty house,
diplaka porphureen, en de throna poikil' epasse.	a purple double-folded robe, and in it she worked embroidered flowers.
	(*Iliad* 22.440–41)

The meaning of *throna* in this passage is not entirely certain, but it seems to refer either to floral patterns or to herbs used as drugs or magic charms (as in Theocritus 2.59). The word here seems to be distinct from *thronos*, "seat" or "chair," hence English "throne." The striking resemblance of the Homeric phrase *throna poikil[a]* to the epithet for Aphrodite in Sappho's "Hymn to Aphrodite," *poikilothron'*, however, reveals a potential layering of meaning in the way that Aphrodite is addressed in Sappho's song; the goddess evidently sits on an elaborately wrought throne, but she also perhaps has access to an elaborate array of drugs or charms that are potentially efficacious in matters of love.[26] In any case, whether it is her throne or her magic charms (or both) that are elaborately wrought, Aphrodite is closely identified in the opening line of the song with the quality of variegation.

The Homeric connection between *poikilia* and elaborately embroidered clothing such as the purple robe that Andromache wears is evident also in at least four of Sappho's fragments in which the adjective occurs. In a tantalizingly short piece of a song in Sapphic stanzas there appears this description of a woman's sandal:

FRAGMENT 39 V.

poda<s> de poikilos masles ekalupte, Ludion kalon ergon	an embroidered sandal was hiding (her) feet, a beautiful piece of Lydian work

Poikilos here may refer to the elaborate tooling of designs in the leather straps of the sandals, evidently imported shoes made in the neighboring country of Lydia.[27] Similarly, the reference in the description of Andromache's dowry in Sappho fragment 44 (see chapter 4) to *poikil' athurmata,* "many-colored adornments," probably includes elaborately wrought clothing and jewelry, occurring as it does in the midst of a catalogue of just such items (fragment 44.8–9).

The importance of *poikilia* in the Sapphic standard of beauty is especially apparent in a relatively lengthy fragment that is preserved in a third-century B.C. papyrus. As Page notes, this papyrus is several centuries older than any other we have containing the poetry of either Sappho or Alkaios, its early date putting it on a par with the third-century B.C. potsherd that preserves a garbled version of fragment 2.[28] The meter in this instance is a three-line stanza that is based on the glyconic (xx-◡◡-◡-); the first two lines are simply the eight-syllable glyconic, and the third line of each stanza is an expanded glyconic:

FRAGMENT 98 V.

a

1   . . . *thos; a gar m' egenna[t*   . . . for my mother [said that]

   s]phas ep' alikias meg[an   in her youth it was indeed a great orna-
   k]osmon ai tis eche phoba<i>s[ment if
4 *porphuroi katelixame[na*   someone had tresses
                                   wrapped in a purple [band].

   emmenai mala touto [But the girl who has hair
   alla xanthotera<i>s eche[brighter than a fiery torch
7 *ta<i>s koma<i>s daidos proph[*

   s]tephanoisin epartia[is   should wear[?] wreaths
   antheon erithaleon; [of blooming flowers.
10 *m]itranan d' artios kl[*

   poikilan apu Sardio[n   Just now a many-coloured
   . . .*] aonias pol(e)is [*   headband from Sardis . . .

b   b

   soi d' ego Klei poikilan [For you, Kleis, I have no
   ouk echo—pothen essetai? [many-colored headband, nor
3 *mitran[an]; alla toi Mutilenaoi[*   do I know where one will come from.
   . . .   But for the Mytilenean . . .
   ] . [

pai. a. eion echen po . [	. . . grows many-colored(?) . . .
6 *aike e poikilask . . . .*	. . . these memories of the exile
tauta tas Kleanaktida [	of the sons of Kleanax . . .
phugas . . . isapolisechei	. . . for they wasted away terribly . . .
9 *mnamat' . ide gar aina dierrue [n*	

Remarkable for its apparent reference to a current political figure, in the phrase "sons of Kleanax" (probably the tyrant Myrsilus, so prominently reflected in the political framework of Alkaios's poetry), this curious fragment provides us with a perfect illustration of the aesthetic described in the present chapter—an aesthetic that values charm, lushness, and variegation over other potential standards of beauty such as evenness, symmetry, and form. The relationship of the apparent political allusion here to the subject of the poem is unclear, but we can guess that perhaps the deprivations of life in exile were somehow contrasted to the images of beauty mentioned earlier in the song— the purple headband, the girl whose shining hair is crowned with flowers, the many-colored (*poikilan*) headband from Sardis and the one (also *poikilan*) that the narrator wishes she had for Kleis. Although the text of line 6 in the (b) portion of the fragment is not at all certain, there appears to be yet another occurrence of a word related to *poikilia,* perhaps an inceptive verb from that might mean "to grow or become many-colored" (*poikilask-*).

While we cannot profitably speculate as to what the central focus of this song was, the attention to the items of physical beauty associated with the females mentioned in the extant scraps is certainly reminiscent of the configuration of desire in fragment 22, where the flow of Gongula's dress inspires the fluttering of *pothos* in Abanthis as she gazes upon her. Whether or not the context in fragment 98 is erotic, the details such as the purple headband, fiery-bright hair, floral wreaths, and the many-colored headband from Sardis represent the kinds of flashes of beauty that Sappho associates with desire: the bright sparkle of Anaktoria's face, for example (fragment 16); the grace (*charis*) radiating from a bride (fragment 112); or wreaths of violets, roses, and saffron and anointings with costly myrrh (fragment 94). Such details of appearance, clothing, and adornment are essential aspects of the Sapphic texture of desire.

If the attribution to Sappho (by Wilamowitz) of the following four-line fragment is correct, even the earth itself displays the quality of variegation that we have seen so intimately bound up with the Sapphic aesthetic:

FRAGMENT 168C V.

poikilletai men	. . . it is many-colored—
gaia polustephanos	the earth, much-garlanded . . .

Quoted by a Hellenistic author named Demetrius (*On Style*) as an example of how beautiful language creates grace (*charis*) in poetry, the fragment seems to describe the earth as a weaver of her own floral embroidery.[29] Crowned with garlands—perhaps at springtime?—the earth's tapestry of colors becomes as one with the many-colored throne of Aphrodite, or the many-colored sandal that hid a woman's foot, or the many-colored headband that was not to be found for Kleis.

Charis and the *Charites, habrosune,* and *poikilia:* these are the distinctive qualities that stand out as hallmarks of Sappho's worldview. It is not a world of self-restraint and denial of material and physical pleasures; rather, it is a sacred space, like the apple grove (full of *charis*) to which Aphrodite is invited in fragment 2, in which one can luxuriate in the grace and beauty that surrounds one. To someone outside that sacred space, such a *Weltanschauung* might smack of Oriental hedonism, of luxurious temptations and frivolous indulgences; to someone who stands within the apple grove, however, the *Charites* seem close at hand, glancing beautifully from beneath their brows and offering the limb-loosening *eros* that drips from their eyes. It is a lush space rich with unfolding erotic possibilities—even, perhaps, the manifestation of Aphrodite herself.

CHAPTER SIX

Sappho's Other Lyric Themes

Despite the unquestionable prominence of Aphrodite, Eros, and woman-centered passions in the songs she composed, Sappho's role as a lyric poet treated a wide range of other themes as well. The present chapter provides an overview of most of the remaining fragments of any substance (i.e., more than three or four connected words) that have not been discussed earlier in this book in an attempt to illustrate what that range most likely was. If we were miraculously to discover a complete copy of the nine books of Sappho's lyrics, we would find songs of prayer, marriage songs, folk songs, festival songs, and no doubt a variety of other kinds of lyric musings on everything from the traditional Greek myths to events of daily life.

Although some of the shorter fragments discussed in this chapter are preserved in tattered papyrus rolls, many of them come from quotations by ancient grammarians or commentators who wrote many centuries after Sappho's time and who were chiefly interested in some peculiarity of dialect or a metrical phenomenon illustrated by the words they chose to quote. Generally speaking, they provide little or no help as to the context of the words quoted. Short of grouping these fragments into five general categories, I have not attempted to supply any missing context. Tempting though it is to try to imagine in what sort of poem the phrase "the black sleep of night [covers] the eyes" (fragment 151 V.) might have occurred, for example, such speculative guesswork is perhaps not as productive as one's simple indulgence in the evocative nature of any fragment. Like the ruins of an ancient temple, these bits and pieces of song stand as hieroglyphic enigmas that stir the imagination without necessarily begging for actual reconstruction.[1] Unlike the ruins of the Parthenon, however, these literary ruins are in no danger of collapse should we choose to let them simply stand as fragments of the original—in most cases no doubt unrecoverable—whole.

Prayers

Not surprisingly, many of the shorter fragments take the same general shape as the "Hymn to Aphrodite" discussed in chapter 1, that is, a prayer addressed to some deity or deities. We have already seen that several fragments open with an address to the *Charites* or to the Muses (see chapter 5), and other deities called upon include Hera, the Nereids, Eos (Dawn), and perhaps Apollo and Artemis.[2] The most substantial among these is the following prayer addressed to the Nereids (and Aphrodite, if, as is likely, the opening of the song has been correctly restored) for the safe return of the speaker's brother following an unspecified journey. We may assume that the poem's journey was by sea, for the daughters of Nereus are sea-goddesses who assist sailors, a role that the Cyprian Aphrodite (whose name reappears toward the end of the fragment), born from the sea, also took on:

FRAGMENT 5 V.

Kupri kai] Nereides, ablabe[n moi	O [Cyprian] and Nereids, grant
ton kasi]gneton d[o]te tuid' ikestha[i	that my brother come hither unharmed
kossa w]oi thumoi ke thele genesthai	and that as many things as he wishes in
4 *panta te]lesthen,*	his heart to come about
	are all brought to pass,
ossa de pr]osth' ambrote panta lusa[i	And that he atones for all his former
kai philois]i woisi charan genesthai	errors,
. . . e]chthroisi, genoito d' ammi	and is a joy to his [friends],
8 *. . . m]ed' eis.*	a [pain] to his enemies; but for us
	let there be no misery.
tan kasig]netan de theloi poesthai	May he wish to do honor to his sister
]timas, [on]ian de lugran	. . . painful suffering . . .
]otoisi p[a]roith' acheuon	
12 *]na*	

]eisaïo[n] to kegchro   . . . millet-seed . . . of the citizens
]lepag [. . .]ai politan   . . .
]llos [. . .]neke d' aut' ou
16   ]kro[ ]

]onaik [ ] eo [ ] i   . . . but you, Cyprian, setting aside
] n su [d]e Kup[ri] . . . na   . . .
]them[en]a kakan [
20   ]i.

Like the "Hymn to Aphrodite" and other songs that made up the opening
book of the Alexandrian edition of Sappho's work, this prayer is composed in
four-line Sapphic stanzas. Voigt and other scholars believe that what we have
left is a skeletal version of the entire song, beginning with the opening address
to Aphrodite and the Nereids in stanza one, and concluding with a repeated
address to Aphrodite in stanza five. Traditionally, the poem has been read auto-
biographically in conjunction with the statements in the historian Herodotus
(2.134 ff.) regarding Sappho's brother Charaxos. Herodotus reports that Charaxos went to Naucratis in Egypt, where he purchased the freedom of a famous
courtesan named Rhodopis with whom he was enamored. When he got home,
Herodotus continues, Sappho mocked him for his actions in one of her poems.
Is fragment 5 that poem? If it is, is our understanding of the fragment likely to
be helped much by the remark of a historian writing some one hundred and
twenty-five years after Sappho's time?

Perhaps it is more to the point to examine the fragment—since we have a
substantial portion of it left—in comparison with other ancient prayers for the
safe return of someone from a journey at sea. Such a poem was known as a
propemptikon, literally a "send-off" song in which the speaker pleads that a friend
or relative will come home safely. If an example by the Roman poet Horace
(65–8 B.C.), who was a great admirer and imitator of Sappho's poetry, is any
indication, such a piece might use the allusion to the departed person's trip as
a taking-off point for other themes as well. In *Odes* 1.3, Horace entreats
Aphrodite and the twins Kastor and Pollux to grant a safe journey to Vergil on
his way home to Italy from Athens. But after the first eight lines, the poem veers
off into philosophical musings (for another thirty-two lines) on the audacity of
human enterprise in seeking to conquer nature—as, for example, in Daedalus's
use of wings for human flight.

In Sappho's song, although the gaps prevent us from knowing exactly what
direction the poem took, it seems clear enough that the actual wish for the
brother's safe return was accomplished within the two opening lines. The re-

maining eighteen lines seem to have enlarged on this wish by setting forth a program for various kinds of reciprocal actions: the speaker prays that the brother will accomplish whatever his heart (*thumos*) desires, but that he will also atone for past mistakes; in addition, according to the conventional Greek morality (along the lines of an eye for an eye), she hopes that he will be a "joy" (*chara*) to his friends and a pain to his enemies. The speaker prays further that no pain will come to themselves, and that the brother will somehow bring honor to his sister. The song thus focuses on the reciprocity of various relation- ships—between the speaker and the addressees, between them and the brother, between the brother and his friends (or enemies), and between the brother and the speaker herself. Like the "Hymn to Aphrodite," the song em- phasizes the bonds between human and divine—and, especially in this frag- ment, between one person and another.

Another, more broken fragment (also in Sapphic stanzas) has been closely linked by scholars to fragment 5, for it appears to contain some of the same language for the notion of atonement, and it mentions a woman named Dori- cha, identified by the first-century A.D. historian Strabo (17.1.33) as the cour- tesan Rhodopis with whom Sappho's brother Charaxos was supposed to have fallen in love. Whether or not this is the case, like fragment 15, this poem, too, seems to be addressed to Aphrodite:[3]

FRAGMENT 15 V.

]*a makai*[*r*		. . . blessed (goddess?)
]*euplo* [		. . .
] *atoska* [		
4]		

]*osth'* [ ]*broteke*[		[May (s)he atone for] as many errors as
]*atais* [ ]*nem*[		(s)he made [before]
] *uchai li* [ ]*enos kl*[		. . .
8 [ ]		

Ku]*pri ka*[*i s*]*e pi*[*krot..*]*an epeur*[*oi*		Cypris, and may Doricha find you
me]*de kauchas*[*a*]*ito tod' enne*[*poisa*		most harsh,
D]*oricha to deu*[*t*]*eron os pothe*[		and may she not boast saying this,
12]*eron elthe.*		how (s)he came a second time [to]
		much-desired *eros.*

Aside from the mention of the feminine name Doricha, the gender of the subjects in this song is not apparent from what is left, but on the basis of Strabo's identification of Doricha with the courtesan Rhodopis, we may perhaps assume a heterosexual context. Evidently the speaker is praying that Aphrodite treat Doricha harshly and not give her assistance in matters of the heart—a plea exactly the opposite of the speaker's request for help in the "Hymn to Aphrodite." In that song, Aphrodite is requested to assist, as she has done many times in the past, with the repetitive, cyclical, and reciprocal aspects of *eros;* here, on the contrary, the goddess is to see to it that the flow of *eros* comes to a dead halt. There is to be no second time.

Another prayer that has survived in skeletal form is fragment 17 V., a five-stanza song (in Sapphic stanzas) that is addressed to the goddess Hera:

FRAGMENT 17 V.

Plasion de m[	Near to me, lady Hera,
potni' (H)era sa ch[	[may your lovely form appear],
tan aratan At[reidai kle-]	whom (famous) kings, the sons of
4 *toi basilees.*	Atreus,
	entreated,
ektelessantes m[	When they had accomplished [many
prota men peri [	labors],
tuid' apormathen[tes	first at Ilium [and then at sea]
8 *ouk edunanto*	setting out to here, they were not able
	[to complete the journey],
prin se kai Di' ant[	Until they [called upon] you and Zeus
kai Thuonas ime[	Antiaios
nun de k[	and the lovely [son] of Thuone.
12 *kat to pal[*	But now kindly [come to my aid]
	according to the custom of old.
agna kai ka[	Holy and beautiful . . .
p]arth[en	maidens . . .
a]mphi [	around . . .
16 *[ ]*	
[ ]	. . . to be . . .
. . . nil [	to come to . . .
emmena[i	
20 *. . . r apike[sthai.*	

Addressed to Zeus's consort Hera, this prayer reminds the goddess of her relationship with earlier Homeric entreaters, namely the Greek kings Agamemnon and Menelaus (the sons of Atreus). In the version told in Homer's *Odyssey* (3.130–83), the two brothers have quarreled and set out separately on the homeward trip after the Trojan War; only Menelaus stops at nearby Lesbos, where he prays to Zeus for guidance in choosing the best route home. In Sappho's account, however, if the supplement in line 3 is correct, both Menelaus and Agamemnon are present, and they pray not only to Zeus but also to Hera and to Dionysos (the son of Thuone, another name for Semele). In any case, it is clear that the allusion to the Homeric story is meant to serve as part of the "reminder" section of the prayer (see chapter 1 above on the reminder section in the "Hymn to Aphrodite").

The mere shreds of the final two stanzas of the song do not permit a reconstruction of what the request to Hera might have been, although the last word of the final line, "to come to" (if the supplement is correct), suggests a journey, perhaps a sea voyage like that of the sons of Atreus. Perhaps Hera is being asked to grant safe passage. Although the song mentions Hera within the context of a trinity of deities especially worshipped on Lesbos (Alkaios fragment 129 V. in all likelihood calls upon the same trinity), Hera is singled out for her especially close relationship to the singer. The goddess is evidently asked to make herself manifest in the singer's very presence—"Near to me." The woman-centered nature of Sappho's poetry is evident even in her theology, for although gods are mentioned, it is the female deities who seem to occupy center stage.

Marriage Songs

I have already mentioned in chapter 5 a few examples of fragments from Sappho's marriage songs (*epithalamia*), but here it is appropriate to discuss other examples in more detail. Some of these fragments seem to center either on the marriage ritual itself, in allusions to the song sung in honor of Hymen (the god of marriage) or on the appearance of the bridegroom. Here is the beginning of one such song, made familiar in the twentieth century through J. D. Salinger's borrowing of the opening words as the title for one of his long short stories (published in 1963):

FRAGMENT 111 V.

Ipsoi de to melathron	Rise high the roof-beams!
umenaon,	Sing the Hymeneal!
aerrete, tektones andres.	Raise it high, O carpenter men!

umenaon.	Sing the Hymeneal!
gambros (eis)erchetai isos Areui	The bridegroom enters, like to Ares,
andros megalo polu mesdon.	by far bigger than a big man.

Some readers have seen an element of risqué humor in the allusion to the size of the bridegroom as "far bigger than a big man," perhaps referring to his ithyphallic state of excitement.[4] Similar humorous exaggeration is evident in the opening of another marriage song that makes fun of the groom's attendant, the doorkeeper:

FRAGMENT 110 V.

Thuroroi podes eptoroguioi,	[At the wedding]
ta de sambala pempeboeia,	the doorkeeper's feet are seven fath-
pissungoi de dek' exeponesan	oms long,
	and his sandals are made of five ox-
	hides,
	and ten shoemakers worked away to
	make them.

Another example in which the groom's appearance is alluded to opens with the following line:

FRAGMENT 115 V.

Tioi s', o phile gambre, kalos eikasdo?	To what, dear bridegroom, may I suit-
orpaki bradinoi se malist'	ably liken you?
eikasdo. . . .	I liken you most to a slender
	sapling. . . .

The description of the groom in this fragment attributed to Sappho by Hephaestion (the second-century A.D. author of a handbook on meter) seems somewhat less than fully heroic, alluding as it may to Odysseus's likening of Nausikaa to the young shoot of a palm tree (*Odyssey* 6.163) and to Thetis's description of her son Achilles "shooting up like a tree" when he was a young child (*Iliad* 18.56). If there is any element of risqué humor here in the possibly phallic overtones of the image, the emphasis on slenderness again reduces the groom to less than heroic proportions.

While such instances of bantering raillery may have been a common feature of Sappho's hymeneals (as indeed they are in later Greek examples of the genre), other scraps of the wedding songs seem to emphasize the beauty of the bride or the poignancy of the impending loss of her girlhood status. Perhaps the most vivid example is the following fragment, which was evidently once part of a song in which the groom was likened to the hero Achilles. The meter is appropriately the dactylic hexameter of Homeric epic:

FRAGMENT 105A V.

oion to glukumalon ereuthetai akroi
    ep' usdoi,
akron ep' akrotatoi, lelathonto de ma-
    lodropees.
ou man eklelathont', all' ouk edunant'
    epikesthai.
	[the bride]
	just like a sweet apple that ripens on
	    the uppermost bough,
	on the top of the topmost; but the
	    apple-gatherers have forgotten it,
	or rather, they haven't altogether
	    forgotten it, but they could not
	    reach it.

Here desire becomes on one level the reach for the unreachable.[5] The young woman is like a beautiful, ripe red apple enjoying privileged access to the rays of the sun high up at the very top of the tree. The apple is perfect—but has only been able to achieve and maintain such a beautiful state because it was just out of the reach of the apple-pickers, who could not fulfill their desire to pluck the ripened fruit. At least within the context of the fragment itself, then, the bride is suspended in time at a moment of utter perfection.

The image of the apple, so high up among apple boughs such as those in Aphrodite's sacred precinct described in fragment 2 (see chapter 1), almost makes us forget that the Achilles-like groom is indeed about to accomplish what the apple-pickers had wanted, but been unable, to do. Indeed, as far as the simile itself is concerned there is no Achilles; at this moment the red apple remains safely on its bough, and desire becomes perhaps not so much the reach for the unreachable as the contemplation of perfect beauty. Even the apple-pickers, though they could not reach the beautiful apple itself, held on to its image. Sappho makes a point of this in the correction of the original statement in line 2 to the effect that they "have forgotten" (lelathonto) the apple; no, she emends, they really have not "entirely forgotten" (eklelathonto) it, for, she implies, they can still see it in the mind's eye.

The enduring significance of the image of the perfect apple in this small fragment of Sappho's work has been well captured in the title of a book by the contemporary American poet Judy Grahn, *The Highest Apple: Sappho and the Lesbian Poetic Tradition*. In her view, the apple stands for "the centrality of women to themselves, to each other, and to their society. That apple remained, intact, safe from colonization and suppression, on the topmost branch, and in the fragmented history of a Lesbian poet and her underground descendants."[6]

Another simile, one that has been attributed to Sappho by modern scholars, also seems to compare someone (possibly a bride) to the beauty of the natural world, in this instance to a mountain hyacinth:

FRAGMENT 105B V.

oian tan uakinthon en oresi poimenes	[the bride?]
andres	like a hyacinth in the mountains which
possi katasteiboisi, chamai de porph-	the shepherd men
uron anthos. . . .	trample with their feet, but the purple
	flower [lying] on the ground. . . .

In this case, not enough of the context remains for us to guess what Sappho's hexameter lines (if indeed they are hers) might have said about the fate of the trampled hyacinth. It is only the resemblance (in meter and general structure) to fragment 105a, the highest apple simile, that has led scholars to presume that these lines, too, were once part of a wedding song by Sappho.

Critics have generally further assumed that the trampled hyacinth may have functioned similarly to the "deflowering" imagery in a wedding song by the Roman poet Catullus (62.39–47), in which the chorus of young girls compare themselves to a wonderful hidden flower nourished by rain and sun, a flower that is about to be plucked and stained, thereby losing all desirability.[7] While it is certainly possible that the flower in fragment 105b functioned as an image of lost virginity (a common enough trope in classical literature), we could just as easily conjecture that it stood for resilience: the hyacinth has been stepped on and some of its blossoms lie on the ground, but after the shepherds have passed it by, its stem, nourished by the mountain air, regains its strength and rises again toward the sun to bloom once more. (If only the ancient grammarian who quoted the lines—without attribution—had quoted one or two more, we would have a better idea as to where the image led!) In other words, it is just possible that the image of the hyacinth, like the image of the perfect apple high up on the tree, performed in some way the role of celebrating a woman's beauty.

A fragment that clearly does belong to the genre of the wedding song, as the remarks of the ancient grammarian who preserved it indicate, is the following dialogue between a bride and her virginity:

FRAGMENT 114 V.

(NUMPHE): *parthenia, parthenia,*	BRIDE: Maidenhood, maidenhood,
poi me lipois' a<p>oichei?	where have you gone and left me?
(PARTHENIA): >*ouketi exo pros*	MAIDENHOOD: No more will I come
se, ouketi exo.	back to you, no more will I come
	back.

The bantering tone of this exchange, with its repetition of the address (*parthenia, parthenia*) for mock-pathetic effect, may suggest a certain disdain on Sappho's part for the conventional notion of the "deflowering" of the bride. "Maidenhood" is something that simply departs, never to return again. It was for this nicety of expression—whereby the figure of speech in the question posed by the bride, who refers metaphorically to *parthenia* as a traveler, is picked up again in *parthenia*'s reply—that the fragment was preserved for us by the ancient grammarian.[8]

Other fragments that can be connected with wedding songs are hardly more than scraps. An ancient commentator on Vergil, Servius, quotes a line from a poem that he says came from Sappho's book entitled *Epithalamia,* no doubt referring to the ninth book of the Alexandrian edition of her poetry, which contained the wedding songs excluded from the other books on the basis of meter:

FRAGMENT 116 V.

Chaire, numpha, chaire, timie gambre,	Farewell, bride, farewell, honored
polla . . .	bridegroom, many . . .

Similarly, Hephaestion quotes what is likely to have been the opening line of a wedding song:

FRAGMENT 117 V.

chairois a numpha, chaireto d' o	May you fare well, bride, and may the
gambros	bridegroom fare well, too.

The same Oxyrhynchus papyrus (1231) that has preserved several significant fragments of the Sapphic stanzas of the first book of Sappho's poems (including the previously discussed fragments 15, 16, 17, 22, 23, and 24a) also contains two rather more substantial, if mutilated, fragments of what appear to be *epithalamia.* These songs were the final two poems in Book 1 of the Alexandrian edition of Sappho's work. The incomplete state of the text leaves much open to guesswork in both cases:

FRAGMENT 27 V.

>]kaip[
>]nos[
> 3]si

]*kai gar de su pais pot[*   For once you, too, [as] a child . . .

]*ikes melpesth' agi tauta[*   . . . come now, sing of these things

]*zalexai, kamm' apu todek[*   . . .

7   a]*dra charissai*   . . . strive after . . . and from . . .

                                                freely grant us *charis* [favor/grace].

s]*teichomen gar es gamon. eu de[*   For we are going to a wedding. And

ka]*i su tout', all' otti tachista[*   you, too,

pa]*r[th]enois appempe, theoi[*   [know?] this well, but as quickly as pos-

11   ]*en echoien*   sible

                                                send away the girls, may the gods

                                                have . . .

]*odos m[e]gan eis Ol[umpon*   [there is no] road to great Olympus

a]*nthro[p] aik [*   for mortals . . .

     . . .

FRAGMENT 30 V.

nukt[ ]   the night . . .

parthenoi d[The girls . . .

pannuchisdoi[s]ai[all night long . . .

san aeidois[i]n ph[ilotata kai num-   singing of your love for the

5   *phas iokolpo.*   violet-bosomed bride.

all' egertheis eïth[e   But wake up and go [to find]

steiche sois umalik[as   the unmarried youths of your own age.

eper osson a ligupho[nos   Let us see as much sleep as

9   *upnon [i]domen.*   the clear-voiced [nightingale?].

The first of these songs (fragment 27 V.) seems to be addressed to someone, perhaps female (the gender is not apparent from the existing grammatical clues), who is bidden to carry out various instructions. In the first more-or-less extant stanza, we note the familiar association of singing with *charis* and its underlying implication of pleasurable exchange (see chapter 5). The request for song seems somehow tied in to the context of a wedding, for the subsequent stanza includes in its opening phrase the conjuction *gar* ("for"), which serves to mark an explanation of what has just preceded. Too many gaps remain to allow the certainty of an explanation like that of one scholar, who argues that the song is addressed to Sappho's rival poet Andromeda; Andromeda, he thinks, is being asked to send back the maidens to Sappho so that they may join in public dance and song.[9]

The second example (fragment 30 V.), the one that concluded Book 1 of the Alexandrian edition, is almost as enigmatic. It appears to be addressed to the bridegroom, who is bidden to go off in search of his fellow bachelors. The song is again one about singing, in this case the all-night singing of the girls about the groom's love for the bride. In what Voigt takes to be the end of the piece, the singer implies further nocturnal celebrations, for she says that they will see as much sleep as some "clear-voiced" creature; the gap at the end of line 8 is usually filled in with *ornis,* "bird," and the allusion is then assumed to be to the proverbially wakeful nightingale. Like the nightingale, the celebrants will forego sleep in favor of singing. The fragment leaves us with only a glimpse of how this book of Sapphic stanzas came to a close—the book that had begun with the powerful "Hymn to Aphrodite." It seems unlikely that the Alexandrian editors, who chose to end Book 1 with two wedding songs, would have been so disparaging of their form and content as one modern editor, Denys Page. Page brands the fragments of the *epithalamia* as "trivial in subject and style."[10] While they may not have carried the emotional force of a song like the "Hymn to Aphrodite" certainly several of these fragments of wedding songs—particularly fragment 105a about the apple on the uppermost bough—suggest a poignant beauty that ought not to be so lightly dismissed.

One other papyrus scrap preserves the end of what could be an *epithalamium* but might also simply be another kind of song meant for nighttime performance, or at least alluding to such performance:

FRAGMENT 43 V.

]ai	
]	
]letai	
] [k]alos	beautiful . . .
] akala klonei	stirs up peaceful (waters) . . .
] kamatos phrena	toil . . . the heart . . .
]e katisdane[i]	sits down . . .
] all' agit', o philai,	But come, my dears,
] agchi gar amera.	. . . for day is near.

The speaker's address to *o philai* (literally, "O dear ones" [feminine gender]) makes clear that the participants in the nighttime ritual or festival (or whatever was described) are other women, who seem to be bidden to depart now that the sun is rising.

Folk Motifs

Another group of short fragments besides the wedding songs are those that contain folk motifs. The beginning two lines of one such poem are preserved for us again by Hephaestion, who reports that the song was in Book 7 of Sappho's collected works:

FRAGMENT 102 V.

Glukea mater, ou toi dunamai kreken	Sweet mother, I am not able to weave
ton iston	at my loom,
pothoi dameisa paidos bradinan di'	overwhelmed with desire for a youth
Aphroditan . . .	because of tender Aphrodite.

Weaving was of course a standard occupation for women all over the Greek world, and in this song the narrator, presumably a girl or young woman, complains to her mother that overwhelming desire for a young man prevents her from carrying out her appointed task.[11] Despite the filial, domestic quality of the setting, with the girl addressing her mother, the language of desire is strong: the girl claims that she is "overwhelmed" or "mastered" by desire (*pothos*), the same word that Sappho uses of sexual desire in fragments 22.11 and 94.23. Thus the opening of the song seems to contain the seeds of both innocence and grand passion at once.

A similar kind of folk element appears in the following fragment addressed to the evening star:

FRAGMENT 104A V.

Espere panta phereis osa phainolis	Hesperus, you bring all that the shining
eskedas' Auos,	Dawn scattered,
phereis oin, phereis aiga, phereis apu	you bring the sheep, you bring the
materi paida.	goat, you bring the child back to its
	mother.

The evening star, described in a related fragment (fragment 104b V.) as *asteron panton o kallistos,* "the most beautiful of all the stars," is here lauded for its reunificatory powers; under its idyllic light, the flocks and the children all return home from the activities of the day.

A tantalizingly brief quotation from an ancient work on figures of speech preserves the following remarkably alliterative bit from one of Sappho's songs; the sentiment expressed seems to be based on a Greek proverb:

FRAGMENT 146 V.

mete moi meli mete melissa	Neither the honey nor the bee for me

Although the context is unknown, the ancient commentators suggest that the proverb refers to the desire to avoid the bad things that inevitably come along with good things; to escape the bee-sting, one may have to give up the bees' honey as well. Might this sentiment have been part of a song about *eros?* We cannot really tell, but we can say that what little evidence remains indicates that folk motifs and proverbial material such as fragment 146 occupied a significant place in Sappho's repertoire of themes.

Mythological Motifs

Another group of short fragments contains mythological figures. In these instances, the fragments are usually too brief to allow any reasonable guesses as to how the myth may have functioned vis-à-vis the major theme of the whole song. In one such song, for example, preserved in a quotation, Sappho describes Hermes as the wine-pourer for the rest of the gods:

FRAGMENT 141 V.

ke d' ambrosias men	There a mixing bowl of ambrosia had
krater ekekrat'	been mixed,
Ermais d' elon olpin theois' eoino-	while Hermes, taking up the jug,
choese.	poured wine for the gods.
kenoi d' ara pantes	These all held their cups and made liba-
karchasi' echon	tions.
kaleibon. arasanto de pampan esla	They prayed for all good things for the
gambroi . . .	bridegroom.

Whether this description of a marriage on Olympus formed part of a wedding song, we cannot tell, despite the preservation of several lines of context. In other cases, we have little left beyond the name of a mythological figure, as in fragment 124 V. referring to the Muse Kalliope, or fragment 123 V. describing "golden-sandaled Dawn" (*chrusopedilos Auos*).

The second-century A.D. scholar Athenaeus preserves two possibly related fragments, the first of which clearly has to do with the story of Leda and the swan (the form taken on that occasion by Zeus), whose union according to some versions in Greek mythology produced two eggs, from which were hatched Kastor, Pollux, Klytemnestra, and Helen:

FRAGMENT 166 V.

phaisi de pota Ledan uakinthinon	Indeed, they say that once Leda found
. . . oïon euren pepukadmenon	an egg, colored like a hyacinth, covered with . . .

FRAGMENT 167 V.

oio polu leukoteron	whiter by far than an egg . . .

Athenaeus preserves another mythological reference in a fragment whose context is known only to the extent that he points out that even in his time free (as opposed to slave) women and girls use the term *hetairai* (literally, "companions") in referring to each other, just as Sappho did in her line:

FRAGMENT 142 V.

Lato kai Nioba mala men philai esan	Leto and Niobe were very dear friends
etairai	

Perhaps the fragment went on to describe the rift between the goddess Leto (mother of the twins Apollo and Artemis) and the Theban queen Niobe, who rashly boasted that as the mother of seven sons and seven daughters, she had been far more productive than Leto. As punishment, Apollo and Artemis struck down all of Niobe's children with their deadly arrows, and Niobe herself was transformed into a perpetually weeping mountain of stone, forever lamenting her dead offspring.

Hephaestion, in his handbook on meter, preserves what is probably the opening line of a song (in ionic meter) addressed to a woman named Eirana (the name occurs also in fragment 91 V.):

FRAGMENT 135 V.

Ti me Pandionis, o Eirana, chelidon	Why, Eirana, does the swallow, daughter of Pandion, [awaken?] me?
. . . ?	

The verb in the question is missing, but the supplement "awaken" seems as likely as any. The myth referred to is the story of Philomela, whose brother-in-law, Tereus, raped her and then cut out her tongue to prevent her telling her sister Procne of his evil deeds. Philomela, however, cleverly wove the story into a tapestry, and when Procne understood what had happened, the two sisters took revenge on Tereus by serving him the flesh of his own son, Itys, for dinner. In the end, all were transformed into birds—Philomela into a swallow, Procne into a nightingale, and Tereus into a pursuing hawk. (In Latin and mediaeval literature, the birds with which the two sisters are identified are sometimes reversed.)

In fragment 135, we note that Philomela (identified as "daughter of Pandion") is already transformed into the wordless swallow, who can communicate only through inarticulate musical sound. Sappho's Philomela-swallow seems even further removed from articulate expression than the Philomela of a lost play by Sophocles (called *Tereus*), in which he referred to her use of "the voice of the shuttle."[12] Unfortunately, however, since so little of Sappho's song remains, we cannot explore further the possibility raised by Patricia Klindienst Joplin that the poet may have given us here "an ominous sign of what threatens the woman's voiced existence in culture."[13] Exactly how the Philomela-swallow functioned in the rest of the song we really cannot tell, but it is certainly tempting to note the irony of the parallels between Philomela's tapestry and the shreds of Sappho's own work, the majority of which must now be read through signs and traces.

One last fragment dealing with mythological figures is more substantial than many, but it cannot be assigned to Sappho with absolute certainty. Although the editors who first published the fragment thought that it was perhaps by Alkaios, Voigt and others attribute the piece to Sappho. Treu, for example, notes the reference in section (b) of the fragment to the Muses and to the *Charites*, so characteristic of Sappho's verse (see chapter 5):[14]

FRAGMENT 44A V.

a

]sanores . . [
Phoiboi chrusoko]mai ton etikte Koo . [
migeisa Kr]onidai megalonumo<i>.
Artemis de theon] megan orkon
    apomose
5   *kepha]lan. aï parthenos essomai*

    ] on oreon koruphais' epi
    ]de neuson eman charin.
eneu]se theon makaron pater
elaphab]olon agroteran theoi

a

[to golden-haired Phoibos], whom the
   daughter of Koios (Leto) bore
after she had slept with the great-
   named son of Cronos.
[But Artemis] swore a great oath [of
   the gods]:
[By your] head, always I will be a
   virgin
   . . . upon the tops of the mountains
   . . .
   . . . grant me this favor.

10] *sin eponumion mega.*	The father of the blessed gods nodded
]*eros oudama pilnatai.*	assent.
. . . *maphobe [ ] ero.*	The gods [called her] far-shooting
	Huntress,
	a great name.
	Eros never draws near to her . . . .

b

b

emm[	The splendid [gifts?] of the Muses . . .
kai [	makes . . . and of the Charites
r e [	slender . . . .
o . . . [	not to forget the wrath . . .
5 *Moisan agla [*	mortals . . .
poei kai Chariton [	
bradinois epeb [	
orgas me 'pilathe [	
thnatoisin. ped. ch[	
10]*dalio [*	

How the story of Apollo and Artemis was tied into the remainder of the song must remain a mystery, but perhaps they were somehow linked to the Muses and the Graces (*Charites*) as inspirers of song. Artemis is mentioned by name in one other fragment of Sappho's (fragment 84 V.), which is otherwise almost totally unintelligible, and Apollo is referred to in fragment 44.33 V. in his roles as both hunter and musician. Neither deity seems to have occupied the place of central importance in Sappho's poetry, which as we have seen was unquestionably held by Aphrodite.

Miscellaneous Short Fragments

We come finally to a small group of fragments that seem to treat a variety of subjects. The most controversial of these is a short papyrus fragment (P. Oxy. 2291, col. I. 1–9) that Voigt prefers to assign to Alkaios. Others assign it to Sappho, sometimes with cautionary notes to the effect that the poem may in fact be by Alkaios.[15] The fragment is badly mutilated but does clearly contain at least one, if not two, references to the sons of Polyanax ("Much-Ruler"), a name that recurs in the following punning line preserved for us in a quotation from Sappho:

FRAGMENT 155 V.

polla moi tan Poluanaktida paida I'm overjoyed to say farewell to you,
  chairen.   Miss Overlord.

In addition to the repetition of the "p" sounds, the pun on *polla* ("much") and *Polu-anaktida* ("child of Mr. Much-Ruler") produces a sarcastic tone that occurs occasionally among Sappho's fragments.[16] In the papyrus fragment in question, however, the allusions to the house of Polyanax occur in far more obscure contexts, quite possibly within two separate poems:

ALKAIOS FRAGMENT 303A V. (= SAPPHO FRAGMENT 99 L.-P.)

a

a

]ga . . eda baio [n] a   After a little . . .

d [ ] oi Poluanakt[id]a . . [. . . the son(s) of Polyanax
. . . aissamiasi . ie . [.]tois . . . . [.] . . .

chordaisidiakreken   to strum on the strings . . . .
5 *olisb. dokois<i> perkath . . . . . enos* receiving the dildo(?) . . .
 . . ou . [. .] si philoph[ro]nos
 ] . . . . d' elelisd[e]tai pr.taneos . . . kindly
 ]onos de dio [. .] o.   it quivers . . . .
  ]. ualod' . [.] . . enete [. .] . ch .

           . . .

           . . .

        [possibly the end of this poem]

b

b

Latos] te kai Di[os] paï [.]   [possibly the beginning of a new poem]
 ] . . e . . . [.] epi[ ]borgian[O child of (Leto) and Zeus,
 Grunean] ulode<n> lipon come . . .
 ] . en chre[s]terion   leaving wooded [Gryneia?]
5 *] . [ ] . eumes [. .] . [.]on* . . . to the oracle
 ] . . . . [. . . . .]   . . .
 ] . . . . . . a [. .] erais sing . . .
 ]rsanon [.] . .rgian   . . . sister
 ]usomen [ ]
10 *]n umne [ ]*
 ka[ ]ena [.]pho . [. . . .]n. adelphean

ospai [ ] . io . [. . .] . [ ]	
.utisde [. . .]kei thele[ ]	show (?) . . . again . . . the sons of
deichnus [. . .] e deute Poluanaktidan	Polyanax . . .
15 *ton margon ondeixai thelo.*	I want to expose the greedy [man?]. . .

The chief reason that these papyrus scraps have attracted so much scholarly attention, despite their wretched state of preservation, is the possible reference in line 5 of part (a) to the word *olisbos,* known from Greek comedy (e.g., Aristophanes, *Lysistrata* 109) to be a leather phallus, or dildo. To those eagerly seeking information about ancient lesbian sexual practices, however, it must be pointed out that even if these fragments could be definitely assigned to Sappho rather than Alkaios, the occurrence of the word *olisbos* here is far from certain; every letter of *olisb-* in line 5 is printed in the Greek editions with a dot underneath, a convention used by editors of papyri to indicate the uncertainty of decipherment. The Sapphic dildo may be a figment of papyrological imagination—and if so, the question then arises as to why scholars have been so eager to find it in an almost illegible fragment of dubious authorship and uncertain context. The elements of scandal and masquerade in the notion of the Sapphic dildo are worth exploring further ("WOMAN POET WEARS FAKE PENIS!"), but I will leave that project aside for now. In any case, we certainly cannot accept Giangrande's glib conclusion that this fragment "leaves us in no doubt as to what Sappho and her companions were up to."[17]

Several of the shorter fragments offer just enough intelligibility to enable us to admire the vividness of the Sapphic imagery while at the same time savoring the multiple range of possibilities of context that each might have come from. Here are four examples that refer in one way or another to the tender, flowerlike qualities of a girl or young woman; had we more context, we might well find that these songs would illustrate some of the qualities of Sapphic *habrosune* (see chapter 5).[18] The first of these is the most famous, for many readers have interpreted it as an autobiographical reference on Sappho's part to her daughter Kleis; others, drawing on the analogy of a male homosexual context, see Sappho's description of Kleis (who is referred to as a *pais,* "child," "boy") as erotic rather than familial:[19]

FRAGMENT 132 V.

Esti moi kala pais chrusioisin an-	I have a child whose beauty
themoisin	resembles golden flowers: beloved
emphere<n> echoisa morphan Kleis	Kleis,
< > agapata,	whom [I would not exchange]
anti tas egoude Ludian paisan oud'	either for all of Lydia or a lovely . . .
erannan . . .	

FRAGMENT 41 V.

tais kalais' ummin <to> noemma
  tomon
ou diameipton

Toward you, beautiful women, my
  thoughts
are not changeable

FRAGMENT 122 V.

anthe' amergoisan paid' agan apalan

[I saw] an exceedingly tender girl pluck-
ing flowers

FRAGMENT 126 V.

dauois(') apalas eta<i>ras en
  stethesin

. . . [a woman]
sleeping on the bosom of a tender companion [hetaira]. . .

Another vivid but tantalizingly incomplete fragment, whose metrical peculiarities perhaps indicate less than precise quotation on the part of the preserver
(Athenaeus), seems to describe the opposite of the aesthetic ideals of *charis,
habrosune,* and *poikilia.* Here the narrator appears to be rebuking someone
(named Andromeda, according to Athenaeus) for succumbing to the charms of
a hayseed, a country-bumpkin:

FRAGMENT 57 V.

tis d' agroïotis thelgei noon . . .
agroïotin epemmena stolan . . .
ouk epistamena ta brake' elken epi ton
  sphuron?

What bumpkin girl charms [your]
  mind . . .
wearing her bumpkin dress . . .
not knowing how to draw her rags
  over her ankles?

The insulting overtones of *agroïotis* are suggested by a fragment from Alkaios,
a relatively lengthy piece complaining of the deprivations of life in exile away
from the center of the action, which in Alkaios's view consists of the politics of
the assembly and the council. The narrator of the song (Alkaios fragment 130b
V.) complains, "I in my wretchedness live the life of a bumpkin's lot, while I
long to hear the assembly being summoned." After complaining further of living
among the "wolf-thickets" in the middle of nowhere, the narrator provides this
curious example of what it means to be away from the urban activities of the
male aristocracy: he keeps out of trouble by going to watch a beauty contest of
the women of Lesbos!

ALKAIOS FRAGMENT 130B.16–20 V.

oikemi k[a]kon ektos echon podas	I survive and keep my feet out of trouble,
oppai L[esbi]ades krinnomenai phuan	where the women of Lesbos with their trailing robes
polent' elkesipeploi, peri de bremei	go up and down as they are being judged for beauty,
acho thespesia gunaikon	while all around there rings the marvelous echo
ira[s o]lolugas eniausias	of the women's sacred cries each year.

Ironically, the Alkaios-narrator illustrates the enforced rustic alienation from the urban political process of the male aristocracy with a description of his own "feminization" at what appears to be an annual religious ritual for women, which, according to various ancient commentators, took place at the precinct of the goddess Hera.[20] No doubt if Sappho alluded to this beauty contest in her songs, it would have been in quite a different context.[21]

Four brief fragments preserved in quotation present puzzles as to what their original context might have been. All are in the form of the first-person statements so characteristic of Sappho's poetry; whether any of these songs featured the named Sappho persona that we have observed in the case of longer pieces such as the "Hymn to Aphrodite" or fragment 94 V., we cannot tell:

FRAGMENT 51 V.

ouk oid' otti theo; duo moi ta noemata	I do not know what to do; my mind is split

FRAGMENT 52 V.

psauen d' ou dokimom' orano dus-pachea(?)	I do not think that I will touch the sky with my two arms(?)

FRAGMENT 121 V.

all eon philos ammin lechos arnuso neo-teron;	But since you are our friend, seek a younger bed.
ou gar tlasom' ego sun <t'> oiken essa geraitera	For I would not dare to live with you, since I am older.

FRAGMENT 120 V.

alla tis ouk emmi paligkoton	But I am not someone resentful in
organ, all' abaken tan phren' echo . . .	my feelings; I have a gentle heart.

A fuller representation of Sappho's lyrics would surely reveal more songs that, like the following fragment, allude self-consciously to the art of song:

FRAGMENT 118 V.

agi de chelu dia moi lege	Come now, divine lyre, speak to me,
phonaessa de gineo	and sounding forth be [my compan-
	ion?] . . .

Preserved (perhaps somewhat inaccurately) through quotation in a later Greek writer named Hermogenes, the lines were cited as an example of what we would call pathetic fallacy, or the attribution of feelings and the the power of judgment to inanimate objects. Evidently, according to Hermogenes, the poem went on to represent the voice of the tortoise-shell lyre actually responding to the poet's apostrophe. We have noted earlier Sappho's fondness for dialogue embedded in her lyrics, as in the "Hymn to Aphrodite" (between the Sappho-narrator and Aphrodite) and in fragment 94 V (between the Sappho-narrator and the departing woman) and fragment 114 V. (between a bride and her virginity). This song addressed to the speaking lyre may have been yet another example of Sappho's enlargement of the lyric scope through the introduction of multiple "voices" within a given poem.

Another short fragment, the text and meter of which are uncertain, seems to refer to "those who serve the Muses," possibly poets:

FRAGMENT 150 V.

ou gar themis en moisopolon	For it is not right for there to be lamen-
<domoi>	tation
threnon emmen' . . . ou k' ammi prepoi	in the house of those who serve the
tade . . .	Muses.
	That would not be suitable for us.

As we have already noted, Sappho frequently opens a song with an address to the Muses, either in conjunction with the *Charites* (see chapter 5) or independently, as in the following beginning of a poem preserved in a quotation in Hephaestion's treatise:

FRAGMENT 127 V.

Deuro deute Moisai chrusion lipoisai	Hither again, O Muses, leaving your
. . .	golden [house] . . .

Three other brief fragments also seem to have to do with the power of song, although the lack of surrounding context makes certainty impossible. In one (in a glyconic meter) Sappho is quoted as praising a young woman (*parthenon*, literally "virgin," or at least an unmarried woman) for her "wisdom" or "skill" (*sophia*), which might be taken to be poetic skill:

FRAGMENT 56 V.

oud' ian dokimomi prosidoisan phaos	I do not think there will be at any time
alio	a woman who looks on the light of the
essesthai sophian parthenon eis oudena	sun
po chronon	with wisdom such as yours
teautan	

Elsewhere, in a two-word quotation, Sappho describes someone as a *parthenon aduphonon* ("sweet-voiced woman," fragment 153 V.), and a papyrus scrap preserves bits of a poem that mentions someone named Mika, a reference to the women of the family of Penthilus (one of the aristocratic Mytilenean families alluded to as well in the poetry of Alkaios), and a "sweet song":[22]

FRAGMENT 71 V.

]misse Mika	Mika . . .
]ela[. .al]la s' egouk easo	. . . but I will not allow you . . .
]n philot[at'] eleo Penthilean[	. . . you preferred the friendship of
]da ka[ko]trop', amma[	the Penthilidae
] mel[os] ti glukeron .[	. . . o mischievous one . . . our . . .
]a mellichophon[os	. . . some sweet song . . .
]dei, ligurai d' ae[	. . . gentle-voiced . . .
] dros[o]essa[	. . . sweet-sounding [breezes?]
	. . . covered with dew . . .

If only we had another papyrus copy of this poem that was torn in different places than in this copy, we might have a better idea of the context of these allusions to song. Those who view Sappho as an official music teacher of young women would regard the fragment as referring to a rival "school," to which Mika has decamped and in so doing has become the object of Sappho's rebuke for her desertion. Of course the fragment may also be interpreted as alluding simply to rival poets or to a rival aristocratic family or to a fiction thereof, without reference to any kind of institutionalized practice.

Another short fragment (again preserved via quotation) seems to promote a "nationalist" concept of the singers of Sappho's homeland. The line is quoted as an example of Sappho's comparison of someone's superior qualities, which surpass the qualities of others by as much as Lesbian singers surpass all other singers:

FRAGMENT 106 V.

perrochos, os ot' aoidos o Lesbios allo-	. . . superior, just as when a Lesbian
dapoisin	singer [outdoes] foreign ones . . .

Aoidos ("singer") is the Homeric word for "bard," a professional singer who (like Phemios and Demodokos in the *Odyssey*) serves as a court musician and can render the latest song for the entertainment of the assembled guests. Here Sappho seems to be claiming a special status for the post-Homeric tradition of singers of which she was a part, and of which we now know so little beyond the scraps of songs written by Sappho herself and by her compatriot Alkaios. "We are the best," she seems to say.

I end this chapter with a beautiful short fragment whose uncertain authorship highlights the tentativeness of nearly everything that can be said about Sappho's poetry. The piece is quoted as a metrical example by Hephaestion, who does not mention the author's name. Since he usually quotes opening lines, we probably have here the beginning of the song. While some modern scholars have rejected the Renaissance attribution of it to Sappho (notably Wilamowitz as well as Lobel and Page), Voigt includes it along with the one complete poem and the two hundred or so fragments of Sappho's work:[23]

FRAGMENT 168B V.

Deduke men a selanna	The moon has set,
kai Pleiades. mesai de	and the Pleiades. The night
nuktes, para d' erchet' ora,	is at its midpoint, the moment passes,
ego de mona kateudo.	and I sleep alone.[24]

One of the arguments for Sapphic authorship is that the fragment seems to be faintly echoed in connection with Sappho in both Horace (*Satires* 1.5.82–83) and Ovid (*Heroides* 15.155–56), although not closely enough in either case to be conclusive. Certainly the piece has a Sapphic ring to it: the description of the natural setting, the allusion to two female-centered celestial phenomena, namely the moon (Selene, or in Sappho's dialect, Selanna) and the Pleiades (seven sisters transformed into the constellation), a dramatic sense of time, and, finally, an implicitly erotic tone centered around the song's narrator, the *ego* of the final extant line. The emphasis on the solitary state of the singer implies that she had perhaps hoped it would be otherwise. It is late at night, for the moon has set, and perhaps it is a cold winter's night to boot—if the reference to the setting of the Pleiades alludes not just to their nightly setting but also to their cosmical setting at the end of the sailing season, in November. However we interpret *ora* at the end of line 3 ("moment," "hour," "season," etc.), the song seems to capture the feeling that *tempus fugit*. The sky turns inexorably onward as the solitary narrator watches. Did the narrator go on to describe her desire for an absent woman? Was this song composed by Sappho, or only by someone imitating Sappho's images and dialect? Like so many questions about the lyrics of this "tenth Muse" of the ancient world, these must remain open ones. But open questions lead to openings, and as I hope to show in the next and last chapter of this book, the openings suggested by the remnants of Sappho's work continue to inspire women writers twenty-six centuries after Sappho's lifetime.

EPILOGUE

Sappho and Modern American Women Poets

Despite the fragmentary state in which Sappho's songs exist today, her work lives on in the writing of recent or contemporary authors of many nationalities. Some, like the Italian poet Giovanna Bemporad, have tried their hand at direct imitation. Here, for example, is Bemporad's sensitive rendering of Sappho fragment 168B V., which was discussed toward the end of the preceding chapter:

> Tramontata è la luna
> e le Pleiadi; a mezzo
> è la notte, già l'ora
> trapassa; io dormo sola.[1]

Other contemporary writers and artists have found inspiration in the remnants of Sappho's songs for their own creative imagination. One might think, for example, of the composer Ned Rorem's *Four Madrigals*, written for mixed chorus a cappella, each of which is set to a translation of one of Sappho's fragments.[2] Most striking among current authors is the fiction of the English writer Jeanette Winterson, in particular her novel titled *Art & Lies: A Piece for Three Voices and a Bawd* (New York: Knopf, 1995). This is undoubtedly the strangest of Winterson's works to date, posing as it does as a novel yet featuring but few of the usual conventions of a novel. The three main characters, such as they are, are Handel (a former priest who is now a surgeon), Picasso (a female painter), and Sappho, who seems to represent the ancient poet of Lesbos. The three are together on a train that is speeding through the present time. Handel and Picasso each have three sections of the book, Sappho two. Chronological time seems to be of little relevance, and the narrative is purposefully disjointed; sometimes the characters speak and other times an impersonal narrator comments. The book ends with several pages of the score from the famous trio (Sophie, the Marschalllin, and Octavian) of Richard Strauss's *Der Rosenkavalier*. In order to whet the reader's appetite to pursue this complex work, I quote here just two short sections from the narrative of the Sappho persona:

> I have a lot of questions, not least, WHAT HAVE YOU DONE WITH MY POEMS? When I turn the pages of my manuscript my fingers crumble the paper, the paper breaks up in burnt folds, the paper colours my palms yellow. I look like a nicotine junkie. I can no longer read my own writing. It isn't surprising that so many of you have chosen to read between the lines when the lines themselves have become more mutilated than a Saturday night whore. (*Art & Lies*, p. 51)

> Only a fool tries to reconstruct a bunch of grapes from a bottle of wine. The world is packed tight with fools. Here, today, spread out in front of me, in numerous learned tomes, is a record of my supposed love-affairs as constructed from my work. Atthis, Andromeda, Gyrinno, Eranna, Mnasidika. They sound like precious stones. They were precious stones but not studded in my heart. They were studies of the imagination. The wind of that day, the purple sea, the copper drum flashing a message off a lovely face, were as much to me as that face. Some I loved, some I dreamed of loving, some were names carved roughly into the rock. It doesn't matter, not now, not then, I was and am still moved by things remote from me. (*Art & Lies*, p. 56)

The book repeatedly addresses the futility of a literalist reading of Sappho's poetry, pointing out in numerous ways that "there's no such thing as autobiography, there's only art and lies" (p. 141).

Sappho's inspiration has also been important in the late twentieth century to communities of women committed to "recreating" a Sapphic lifestyle, not unlike the attempts early in the century by Renée Vivien and Natalie Barney to reestablish what they saw as Sappho's circle of women on Lesbos. One such community was in Yellow Springs, Ohio, an unconventional little village that is the home of Antioch College. Members of the lesbian community tell me that in the radical days of the 1970s, many Yellow Springs residents used to read Mary Barnard's translation of Sappho almost every day as if it were a book of affirmations to help them come to terms with their own sexual identities. Community members remember frequent social gatherings at each other's Victorian houses in an atmosphere charged with romantic involvement and sexual tension. In wintertime, they recall, especially after a heavy snowfall, the light of the sun seemed to shine through the windows of the old brick houses with a special slant. Lovers took walks through the snow along the paths of the forested ravines in the nearby park known as Glen Helen. Everyone in the community thought constantly about their emotions, and work was something one did on the side when it was necessary. The important question in life was "With whom are you in love *this* week?" All else took a subordinate role in the daily life of the Yellow Springs lesbian community during its heyday in the comfortable economic climate of the 1970s.

I want now to demonstrate briefly how our reading of recent and contemporary lesbian poetry can be enriched by an awareness of Sappho's influence.[3] If we take note of the special slant of Sappho's light as it shines on writers of the twentieth century, we will read their works with a greater sensitivity toward the nuances of their images. A thorough study of Sappho's continuing effect on modern literature would require a separate book-length treatment, as evidenced by Joan DeJean's *Fictions of Sappho, 1546–1937*, which deals only with the Sapphic tradition in French literature and only during the period specified. Here I have chosen to focus—by way of a brief sampling—on three twentieth-century American women poets in whose work we can detect the influence of Sappho, whether in the form of general imitation of subject matter and style, of direct or indirect allusion, or of direct quotation. This brief overview includes Amy Lowell (1874–1925), Hilda Doolittle (H.D., 1886–1961), and Olga Broumas (b. 1949).

Particularly in the case of H.D. and Broumas, the intertextuality is based on the authors' direct knowledge of Sappho's fragments in the original Greek, so that our reading of their work is considerably enriched by a conscious awareness of their close relationship to the ancient poet. In these three poets we find many of the same qualities we have observed in the case of Sappho: a strong sense of self-definition; a display of independence within a poetic tradition (rather than a separatist approach); a relishing of the erotic and the sensual; and an emphasis on the mutuality of desire and a blurring of the gaze in such a way as to disrupt the hierarchy of subject versus object. I leave to others the task of extending such a study to include other twentieth-century writers of various nationalities.

Amy Lowell (1874–1925)

I will not rehearse the well-known details of Amy Lowell's life as a member of the wealthy and prestigious Lowell family, but only note that the lesbian aspect of her love poetry provoked a hostile critical response both during and immediately after her lifetime.[4] Despite the high quality of much of her poetry, not to mention her place in literary history as a founder of the Imagist movement and her creative use of Eastern models such as *haiku*, her reputation has fallen into decline. In general, critics have minimized her contributions to the group of modernist poets that included Ezra Pound, Hilda Doolittle (H.D.), William Carlos Williams, and Richard Aldington.[5]

Since Lowell did not receive a formal education beyond the age of seventeen, we have no evidence of a specific curriculum that she followed in her youthful reading or of any particular exposure to classical literature. However, her own reference to Sappho in a long poem entitled "The Sisters," as well as the nature of Lowell's poetry itself, suggests a certain familiarity with the work of the ancient poet, at least in English translation. Indeed, I would go so far as to argue that Lowell's increasing interest in writing short poems that focus on a specific image was influenced not only by Japanese *haiku* but also by the short fragments of Sappho preserved in quotations by later writers—the hyacinth trampled by the shepherds, the apple ripening on the topmost branch, Eros shaking one's heart like the wind blowing against the mountain oaks. In "The Sisters" Lowell opens her musings about her poetic foremothers (including, besides Sappho, Elizabeth Barrett Browning and Emily Dickinson) with a statement about the peculiar status of women poets and an expression of her own desire to interrogate Sappho regarding the nature of her poetry:

> Taking us by and large, we're a queer lot
> We women who write poetry. And when you think
> How few of us there've been, it's queerer still.
> I wonder what it is that makes us do it,
> Singles us out to scribble down, man-wise,
> The fragments of ourselves. Why are we
> Already mother-creatures, double-bearing,
> With matrices in body and in brain?
> I rather think that there is just the reason
> We are so sparse a kind of human being;
> The strength of forty thousand Atlases
> Is needed for our every-day concerns.
> There's Sapho, now I wonder what was Sapho.
> I know a single slender thing about her:
> That, loving, she was like a burning birch-tree
> All tall and glittering fire, and that she wrote
> Like the same fire caught up to Heaven
>   and held there,

> A frozen blaze before it broke and fell.
> Ah, me! I wish I could have talked to Sapho,
> Surprised her reticences by flinging mine
> Into the wind. This tossing off of garments
> Which cloud the soul is none too easy doing
> With us to-day. But still I think with Sapho
> One might accomplish it, were she in the mood
> To bare her loveliness of words and tell
> The reasons, as she possibly conceived them,
> Of why they are so lovely. Just to know
> How she came at them, just to watch
> The crisp sea sunshine playing on her hair,
> And listen, thinking all the while 'twas she
> Who spoke and that we two were sisters
> Of a strange, isolated little family.

The narrator's sense of identification with—and awe in the face of—the ancient poet come through forcefully in these lines, along with the feeling of isolation as a woman poet who is one among a "queer lot." Lowell's appreciation of Sappho as an erotic poet is clear from her description of the "single slender thing" she claims to know about Sappho: "That, loving, she was like a burning birch-tree." Lowell's poem goes on to contrast the fiery emotions of Sappho's poetry with the restrained conventions evident in the work of "Mrs. Browning":[6]

> And she is Sapho—Sapho—not Miss or Mrs.,
> A leaping fire we call so for convenience;
> But Mrs. Browning—who would ever think
> of such presumption as to call her "Ba."
> Which draws the perfect line between sea-cliffs
> And a close-shuttered room in Wimpole Street.
> Sapho could fly her impulses like bright
> Balloons tip-tilting to a morning air
> And write about it. Mrs. Browning's heart
> was squeezed in stiff conventions. So she lay
> Stretched out upon a sofa, reading Greek
> And speculating, as I must suppose,
> In just this way on Sapho.

Later in this lengthy narrative, the poet decries the effects of Victorian restraints and the consequent likely formality of an imagined encounter with "Mrs. Browning," complaining, "Convention again, and how it chafes my nerves, / For we are such a little family / Of singing sisters." Soon the narrator introduces a third "sister," Emily Dickinson. She describes the contrasts among the three in financial terms:

> Strange trio of my sisters, most diverse,
> And how extraordinarily unlike
> Each is to me, and which way shall I go?
> Sapho spent and gained; and Mrs. Browning,
> After a miser girlhood, cut the strings
> Which tied her money-bags and let them run;
> But Emily hoarded—hoarded—only giving
> Herself to cold, white paper.

A few lines later the narrator bids farewell to these "marvellously strange" sisters, hoping that she herself will someday serve as an interlocutor for "some other woman with an itch for writing." By the end of the poem the "strange trio" has become familiar, and in a concluding statement the narrator revises her earlier assessment:

> No, you have not seemed strange to me, but near,
> Frightfully near, and rather terrifying.
> I understand you all, for in myself—
> Is that presumption? Yet indeed it's true—
> We are one family. And still my answer
> Will not be any one of yours, I see.
> Well, never mind that now. Good night! Good night!

This poem about poetry—and in particular about writing as a woman poet—suggests a full appreciation on Lowell's part for the apparent freedom with which Sappho was able to let her poetic imagination soar. Although the narrator of "The Sisters" on one level separates herself from any of the three poetic models, proclaiming the uniqueness of her own voice, she seems to feel a greater connection to Sappho than to either Browning or Dickinson, to the point that she can at least dream of communicating directly with her. The narrator seems to appreciate the robust eroticism, expressed without restraints of the sort that affected Browning or Dickinson, that permeates the songs of Sappho. We can probably safely assume that this expository poem, published posthumously in the volume entitled *What's O'Clock*, represents Lowell's own views on her art toward the end of her life. Although Lowell herself certainly did not attempt to imitate the erotic qualities of Sappho's verse, her love poetry is nevertheless remarkably direct and "uncoded," given the time at which it was written, as we can see in some of the examples that follow.

Unlike Sappho, who gives her cast of characters names—including, of course, her own self—Lowell's more personal poems operate within the framework of an anonymous "I" and an unnamed "you." Even without the abundance of biographical information about Lowell, however, including her long-term relationship with the actress Ada Dwyer Russell, with whom she lived from 1914 until her death in 1925, it would not be difficult to discern the woman-centered basis that underlies her love poems.[7] An example from her first published volume, *A Dome of Many-Coloured Glass* (1912), opens with a moonlit landscape and floral imagery that echo Sappho and at the same time presage Lowell's later imagistic poetry. The poem is entitled ΔΙΨΑ, the Classical Greek word for "thirst":

> Look, Dear, how bright the moonlight is to-night!
> See where it casts the shadow of that tree
> Far out upon the grass. And every gust
> Of light night wind comes laden with the scent
> Of opening flowers which never bloom by day:
> Night-scented stocks, and four o'clocks, and that
> Pale yellow disk, upreared on its tall stalk,
> The evening primrose, comrade of the stars.
> It seems as though the garden which you love
> Were like a swinging censer, its incense
> Floating before us as a reverent act
> To sanctify and bless our night of love.

The piece goes on to declare the narrator's love, comparing the narrator to a priest and the anonymous "Dear Heart" to a holy shrine. The addressee, further described as "beautiful" and "lovely," is urged, "Yes, yes, once more / Kiss me, and let me feel you very near / Wanting me wholly, even as I want you." Like Sappho fragment 96 V., which compares the woman who has gone away to Sardis to the rosy-fingered moon (see chapter 3), Lowell's poem makes the natural landscape the locus of eroticism—shadows in the moonlight, winds bearing floral scents, flowers opening up their petals by night rather than by day, the whole garden becoming a sacred space (as if it were a censer of incense in a religious rite) in which the lovers are blessed by nature. It is the same kind of space that surrounds Aphrodite's precinct amidst the apple groves in Sappho fragment 2 V. (see chapter 1).

Some twenty poems within the volume entitled *Sword Blades and Poppy Seeds* (1914) celebrate an unnamed "beloved," again often making use of images of moonlight and flowers, as in the following two examples:

ABSENCE

My cup is empty to-night,
Cold and dry are its sides,
Chilled by the wind from the open window.
Empty and void, it sparkles white in the moonlight.
The room is filled with the strange scent
Of wistaria blossoms.
They sway in the moon's radiance
And tap against the wall.
But the cup of my heart is still,
And cold, and empty.

When you come, it brims
Red and trembling with blood,
Heart's blood for your drinking;
To fill your mouth with love
And the bitter-sweet taste of a soul.

A GIFT

See! I give myself to you, Beloved!
My words are little jars
For you to take and put upon a shelf.
Their shapes are quaint and beautiful,
And they have many pleasant colours and lustres
To recommend them.
Also the scent from them fills the room
With sweetness of flowers and crushed grasses.

When I shall have given you the last one,
You will have the whole of me,
But I shall be dead.

In both these short poems, the narrator views herself as a vessel—in "Absence" she is an empty cup sitting in the moonlight until the beloved arrives and causes the cup to overflow its brim with "heart's blood," and in "A Gift" a series of colorful little jars filled with floral scents—jars that seem to represent both the words and the very essence of the narrator. She will give these magical word-jars to the beloved as long as she lives.

Once Lowell's Imagistic period was in full swing, many of her short poems, such as those in *Pictures of the Floating World* (1919), read almost like translations of some of the fragments of Sappho's poetry preserved for us by later ancient writers who were interested in a particular image or expression that the poet of Lesbos had used. There are no deliberate quotations from Sappho, but the pieces (in addition to their obvious indebtedness to Japanese *haiku*) have a Sapphic ring about them. In "Shore Grass" we can hear an echo of Sappho fragment 1 6 8B V. (see chapter 6) about the moon and the Pleiades, and the narrator lying alone at midnight:

Shore Grass

The moon is cold over the sand-dunes,
And the clumps of sea-grasses flow and glitter;
The thin chime of my watch tells the quarter
   after midnight;
And still I hear nothing
But the windy beating of the sea.

The pleasure offered by the sight of the beloved expressed in Sappho fragment 3 1 V. (see chapter 2) is described (in considerably tamer terms, to be sure) by Lowell in "A Sprig of Rosemary":

I cannot see your face.
When I think of you,
It is your hands which I see.
Your hands
Sewing,
Holding a book,
Resting for a moment on the sill of a window.
My eyes keep always the sight of your hands,
But my heart holds the sound of your voice,
And the soft brightness which is your soul.

In a similar celebration of the beloved's appearance, in which she is compared to the goddess Diana, the narrator describes listening to her voice and watching her in a garden. The title of this poem in rhymed couplets (published in *What's O'Clock*) comes from the Italian name of the musical instrument (similar to a viola) that translates "viola of love," and at the same time suggests (through the Latin *viola*) violets:

Song for a Viola D'Amore

The lady of my choice is bright
As a clematis at the touch of night,
As a white clematis with a purple heart

When twilight cuts earth and sun apart.
Through the dusking garden I hear her voice
As a smooth, sweet, wandering, windy noise,
And I see her stand as a ghost may do
In answer to a rendez-vous
Long sought with agony and prayer.
So watching her, I see her there.

I sit beneath a quiet tree
And watch her everlastingly.
The garden may or may not be
Before my eyes, I cannot see.
But darkness drifting up and down
Divides to let her silken gown
Gleam there beside the clematis.
How marvellously white it is!
Five white blossoms and she are there
Like candles in a fluttering air
Escaping from a tower stair.

Be still you cursed, rattling leaf,
This is no time to think of grief.

The night is soft, and fire-flies
Are very casual, gay, and wise,
And they have made a tiny glee
Just where the clematis and she
Are standing. Since the sky is clear,
Do they suppose that, once a year,
The moon and five white stars appear
Walking the earth; that, so attended,
Diana came and condescended
To hold speech with Endymion
Before she came at last alone.

The lady of my choice is bright
As a clematis at the fall of night.
Her voice is honeysuckle sweet,
Her presence spreads an April heat
Before the going of her feet.
She is of perfectness complete.

The lady whom my heart perceives
As a clematis above its leaves,
As a purple-hearted clematis.
And what is lovelier than that is?

Unlike what happens in most of Lowell's love poetry, the gender of the be-loved is here marked from the outset—"the lady of my choice." In an echo of Sappho's fragments 31 V. and 22 V., the focus of the poem is on the narrator's perceptions of the beloved, especially her voice and her gown. The beloved is compared to Diana, the Roman goddess identified with Artemis but also having some of the characteristics of Selene, the moon-goddess, who was married to the mortal Endymion. By the end of the poem, the narrator returns to the initial floral comparison; the beloved has truly become, as the title suggests, a "violet of love."

The lover's sense of restful fulfillment is vividly conveyed in "A Decade," which seems to celebrate the maturation of the relationship between narrator and the beloved. In a poem that might have gone in the direction of the intensity of physical reactions described in Sappho fragment 31, Lowell instead turns to the transformation of passion into satisfied contentment:

A DECADE

When you came, you were like red wine and honey,
And the taste of you burnt my mouth with its sweetness.
Now you are like morning bread,
Smooth and pleasant.
I hardly taste you at all for I know your savour,
But I am completely nourished.

In a lengthy ode celebrating the beloved entitled "In Excelsis" (in *What's O'Clock*), Lowell returns to images drawn from nature to convey the narrator's sense of the cosmic importance of the beloved to the narrator and to her words, which, as a consequence of the feelings of the narrator for the beloved, turn out to be "rubies mortised in a gate of stone." As in Sappho's songs, *eros* and poetry are closely linked:

IN EXCELSIS

You—you—
Your shadow is sunlight on a plate of silver;
Your footsteps, the seeding-place of lilies;
Your hands moving, a chime of bells across a
    windless air.

The movement of your hands is the long,
　golden running of light from a rising sun;
It is the hopping of birds upon a garden-path.

As the perfume of jonquils, you come forth
in the morning,
Young horses are not more sudden than your thoughts,
Your words are bees about a pear-tree,
Your fancies are the gold-and-black striped
　wasps buzzing among red apples.
I drink your lips,
I eat the whiteness of your hands and feet.
My mouth is open,
As a new jar I am empty and open.
Like white water are you who fill the
　cup of my mouth,
Like a brook of water thronged with lilies.

You are frozen as the clouds,
You are far and sweet as the high clouds.
I dare reach to you,
I dare touch the rim of your brightness.
I leap beyond the winds,
I cry and shout,
For my throat is keen as a sword
Sharpened on a hone of ivory.
My throat sings the joy of my eyes,
The rushing gladness of my love.

How has the rainbow fallen upon my heart?
How have I snared the seas to lie in my fingers
And caught the sky to be a cover for my head?
How have you come to dwell with me,
Compassing me with the four circles of your
　mystic lightness,
So that I say "Glory! Glory!" and bow
As to a shrine?

Do I tease myself that morning is morning
　and a day after?

Do I think the air a condescension,
The earth a politeness,
Heaven a boon deserving thanks?
So you—air—earth—heaven—
I do not thank you,
I take you,
I live.
And those things which I say in consequence
Are rubies mortised in a gate of stone.

Lowell returns here to her themes of the beloved as part of nature—lilies, bees, apples—and the lover as an empty jar that can only be filled by the beloved. The exclamation "Glory! Glory!" suggests the notion of "Gloria in Excelsis" contained in the title of the poem, and again suggests the metaphor of the lover as a priest or worshipper at the shrine of the beloved. Despite the reticence owing to the omission of any explicit gender references, a reading of this poem based on the assumption (not seriously questioned by any scholars today) that both narrator and addressee are women reveals a bold assertion of the all-encompassing effects of the passion between them. The narrator drinks the lips of the beloved, is filled and fulfilled, and in so taking the air-earth-heaven of the beloved, yields up gems of words. It would seem that Lowell, like her projected vision of Sappho, was able to achieve what she thought Sappho herself had achieved: "Sapho could fly her impulses like bright / Balloons tip-tilting to a morning air / And write about it."

H.D. (Hilda Doolittle, 1886–1961)

Amy Lowell helped to introduce to the American public the work of a younger poet from among the "queer lot" of writing sisters—Hilda Doolittle, whom she described rather exotically as having "a strange, faun-like, dryad-like quality."[8] Although H.D. was revered in her early years (partly through the influence of Lowell) as the ideal exponent of the Imagist movement, her reputation as a poet lapsed into obscurity during the second half of her still-prolific writing career, and it is only within the last decade or so that scholars and critics have focused their attention on the body of her poetry, stories, novels, and essays, some of them not published until well after her death.

Renewed interest in her poetry has spawned several recent biographies, which clearly establish the main facts of her life: her birth in Bethlehem, Pennsylvania, in 1886; her classical education at Bryn Mawr; her engagement to the poet Ezra Pound and her marriage to the English poet Richard Aldington (from whom she was separated in 1919 and divorced in 1938); her analysis with Freud in 1933–1934; the birth of her daughter Perdita in 1919 by a man whom she declined to name; her long association with the wealthy English lesbian writer Winifred Ellerman, alias Bryher, with whom she lived and traveled (including to Greece) off and on for the better part of her adult life; and her death in Switzerland in 1961.[9] Less easy to establish is any fixed definition of her sexual identity, and certainly her poetry eludes facile explanation. Still, the renewal of interest in her work has led several scholars to offer useful guides to the interpretation of her writing, among them Alicia Ostriker, Gary Burnett, and particularly Susan Stanford Friedman.[10]

Here I want to reinforce the views of critics who have sensed that H.D.'s poetry, steeped as it is in references to the classical myths, relies on one essential underpinning: the lyrical fragments of Sappho, surviving over the centuries like rocks, as H.D. calls them, amidst which the flowers of later poets like herself may blossom. In dealing with such a substantial and complex corpus of poetry and prose, I can only hope to touch the surface in an attempt to show how pervasive Sappho's influence on H.D. has been, and how reading H.D. against the text of Sappho leads one to appreciate the layers of meanings in H.D.'s verse.

H.D.'s poetry cannot be read without some knowledge of Greek mythology and literature, for her own study of Classical Greek led her deeply into the ancient past. Just as her Hellenism served to reinforce her popularity in pre-World War I England (as Barbara Guest puts it, "Greekness was everywhere"), so in post-World War II America it has no doubt had the effect of distancing an increasingly nonclassical audience of readers.[11] H.D.'s Hellenism has posed a problem even for those who appreciate her knowledge of Homer, Sappho, and Euripides, for many critics have viewed it as a mask or disguise or some sort of escape—something that interferes with her poetic expression rather than enables it. More recently, however, through the influence of intertextual theory, others have seen her use of the ancient material as a "collaboration," a way of engaging in a three-way dialogue among ancient author, the modern interpreter—or H.D. as poet-prophet—and the modern reader.[12]

I myself would argue for a position that perhaps lies somewhere between these two extremes, namely, the notion that H.D.'s work is a palimpsest, a term that she herself used as the title of a novel written c. 1923–1924.[13] "Palimpsest," as a palaeographical term that refers to a parchment on which one layer of writing has been scraped off—so that it is all but invisible—to allow a nearly clean surface on which new writing may be set down, implies that faint traces of the original writing remain, a precious record of what was deemed obsolete and therefore erased to make way for what was in demand. Indeed, several major works of classical literature, most notably Cicero's *De Republica*, owe their survival to just such a ghostly existence. In the case of H.D., the Greek poets, especially Homer, Sappho, and Euripides, continually float up from the underlying surface on which she layers her meanings, and layer interacts with layer to create an ever-shifting pattern of text.

As far as Sappho in particular is concerned, as we shall see, the ancient poet of Lesbos is the foundation for H.D.'s poetic voice as a desiring woman. To borrow Gubar's phrase, Sappho's lesbianism becomes an "imaginative force" that empowers H.D. to articulate female desire, whether for a man or a woman.[14] H.D.'s stance toward Sappho is expressed in prosaic terms in an essay—actually more a meditation—on "The Wise Sappho," probably written in 1919 but not published until 1982, more than twenty years after her death. In these short musings, the poet reveals her utter captivation with Sappho. Taking off from Meleager's first-century B.C. assessment of Sappho in the *Greek Anthology* to the effect that Sappho's poems are scant but all "roses," H.D. weaves her own variations on the theme of Sappho's divine perfection as a poet. First likening Sappho's songs to orange blossoms (rather than roses), she goes on to compare them rather to a magical kind of white lightning, then to all the colors in the spectrum, and finally to imperishable rocks:

> "Little, but all roses." I think, though the stains are deep on the red and scarlet cushions, on the flaming cloak of love, it is not warmth we look for in these poems, not fire nor sunlight, not heat in the ordinary sense, diffused, and comforting (nor is it light, day or dawn or light of sunsetting), but another element containing all these, magnetic, vibrant; not the lightning as it falls from the thunder cloud, yet lightning in a sense: white, unhuman element, containing fire and light and warmth, yet in its essence differing from all these, as if the brittle crescent-moon gave heat to us, or some splendid scintillating star turned warm suddenly in our hand like a jewel, sent by the beloved.
>
> I think of the words of Sappho as these colours, or states rather, transcending colour yet containing (as great heat the compass of the spectrum) all colour. And perhaps the most obvious is this rose colour, merging to richer shades of scarlet, purple or Phoenician purple. To the superficial lover—truly—roses!
>
> Yet not all roses—not roses at all, not orange blossoms even, but reading deeper we are inclined to visualize these broken sentences and unfinished rhythms as rocks—perfect rock shelves and layers of rock between which flowers by some chance may grow but which endure when the staunch blossoms have perished.[15]

Like almost all of H.D.'s prose, these words reveal her poet's eyes and ears, which see and hear more acutely than those of most people. She plays with her words, searching for a way to express how Sappho's poetry should be described, how its force should be conveyed. Although H.D. was no literary theoretician, nor did she likely make a conscious effort to see that her poetry enacted the ideas of her essays, we can still find evidence in her poems that indicates how Sappho's poetic landscape informed H.D.'s own.

Among the more obvious echoes of Sappho in H.D.'s *oeuvre* are six poems that present themselves as takeoffs from fragments of Sappho, each of which is at least partially quoted as an epigraph for the poem it inspired. These include the following six pieces, in which H.D. refers to a numbering system for Sappho's fragments (Henry T. Wharton's) that is no longer used: "Fragment 113" (Sappho fragment 146 V.); "Fragment Thirty-six" (Sappho fragment 51 V.); "Fragment Forty" (Sappho fragment 130 V.); "Fragment Forty-one" (Sappho fragment 130 V., 131 L.-P.); "Fragment Sixty-eight" (Sappho fragment 55 V.); and "Calliope" (Sappho fragment 124 V.).[16] Since most of these are relatively lengthy poems—ironically, perhaps, since all but one bear the word "fragment" in the title—I will treat only one of them as an example. This poem is especially important because it presents the lyric narrator in a direct relationship to the goddess Aphrodite (named in stanza five of section 1), much as the Sappho-narrator of the "Hymn to Aphrodite" sings of her relationship with the goddess:

FRAGMENT FORTY-ONE

. . . *thou flittest to Andromeda.*
—SAPPHO

I

Am I blind alas,
am I blind?
I too have followed
her path.
I too have bent at her feet.
I too have wakened to pluck
amaranth in the straight shaft,
amaranth purple in the cup,
scorched at the edge to white.

Am I blind?
am I the less ready for her sacrifice?
am I the less eager to give

what she asks,
she the shameless and radiant?

Am I quite lost,
I towering above you and her glance,
walking with swifter pace,
with clearer sight,
with intensity
beside which you two
are as spent ash?

Nay, I give back to the goddess the gift
she tendered me in a moment
of great bounty.
I return it. I lay it again
on the white slab of her house,
the beauty she cast out
one moment, careless.

Nor do I cry out:
"why did I stoop?
why did I turn aside
one moment from the rocks
marking the sea-path?
Aphrodite, shameless and radiant,
have pity, turn, answer us."

Ah no—though I stumble toward
her altar-step,
though my flesh is scorched and rent,
shattered, cut apart,
slashed open;
though my heels press my own wet life
black, dark to purple,
on the smooth, rose-streaked
threshold of her pavement.

2

Am I blind alas, deaf too
that my ears lost all this?

nay, O my lover,
shameless and still radiant,
I tell you this:

I was not asleep,
I did not lie asleep on those hot rocks
while you waited.
I was not unaware when I glanced
out toward the sea
watching the purple ships.

I was not blind when I turned.
I was not indifferent when I strayed aside
or loitered as we three went
or seemed to turn a moment from the path
for that same amaranth.

I was not dull and dead when I fell
back on our couch at night.
I was not indifferent when I turned
and lay quiet.
I was not dead in my sleep.

3

Lady of all beauty,
I give you this:
say I have offered small sacrifice,
say I am unworthy your touch,
but say not:
"she turned to some cold, calm god,
silent, pitiful, in preference."

Lady of all beauty,
I give you this:
say not:
"she deserted my altar-step,
the fire on my white hearth
was too great,
she fell back at my first glance."

Lady, radiant and shameless,
I have brought small wreaths,
(they were a child's gift,)
I have offered myrrh-leaf,
crisp lentisk,
I have laid rose-petal
and white rock-rose from the beach.

But I give now a greater,
I give life and spirit with this.
I render a grace
no one has dared to speak,
lest men at your altar greet him
as slave, callous to your art;
I dare more than the singer
offering her lute,
the girl her stained veils,
the woman her swathes of birth,
or pencil and chalk,
mirror and unguent box.

I offer more than the lad
singing at your steps,
praise of himself,
his mirror his friend's face,
more than any girl,
I offer you this:
(grant only strength
that I withdraw not my gift,)
I give you my praise and this:
the love of my lover
for his mistress.[17]

Despite its carefully marked heterosexuality, with a female narrator and a male lover who has rejected her in favor of his "mistress," several features of this poem call up a Sapphic landscape. Like the dialogue between Aphrodite and speaker in Sappho's "Hymn to Aphrodite," the dialogue here too is in the speaker's mind, here cast in the form of polite prohibitions ("say . . . but say not"). The theme of the bittersweetness of *eros* and the pain of jealousy suggested by the epigraph is underscored by the narrator's self-description, one worthy of Sappho fragment 31 V. in its intensity: her flesh is "scorched and rent, / shattered, cut apart, / slashed open." The effects of *eros* are overwhelming.

As in Sappho's poem about the narrator looking at the woman talking and sweetly laughing, much of the focus of this poem is on the emotional state of the narrator, not on the object of her love. Despite the shocking ending, the impact of which is heightened by the repeated delays in specifying exactly what it is that the H.D.-narrator will make as offering to the goddess, the overall effect is hardly one of virginal renunciation. Read against the background of Sappho, for whom Andromeda is but one of many names associated with *eros* in her songs, we can assume that Aphrodite will respond appropriately to the supremely great gift that the speaker offers her: the love of the rejecting lover for his new lover. The speaker will not desert the goddess's altar-step, and she will survive to pluck again the unfading flower of purple amaranth. The speaker offers back this particular love, but in the *quid-pro-quo* ambience of the Sapphic landscape, we must assume that her sacrifice will be met with rewards in the future.

"Fragment Forty-one," then, despite its Sapphic epigraph, is by no means an adaptation of Sappho or even a loose imitation. It is rather a reflection of the color and intensity of Sappho's lyrics, as well as a reassertion of the validity of the female lyric voice. The rhetorical questions of the narrator in section 1, all in the first person, are reinforced by the first-person assertions addressed to the lover in section 2. By the final section of the poem, the speaker addresses only the goddess herself, resplendent in her shrine that seems to be reached by a rocky path from the sea. Other than the general theme of a rival lover, there is no specific allusion to Sappho, and yet everywhere in this poem bits of Sappho float across the page: the sacred space of the goddess; the purple flowers; the sea; the altar; hot rocks; roses and myrrh; and above all, the overriding power of Aphrodite and the close relationship between singer and goddess.

Similar observations could be made about the remaining poems in the Sappho-epigraph group, each of which derives additional layers of meaning when read against the ancient poet's fragments. "Fragment 113," taking off from "Neither honey nor bee for me" (Wharton's translation), presents the narrator's new kind of white-heat desire that is like "fiery tempered steel." "Fragment Thirty-six," prefaced by "I know not what to do: my mind is divided," considers the seeming dichotomy between domestic love and the profession of poet: "is song's gift best? / is love's gift loveliest?" "Fragment Forty," with its epigraph simply as "Love . . . bitter-sweet," meditates on the "honey and salt" of *eros*.

"Fragment Sixty-eight" (". . . even in the house of Hades") is on one level concerned with the pain of love, but in view of the Sappho fragment's allusion to the mortality of one who is outside the realm of poetry (the ignorant woman whose ghost will flit about invisibly in Hades), this poem, too, may have to do with artistic vocation. Finally, "Calliope," prefaced by a complete translation of a very short fragment ("And thou thyself, Calliope")—which refers to the muse of epic poetry—presents a dialogue between two speakers who seem to articulate another version of the same dichotomy posed in "Fragment Thirty-six": one lyric voice argues for "unimpeded rapture," while the other (perhaps Calliope?) eschews the flesh in favor of "the host of the immortals." In all of these we find the same palimpsest quality, for in all of them Sappho is both erased and present at the same time.

Less obvious but no less real is the erasure-and-presence of Sappho in H.D.'s earliest collection of poetry, *Sea Gardens*, published in 1916. As Eileen Gregory has demonstrated in detail, H.D. in this collection "attempts to recover the imagination of goddess-centered Lesbos."[18] There is no poem among these that bears any direct resemblance to the fragments of Sappho, nor any bearing Sapphic epigraphs. Only one piece in the collection hints directly at the Sapphic inspiration, the second stanza of "Pursuit" (*Collected Poems*, pp. 11–12):

> But here
> a wild-hyacinth stalk is snapped:
> the purple buds—half-ripe—
> show deep purple
> where your heel pressed.

The reference to Sappho's trampled hyacinth (fragment 105b V.) is easily discerned.[19]

Yet despite the dearth of direct Sapphic allusions, Sappho becomes, as Gregory has shown, "the mythic figure at the ground of H.D.'s world of fragile sea- and rock-roses. She is the goddess who guards it, the sea that washes it, and the spirit informing the poet who suffers her ecstasies within it."[20] H.D.'s "Sea Garden" is indeed a garden of flowers, herbs, and flowering trees—violets, hyacinths, roses, pear trees, myrrh, and lilies recur again and in again in these pieces—but it is always a garden whose sweetness and comfort is tempered by sea-salt and rock, by sand and wind. There is always the undertow of bitterness to counter the honeyed delight of the flowers—the *glukupikron* ("sweet-bitter") element of *eros* with which Sappho is so constantly preoccupied.

Aside from an occasional mention of Hermes, Dictaeus, or dryads, references to names from Greek myth are surprisingly sparse in these poems, as is any description of specifically Greek landscapes. In "The Shrine" (*Collected Poems*, pp. 7–10), for example, no goddess is named outright, and yet the unattributed epigraph "She watches over the sea" suggests Aphrodite, born from the sea-foam and often identified in classical Greek literature as a protector of sailors. As the narrator asserts, "honey is not more sweet / than the salt stretch of your beach," again suggesting the bittersweetness of love. What is present throughout *Sea Garden*, however, is either the lyric voice of the poet-prophet, proclaiming her visionary insights into ecstatic or anguishing experience, or a collective voice, a plural narrator who refers to the protected environment in which this female group (only vaguely marked as female) enjoys its own rituals apart from outside interference; as it is put in "The Helmsman" (*Collected Poems*, pp. 5–7), "We worshipped inland— / we stepped past wood-flowers, / we forgot your tang, / we brushed wood-grass." Through such indirect means, H.D. repeatedly creates her Sapphic palimpsest.

What might be read as a helpless cry of abandonment and hopeless frustration, when read against Sappho fragment 31 V., for example, will become an assertion of the validity of self-knowledge through painful experience, of the rocks that (like Sappho's poems) yet may permit a tiny flower to grow:

MID-DAY

The light beats upon me.
I am startled—
a split leaf crackles on the paved floor—
I am anguished—defeated.

A slight wind shakes the seed-pods—
my thoughts are spent
as the black seeds.
My thoughts tear me,
I dread their fever.
I am scattered in its whirl.
I am scattered like
the hot shrivelled seeds.

The shrivelled seeds
are split on the path—
the grass bends with dust,
the grape slips
under its crackled leaf:
yet far beyond the spent seed-pods,
and the blackened stalks of mint,
the poplar is bright on the hill,
the poplar spreads out,
deep-rooted among trees.

> O poplar, you are great
> among the hill-stones,
> while I perish on the path
> among the crevices of the rocks.

The image of the narrator being scattered like a crackling seedpod blown in the wind perhaps calls to mind some of Sappho's descriptions of the force of *eros* (which can shake the lover's mind like the wind falling on mountain oaks, see Sappho fragment 47 V.), but what is even more remarkable is simply the poem's total absorption with the lyric persona of the narrator; even the poplar tree at the end of the piece—the result of just such blowing seedpods—is seen only in terms of the contrast between its strength and the narrator's spent condition. Yet the reference in the final two lines to her perishing among the rocks is surely no more literally meant than Sappho's wishes for death. When this narrator says, "My thoughts tear me, / I dread their fever. / I am scattered in its whirl," we can hear the ghost of the Sappho-singer crying, "Cold sweat covers me, trembling / seizes my whole body, I am more moist than grass; / I seem to be little short / of dying."

The two narrators seem to be combined in the following poem, in which the first-person voice speaks on behalf of the collective voice in the repeated request "spare us from loveliness":

ORCHARD

> I saw the first pear
> as it fell—
> the honey-seeking, golden-banded,
> the yellow swarm
> was not more fleet than I,
> (spare us from loveliness)
> and I fell prostrate
> crying:
> you have flayed us
> with your blossoms,
> spare us the beauty
> of fruit-trees.
>
> The honey-seeking
> paused not,
> the air thundered their song,
> and I alone was prostrate.

O rough-hewn
god of the orchard,
I bring you an offering—
do you, alone unbeautiful,
son of the god,
spare us from loveliness:

these fallen hazel-nuts,
stripped late of their green sheaths,
grapes, red-purple,
their berries
dripping with wine,
pomegranates already broken,
and shrunken figs
and quinces untouched,
I bring you as offering.

Ripeness and delicious beauty are everywhere in this poem: just-fallen pears sought by swarms of bees, their buzzing making a thundering song in the air; an orchard in blossom, grapes already—it seems—teeming with the wine they will produce; pomegranates split open to reveal their plethora of seeds. Even though it is a male god who is addressed, not Aphrodite, how far away can she be? "Hither to me from Crete, to this holy / temple, where your lovely grove / of apple trees is" (Sappho fragment 2 V.). The loveliness of the place is overwhelming even to the point of being frightening. The request to the god to "spare us from loveliness" is ambiguous; does it mean that the collective "we" is so struck by the beauty of the orchard as not to be able to bear it? Or do they wish to avoid being seen as lovely themselves in order to be spared the fate of the fallen pear—attacked as it is by a thundering swarm of bees? Surely in these lines we can hear echoes of "just like a sweet apple which ripens on the uppermost bough" (Sappho fragment 105a V.).

One final example from *Sea Garden* will illustrate again H.D.'s fondness for what we might call Sappho's roses among the rocks—for the honey and its inevitable companions, the honey-bee and its sting. The force of *eros* and its heat come across with Sapphic intensity, despite the complete absence of any details about any persons or situations; all we see is the rose, "cut in rock," frozen in the heat, as frozen as the narrator who is unable to bestir herself in heat so intense and thick that even fruit cannot fall from the trees. As Friedman has observed, "[as] in Georgia O'Keeffe's flower paintings of the 1920s, the flowers in *Sea Garden* pulsate with an ecstatic eroticism whose power comes precisely from its elusive, impersonal expression."[21]

GARDEN

I

You are clear
O rose, cut in rock,
hard as the descent of hail.

I could scrape the colour
from the petals
like spilt dye from a rock.

If I could break you
I could break a tree.

If I could stir
I could break a tree—
I could break you.

II

O wind, rend open the heat,
cut apart the heat,
rend it to tatters.

Fruit cannot drop
through this thick air—
fruit cannot fall into heat
that presses up and blunts
the point of pears
and rounds the grapes.

Cut the heat—
plough through it,
turning it on either side
of your path.

It is only in H.D.'s later poems that the oxymoronic quality of passion—its sweetness and sting, its heat and hailstones—takes on a more specifically gendered marking. As she proclaims in a long poem generally taken to have been inspired by her analysis with Freud, "The Master" (*Collected Poems*, pp. 451–61):[22]

for a woman
breathes fire
and is cold,
a woman sheds snow from ankles
and is warm;
white heat
melts into snow-flake
and violets
turn to pure amethysts,
water-clear. . . .

She is a woman,
yet beyond woman,
yet in woman,
her feet are the delicate pulse of the narcissus bud,
pushing from earth. . . .

there is a rose flower
parted wide,
as her limbs fling wide in dance
ecstatic
Aphrodite,
there is a frail lavender flower
hidden in grass;

O God, what is it,
this flower
that in itself had power over the whole earth?
for she needs no man,
herself
is that dart and pulse of the male,
hands, feet, thighs,
herself perfect.

Olga Broumas (b. 1949)

A native of a Greek island herself (although she has lived in the United States since 1967), Broumas seems to have been drawn to the Lesbian poets both ancient and modern. Besides her obvious affinities with Sappho, which I will explore below, Broumas has published two translations from the Nobel Prize-winning poet Odysseas Elytis, who was born on Lesbos: *What I Love: Selected Poems of Odysseas Elytis*, (Port Townsend: Copper Canyon Press, 1986) and *The Little Mariner* (also Copper Canyon Press, 1988). In her most recent work, *Sappho's Gymnasium* (coauthored with T Begley [sic]), she wryly refers to Elytis as "the second great Lesbian" (p. viii).

The volumes of original work published by Broumas vary considerably in both style and content, ranging from short lyrical reminiscences of her childhood in Greece to a series of prose poems interspersed with translations from Pierre Louÿs's Sapphic imitations, *Les Chansons de Bilitis*. In almost all of her poetry, women are the central focus and the world is viewed through the female body. Although a few of her pieces treat political or moral themes, most could be said in one fashion or another to deal with love, *eros*, and the body of woman. Her first published work, *Beginning with O*, and her most recent volume, *Sappho's Gymnasium*, are the most self-consciously Sapphic of her works to date, and for that reason I will concentrate on examples from these two collections.

Broumas's career as a poet was launched in 1977 with the publication of the volume that had won her the seventy-second Yale Series of Younger Poets Award, *Beginning with O*.[23] The title proclaims her radical vision, for the *O* referred to is the Greek letter *omega*, the final letter of the Greek alphabet. Thus, in an oxymoronic twist, what is usually seen as the end becomes the beginning, the horseshoe-shaped, womblike Ω The meaning of the volume's title becomes clear in the poem entitled "Artemis," the last in a series of pieces called "Twelve Aspects of God":

ARTEMIS

Let's not have tea. White wine
eases the mind along
the slopes
of the faithful body, helps

any memory once engraved
on the twin
chromosome ribbons, emerge, tentative
from the archaeology of an excised past.

I am a woman
who understands
the necessity of an impulse whose goal or origin
still lie beyond me. I keep the goat

for more
than the pastoral reasons. I work
in silver the tongue-like forms
that curve round a throat

an arm-pit, the upper
thigh, whose significance stirs in me
like a curviform alphabet
that defies

decoding, appears
to consist of vowels, beginning with O, the O-
mega, horseshoe, the cave of sound.
What tiny fragments

survive, mangled into our language.
I am a woman committed to
a politics
of transliteration, the methodology

of a mind
stunned at the suddenly
possible shifts of meaning—for which
like amnesiacs

in a ward on fire, we must
find words
or burn.

Unlike the Artemis of ancient Greece, the virgin huntress and twin of Apollo, this Artemis seems to be a goddess of carefully articulated erotic desire. The language of *eros* here, beginning with the *"omega"* of the female body, can only be found through a kind of primordial memory and through excavations into a bygone era that has been largely erased—that is, through "the archaeology of an excised past." If we read Broumas in the light of Sappho, we can see an allusion to Sappho's erotic language in the assertion "What tiny fragments / survive, mangled into our language." The "transliteration" to which the narrator is committed, then, is the transliteration of *omega* into our *O* and of Sappho's Greek text into a modern text celebrating the female body and woman-centered *eros*.

From the outset, "Artemis" emphasizes the primacy of the "faithful body" and its imprinted chromosomes. The narrator becomes a kind of artisan sculpting the curves of the female body, the meaning of which is only beginning to be apparent: the curves of the body are compared to a "curviform alphabet" that cannot quite be deciphered but that contains an abundance of round vowel sounds. In these middle stanzas of the poem, the tongue (as in "tongue-like forms")—the instrument of speech— the body of woman, and the as-yet undecoded language become closely intertwined. It is only through the reliance on the primacy of the body that the mind, in the next-to-last stanza, is free to perceive the radical reinterpretation of the mangled present-day remnants of the lost primal language.

The artisan-narrator of "Artemis" also seems to be a goatherd, who keeps her goat "for more than the pastoral reasons." She seems to be saying that tending the goat has a deeper significance than merely as part of leading the idyllic countryside life. This is no peaceful Arcadia, but a world of primal instincts and deeply imprinted urges. The goat as a sacrificial animal perhaps suggests this underlying layer of primitive—and primary—impulses toward the female world symbolized by Artemis, mistress of wild animals and goddess of the hunt. The goat, like the wine of the opening stanza—Dionysiac liquid that helps ease forth the bodily traces of the past—is an earthy link to the alphabet of the female body, to the womblike curves of the *omega*, the end that is the beginning of all things.

Like Sappho in her treatment of the Helen myth (fragment 16 V.), Broumas, too, feels free to rewrite the ancient myths to suit her own purposes. In Broumas's case, such rewriting may take the form of gender-bending experiments, as in her "Leda and her Swan," the opening piece in the series "Twelve Aspects of God." Here Broumas transforms what is essentially a patriarchal story of the rape of Leda by Zeus in the form of a swan into a story of mutually passionate lovemaking in which both Leda and her swan are female:

Leda and Her Swan

You have red toenails, chestnut
hair on your calves, oh let
me love you, the fathers
are lingering in the background
nodding assent.

I dream of you
shedding calico from
slow-motion breasts, I dream

of you leaving with
skinny women, I dream you know.

The fathers are nodding like
overdosed lechers, the fathers approve
with authority: Persian emperors, ordering
that the sun shall rise
every dawn, set
each dusk. I dream.

White bathroom surfaces
rounded basins you
stand among
loosening
hair, arms, my senses.

The fathers are Dresden figurines
vestigial, anecdotal
small sculptures shaped
by the hands of nuns. Yours

crimson tipped, take no part in that
crude abnegation. Scarlet
liturgies shake our room, amaryllis blooms
in your upper thighs, water lily
on mine, fervent delta

the bed afloat, sheer
linen billowing
on the wind: Nile, Amazon, Mississippi.

The recurring "father figures" of the first and third stanzas, who represent
the traditional patriarchal grounds of authority, are reduced by the fifth stanza
to frozen and fragile Dresden figurines of marginal significance. This Leda is no
object of vicarious patriarchal enjoyment. Instead, in the final two stanzas a
burst of floral images describes the ecstasies of the two women, in the midst of
which the bed of lovemaking becomes a ship sailing the great rivers of the whole
world. The "delta" of the women's bodies suggests the delta of the Nile in the
final list, in which "Amazon" serves a double function as both the great river of
South America and the name of the legendary tribe of female warriors of Greek
mythology. The final river, Mississippi, forms a cosmic link between the ancient

rivers of Egypt, South America, and North America. This is no small odyssey on which Leda and her swan have embarked.

Like the narrator in Sappho fragment 3 1 V., the narrator here focuses on her own reactions to Leda as the patriarchal figures recede (as does the godlike man sitting beside the woman in Sappho's poem). The narrator dimly notices the nodding "fathers," but her attention is fixed primarily on particular details of Leda's body—her red toenails, the chestnut hair of her legs, the image of her breasts moving beneath clothing. The narrator repeatedly emphasizes her dreams of Leda's body, which suddenly become concretized as Leda loosens her hair—and simultaneously the swan-narrator's senses. The cool white porcelain of the basins where Leda is standing ironically becomes a veritable hothouse of color and blossoms that shake the room with their intensity as the women make love. By taking over and completely transforming the role of Zeus, the female narrator in this piece effectively creates an entirely new perspective from which to view the traditional story. It is an example of the "transliteration" to which Broumas refers in "Artemis," an attempt to rediscover the primal language of woman-centered desire.

Another poem in the same series, "Triple Muse," reinforces its central theme by its tripartite structure. Alluding like many of Sappho's poems to song and performance, this piece boldly asserts that the three women friends and performers who constitute the collective narrator are in fact themselves the muses of their own inspiration, "tuning / our instruments to ourselves":

I

Three of us sat
in the early summer, our instruments
cared for, our bodies dark

and one stirred the stones on
the earthen platter, till the salt
veins aligned, and she read the cast:

Whatever is past
and has come to an end
cannot be brought back by sorrow.

II

False things
we've made seem true, by charm, by music. Faked
any trick when it pleased us

and laughed, faked
too when it didn't. The audience couldn't tell, invoking
us absently, stroking their fragile beards, waiting

for inspiration
served up like dinner, or sex. Past. Here
each of us knows, herself, the mineral-bright pith.

III

It's been said, we are of one mind.
It's been said, she is happy whom
we, of the muses, love.

Spiral Mountain: the cabin
full of our tools: guitar, tapedeck, video
every night

stars we can cast the dice by. We are
of one mind, tuning
our instruments to ourselves, by our triple light.

Unlike the performers' audience, marked as male by the allusion to their beard-stroking pose, the performers themselves form a self-contained world in which their bodies and their "instruments" (updated from mere guitars—the word being derived from the ancient Greek word *kithara*—to include taped-ecks and videos) are all that they need. Like the Muses of Hesiod's *Theogony* to whom Broumas alludes in the opening stanza of section II above, who tell the Greek poet

> We know how to say many false things that are similar to truth,
> But we also know, whenever we wish, to utter true things
>
> (Hesiod, *Theogony* 27–28)

these Muses can make false things seem true through the power of their music. They are masters at the art of illusion, but they also know directly the inner core—the pith—of everything. Without intermediaries, they can read the signs contained in the stones and the salt of the earth. Unlike the audience, they need no external agents to deliver to them sustenance or sex. As Carruthers has observed with regard to this poem and to Broumas's creation of a feminized world, "the muses . . . do not visit or inspire her, they *are* her and her friends."[24]

Elsewhere in the "Twelve Aspects of God" series, however, Broumas makes clear that her feminized world does owe much to the inspiration of other women poets. In her "Demeter," as she spins a poem around the mother-daughter theme that is the central focus of the Demeter and Persephone myth, she alludes to some of her own literary mother figures, "Anne. Sylvia. Virginia. / Adrienne the last, magnificent last," referring to Sexton, Plath, Woolf, and Rich. Her indebtedness to Sappho in *Beginning with O* is paramount to the point that she hardly even needs to mention her by name. Besides the kind of re-creation of the sacred space of Sappho's apple grove in the poems we have examined so far, Broumas also alludes to some of Sappho's songs in more direct fashion, as in a lengthy poem entitled "Betrothal / the bride's lament." A line near the poem's beginning, "we make the roof high stud the crossbeams with hooks," is a twisted allusion to Sappho fragment 111 V., the wedding song beginning "Raise high the roof-beams!" Broumas's poem goes on to paint a grim picture of a rough and splintery structure that turns out to be a trap rather than a place of shelter and refuge: "when the latch slips its lock this time / past our linked fingers / more doors than this / one are closing."

Another poem in this volume, "Bitterness," is prefaced by an epigraph assigned by Broumas to Sappho:

> She who loves roses must be patient
> and not cry out when she is pierced by thorns.

However, when one reads the notes printed at the back of the volume, one finds the following curious annotation:

> The epigraph appears in the middle of a page of notes on Sappho. I have been unable to locate it in any of her works. It is possible that I wrote it myself, under her influence, or that it might be from some lyric in the *Greek Anthology*, though here again my efforts to locate it have been unfruitful. At the risk of mysticism, I feel the couplet to be hers, regardless of its actual provenance.[25]

The fragment about the roses and the thorns is indeed not attributable to Sappho, although its apparent allusion to the bittersweetness of love is certainly reminiscent of Sappho fragment 130 V. about Eros as a *glukupikron* ("sweet-bitter") creature. Broumas's remark about the provenance of the sentiment displays her own sense of connection with the ancient poet, who is clearly the source of her own bold assertion of an unabashedly female-oriented erotic view of the world.

More pieces from *Beginning with O* would bear a close reading in order to demonstrate affinities with Sappho, but for the sake of space I single out just a few excerpts. These poems show a constant preoccupation with the remnants of the lost female language and the need to redefine our way of speaking about the love between women. In "Rumplestiltskin," for example, Broumas asserts that "the words we need are extinct. / Or if not extinct / badly damaged." Similarly, like the allusion to the imprinted chromosomes in "Artemis," Broumas frequently refers signs of a lost past—to "a loop of memory" (in "Rapunzel"), to "fossils" (in "Sleeping Beauty"), and to "archaeologists" ("Rumplestiltskin"). Broumas constantly pursues her project of transliteration, of finding the words to express what Sappho before her had expressed. Unlike Sappho, who seems to take the female-centeredness of her poetic world for granted, Broumas is always alert to the radical nature of her vision in the terms forced on everyone in late-twentieth-century American society. As she comments in "Rumplestiltskin,"

> Two
> women, laughing
> in the streets, loose-limbed
> with other women. Such things are dangerous.
> Nine million
>
> have burned for less.

The radical element in Broumas's vision—an excitement in the recovery of the lost connections between women combined with a sense of danger in the living out of that connection—is nowhere more clearly expressed than in the conclusion to "Sleeping Beauty":

> City-center, mid-
> traffic, I
> wake to your public kiss. Your name
> is Judith, your kiss a sign
>
> to the shocked pedestrians, gathered
> beneath the light that means
> stop
> in our culture
> where red is a warning, and men
> threaten each other with final violence: *I will drink
> your blood.* Your kiss
> is for them

a sign of betrayal, your red
lips suspect, unspeakable
liberties as
we cross the street, kissing
against the light, singing, *This*
is the woman I woke from sleep, the woman that woke
me sleeping.

As Judy Grahn has noted, this bold description of a public kiss between the two women marks a distinct difference in the way in which the "island of women" (to use Grahn's term) is presented in the poetic medium in American literature. No longer is the island "perched in the rarified air of the upper class with Low-ell, nor exiled in the safety of Switzerland with H.D. and Bryher; now the love is public, is out in the open in America. It is in the world."[26]

Broumas's sense of connection with Sappho is of course acknowledged in the title of her most recent collection of poetry, *Sappho's Gymnasium*, coauthored with T Begley. The proem to the collection begins with a partial quotation from Sappho fragment 150 V., which the authors translate as "Tears unbecome the house of poets." (The Greek text of the fragment, preserved in a quotation, has metrical problems and is therefore open to debate as to its exact wording.) Other sources of inspiration alluded to in this proem include Odysseas Elytis, Adrienne Rich, and W. S. Merwin. The volume is divided into ten sections, the final one of which bears the book's title and is the most self-consciously Sapphic in tone. All the poems in this final section of the volume read like translations of cryptic fragments, often consisting of only a dozen or so words and written without punctuation. One of the pieces is in fact "intuited" from Sappho fragment 132 V. (see Broumas's note on p. 185):

FRAGMENT 132 V.

Esti moi kala pais chrusioisin	I have a child whose beauty
anthemoisin	resembles golden flowers: beloved
emphere<n> echoisa morphan Kleis	Kleis,
< > agapata,	whom [I would not exchange]
anti tas egoude Ludian paisan oud'	either for all of Lydia or a lovely . . .
erannan . . .	

Here is the Broumas-Begley version (p. 172):

"I have a young girl good as blossoming gold
her ephemeral face I have formed of a key
dearer than skylark homelands"

Aside from the opening line, it bears only slight resemblance to the existing fragment, but the image of the "blossoming gold" is a felicitous rendition of the original's comparison of the girl to "golden flowers." The deliberate re-creation of fragmentary images in this portion of "Sappho's Gymnasium" produces some startling lines, many of which carry a faint echo of the Sapphic voice, and mention of "Lesvos" (the modern Greek pronunciation of Lesbos), "Lesbian," "olive groves," and "Pansappho" sprinkled here and there in the lines helps create a Sapphic ambience. For example, to Sappho fragment 130 V. (see chapter 1) and perhaps fragment 57 V. we may compare the following (p. 174):

> Limblooser sweetbitter's scale holds the hem
> kitesilk the mind at your ankles

The force of Sappho fragment 47 V. (see chapter 1) is conveyed in the following Broumas-Begley "fragment" (p. 176):

> Spasm my brakes
> downhill oaks
> eros wind

Syntax and grammatical sense are of little import in any of the pieces in this volume, which seem to serve as fragments of the primal female memory of which Broumas spoke in *Beginning with O*. Their semantic obscurity is seemingly contradicted by the vividness of the images and the forcefulness of individual words and their sound effects, as in

> Preumbilical eros preclassical brain   (p. 172)

> Horizon helicoptera
> Lesbian your cups   (p. 173)

> Hermaphrodyte phototaxis   (p. 173)

The final three pieces in the "Sappho's Gymnasium" section bear no specific correspondence to the fragments of Sappho's songs, but they do convey something of Sappho's confidence in the eternal power of poetry to effect transformation (pp. 183–84):

> In the dark before the candle
> where the archetypes take our unconscious to build
> this work is forever

> Wanderer gathers dusk in mountains
> to its end the wind the stream
> only riverbank hurry me
>
> Only poetry

In *Sappho's Gymnasium* Broumas and Begley have indeed subjected Sappho's lyrics to an athletic transformation to serve their own purposes in the late twentieth century. Although these two poets are clearly steeped in the Sapphic tradition, their jointly produced volume is in no way an attempt at imitation of Sappho, nor does it try to use Sapphic references as a kind of safe code for describing erotic connections between women. Bold and forthright in their eroticism, these mystical poems—these fragments of memory—repeatedly proclaim the positive power of song:

> Honey of clarity and strength laboring light
> the yes of song and its relentless ear
> the actual words   (p. 89)

By reading the "actual words" of modern American women poets in the strength of Sappho's light, we can truly see how the "yes of song" continues to be felt across the span of twenty-six centuries since the time that Sappho sang her songs on the island of Lesbos. In those songs, or in what they might have been, Lowell, H.D., and Broumas, among many others, have found an authoritative paradigm for the passionate female voice that speaks in their own lyrics.

APPENDIX ONE

A Guide to the Transliteration

	GREEK	ROMAN
alpha	α	a
beta	β	b
gamma	γ	g (γγ = ng)
delta	δ	d
epsilon	ε	e (short)
zeta	ζ	z
eta	η	e (long)
theta	θ	th
iota	ι	i
kappa	κ	k
lambda	λ	l
mu	μ	m
nu	ν	n
xi	ξ	x
omicron	ο	o (short)
pi	π	p
rho	ρ	r
sigma	c (σ, ς)	s
tau	τ	t

upsilon	υ	u
phi	φ	ph
chi	χ	ch
psi	ψ	ps
omega	ω	o (long)
digamma	Ϝ	w

APPENDIX TWO

THE GREEK TEXT

Greek text from the edition by Eva-Maria Voigt, *Sappho et Alcaeus: Fragmenta* (Amsterdam: Athenaeum-Polak and Van Gennep, 1971). A list of the ancient source(s) for each fragment, similar wording from elsewhere in Greek literature, and further bibliography (including suggestions for alternate readings of the Greek text) may be found in her critical apparatus.

Largely unintelligible fragments have been left untranslated below. The symbol ⊗ in the Greek text indicates the likely beginning or ending of a poem. The annotation in Latin following each number identifies the type of meter in a given fragment. The numbering is not always consecutive since Voigt omits a few fragments that had previously been included in an earlier edition of the Greek text of Sappho.

1 (1)   METRUM: STROPHA SAPPHICA

⊗ Ποι꜀κιλόθρο꜀ν᾽ ἀθανάτ᾽Ἀφρόδιτα,
    παῖ꜀ Δ꜀ί꜀ος δολ꜀όπλοκε, λίccομαί
      ce,
    μή μ᾽꜀ ἄcαιcι ꜀μηδ᾽ ὀνίαιcι δάμνα,
4   πότν꜀ια, θῦ꜀μον,

O immortal Aphrodite of the many-
    colored throne,
child of Zeus, weaver of wiles, I be-
    seech you,
do not overwhelm me in my heart
with anguish and pain, O Mistress,

ἀλλὰ τυίδ᾽ ἔλιθ᾽, αἴ ποτα κάτ-
  έρωτα
τὰ‿ϲ ἔμαϲ αὔιδαϲ ἀίοιϲα πήλοι
ἔκꜗλυεϲ, πάτροιϲ δὲ δόμον λίποιϲα
8   χϳρύϲιον ἦλθιεϲ

But come hither, if ever at another
  time
hearing my cries from afar
you heeded them, and leaving the
  home of your father
came, yoking your golden

ἄρϳμ᾽ ὐπαϲδειύξαιϲα· κάλοι δέ ϲ᾽
  ἆγον
ὤꜗκεεϲ ϲτροῦιθοι περὶ γᾶϲ
  μελαίναϲ
πύϳκνα δίνινεντεϲ πτέρ᾽ ἀπ᾽
  ὠράνω‿ αἴθε-
12   ροϳϲ διὰ μέϲϲω·

Chariot: beautiful, swift sparrows
drew you above the black earth
whirling their wings thick and fast,
from heaven's ether through mid-air.

αἶϳψα δ᾽ ἐξίκοιντο· cὺ δ᾽, ὦ μά-
  καιρα,
μειδιαίϳϲαιϲ᾽ ἀθανάτωι προϲώπωι
ἤϳρε᾽ ὄττι δηὖτε πέπονθα κὤττι
16   δηϳὖτε κϳάλιηϳμμι

Suddenly they had arrived; but you, O
  Blessed Lady,
with a smile on your immortal face,
asked what I had suffered again and
why I was calling again

κϳὤττι ϳμοι μάλιϲτα θέλω γένεϲθαι
μϳαινόλαι ιθύμωι· τίνα δηὖτε
  πείθω
.ϳ.ϲάγην ιἐϲ ϲὰν φιλότατα; τίϲ ϲ᾽, ὦ
20   Ψάϳπφ᾽, ιἀδίκηϲι;

And what I was most wanting to happen for me
in my frenzied heart: "Whom again
  shall I persuade
to come back into friendship with you?
  Who,
O Sappho, does you injustice?

καϳὶ γιὰρ αἰ φεύγει, ταχέωϲ διώξει,
αἰ δὲ δῶρα μὴ δέκετ᾽, ἀλλὰ δώϲει,
αἰ δὲ μὴ φίλει, ταχέωϲ φιλήϲει
24   κωὐκ ἐθέλοιϲα.

"For if indeed she flees, soon will she
  pursue,
and though she receives not your gifts,
  she will give them,
and if she loves not now, soon she will
  love, even against her will."

ἔλθε μοι καὶ νῦν, χαλέπαν δὲ λῦϲον
ἐκ μερίμναν, ὄϲϲα δέ μοι τέλεϲϲαι
θῦμοϲ ἰμέρρει, τέλεϲον, cὺ δ᾽ αὔτα

Come to me now also, release me
  from
harsh cares; accomplish as many things

28   cύμμαχοc ἔccο.   ⊗   as my heart desires
to accomplish; and you yourself
be my fellow soldier.

2 (5)   METRUM: STROPHA SAPPHICA

1ᵃ . .ανοθεν κατιου[c]-

1   †δευρυμμεκρητεcιπ[.]ρ[   ]|.†
      ναῦον

    ἄγνον ὄππ[αι   ]| χάριεν μὲν
      ἄλcοc

    μαλί[αν],| βῶμοι δ᾽ ἔ⟨ν⟩ι θυμιάμε-

4   νοι [λι]||βανώτω⟨ι⟩·

Hither to me from Crete, to this holy
temple, where your lovely grove
of apple trees is, and the altars
smoke with frankincense.

    ἐν δ᾽ ὕδωρ ψῦχρο[ιν]| κελάδει δι᾽
      ὔcδων

    μαλίνων,| βρόδοιcι δὲ παῖc ὀ
      χῶρος

    ἐcκί|αcτ᾽, αἰθυccομένων δὲ φύλλων|

8   κῶμα †καταιριον·

Herein cold water rushes through
apple boughs, and the whole place is
   shaded
with roses, and sleep comes down
from rustling leaves.

    ἐν δὲ λείμων| ἰππόβοτοc τέθαλε

    †τωτ. . .(.)ριν|νοιc† ἄνθεcιν, αἰ ⟨δ᾽⟩
      ἄηται

    μέλλι|χα πν[έο]ιcιν [

12   [   ]

Herein a meadow where horses graze
blooms with spring flowers, and the
   winds
blow gently . . .

    ἔνθα δὴ cὺ †cυ.αν†| ἔλοιcα Κύπρι

    χρυcίαιcιν ἐν κυ|λίκεccιν ἄβρωc

    ⟨ὀ⟩μ⟨με⟩μεί|χμενον θαλίαιcι|
      νέκταρ

16   οἰνοχόειcα

Here, O Cyprian, taking [garlands],
in golden cups gently pour forth
nectar mingled together with our festivities. . . .

3 (23)   METRUM: STROPHA SAPPHICA

      ]δώcην

    κλ]ύτων μέντ᾽ ἐπ[

    κ]άλων κᾰcλων, c[

    ˙]λοιc, λύπηc τέμ[

5   ]μ᾽ ὄνειδοc

      ]οιδήcαιc. ἐπιτα[

].ͅαν, ἄσαιο. τὸ γὰρ .[

]μον οὐκοὖτω μ[

9] διάκηται,

]μηδ[   ].αζε,

]χις, cυνίημ[ι

].ης κακότατο[c

13]μεν

]ν ἀτέραιc με[

]η φρέναc, εὖ[

]ατοιc μακα[

17]

]α[

4 (24) METRUM: STROPHA SAPPHICA

]θε θῦμον

]μι πάμπαν

] δύναμαι,

4]

]αc κεν ἦ μοι

]cαντιλάμπην

]λον πρόcωπον.

8]

]γχροΐcθειc,

]΄[. .]ροc

5 (25) METRUM: STROPHA SAPPHICA

⊗ Κύπρι καὶ] Νηρήϊδεc, ἀβλάβη[ν μοι	O [Cyprian] and Nereids, grant
τὸν καcί]γνητον δ[ό]τε τυίδ᾿ ἴκεcθα[ι	that my brother come hither unharmed
κὤccα Ϝ]οι θύμω⟨ι⟩ κε θέλη γένεcθαι	and that as many things as he wishes in his heart to come about
4 πάντα τε]λέcθην,	are all brought to pass,
[—]	
ὄccα δὲ πρ]όcθ᾿ ἄμβροτε πάντα λῦcα[ι	And that he atones for all his former errors,
καὶ φίλοιc]ι Ϝοῖcι χάραν γένεcθαι	and is a joy to his [friends],

. . . . . . .ἔ]χθροιϲι, γένοιτο δ᾽ ἄμμι   a [pain] to his enemies; but for us

8   . . . . . .μ]ηδ᾽ εἶϲ·   let there be no misery.

[—]

τὰν καϲιγ]νήταν δὲ θέλοι πόηϲθαι   May he wish to do honor to his sister

]τίμαϲ, [ὀν]ίαν δὲ λύγραν   . . . painful suffering . . .

]οτοιϲι π[ά]ροιθ᾽ ἀχεύων

12].να

]. ειϲαΐω[ν] τὸ κέγχρω   . . . millet-seed . . . of the citizens . . .

]λεπαγ[. . ῳ̂]αι πολίταν

]λλωϲ[. . .]νηκε δ᾽ αὖτ᾽ οὐ

16]κρω[ ]

]οναικ[   ]εο[   ]. ι

]. . [.]ν· ϲὺ [δ]ὲ̀ Κύπ̣[ρι]. .   . . . but you, Cyprian, setting aside . . .

[. . (.)]να

]θεμ[έν]α κάκαν [

20]ι.   ⊗

6   METRUM: FORT. STROPHA SAPPHICA

ὼϲ δα.[

    κακ̣κ̣[

—

ατρι[

κτα̣.[

5   .].[

    θα[

—

⊗   Ϲτεῖχ[

ὼϲ ἰδω[

τὰϲ ἐτ.[

10   ποτνια.[

—

χρυϲοπ̣[

καππο[

.ανμ[

    κ̣ᾶρα.[

15   ].[

7   METRUM: STROPHA SAPPHICA

Δωρί]χ̣αϲ. [. . . . .] . [

]κην κέλ̣ετ̣᾽, οὐ γὰρ̣ [

3   ]αιϲ
]κάνην ἀγερωχία[
]μμεν᾽ ὄαν νέοιϲι[
]. αν φ[ι]λ[. . . . . .]. [
7   ]μα. [

8

].ν.ọ.[
]ạμφ.[
Ἄ]τθι· co.[
].νέφ[
5   ] [

9   METRUM: STROPHA SAPPHICA

]αρκαλειοιταϲε.[
]παν οὐκεχη[
3   ]ερ ἑόρταν
]μαν [Ἤ]ραι τελε[
].ωνέμ[
].. ᾶϲ ἄ.[
7   ]υϲαι[
].οϲδε̣[
]ν.[

12   METRUM: STROPHA SAPPHICA

]. . .[
]ϲ̣θε.[
3   ] [
]ỵọημ̣[
].απεδ[
᾽].ηνεο[
7   ] [
]. .ρις.[
].ι̣φ[

15 (26)   METRUM: STROPHA SAPPHICA

b

]ạ μάκαι̣[ρ   . . . blessed (goddess?)
]ε̣υπλο.᾽[

a   ]. ατοςκα[

4   ]

]οϲθ᾽[   ]βροτεκη[. . .

]αται̣ϲ[   ]ν̣εμ̣[[May (s)he atone for] as many errors as

]. ύχαι λι.[   ]ε̣νοϲ κλ[(s)he made [before]

8   ].[   ]

[—]   . . .

Κύ]πρι κα[ί ϲ]ε πι[κροτ᾽. .]α̣ν   Cypris, and may Doricha find you

ἐπεύρ[οι   most harsh,

μη]δὲ καυχάϲ[α]ι̣το τόδ᾽ ἐν-   and may she not boast saying this,

νέ[ποιϲα   how (s)he came a second time [to]

Δ]ωρίχα τὸ δεύ[τ]ερον ὠϲ ποθε[much-desired *eros.*

12   ]ερον ἦλθε.   ⊠

16 (27)   METRUM: STROPHA SAPPHICA

⊠Ο]ι μὲν ἱππήων ϲτρότον, οἰ δὲ   Some say that the most beautiful thing

πέϲδων,   upon the black earth is an army of

οἰ δὲ νάων φαῖϲ᾽ ἐπ[ὶ] γᾶν μέλ-   horsemen:

αι[ν]αν   others, of infantry, still others, of

ἔ]μμεναι κάλλιϲτον, ἔγω δὲ κῆν᾽ ὄτ-   ships;

τω τιϲ ἔραται·   but I say it is what one loves.

4   [—]

πά]γχυ δ᾽ εὔμαρεϲ ϲύνετον πόηϲαι   It is completely easy to make this

π]άντι τ[ο]ῦτ᾽, ἀ γὰρ πόλυ περϲ-   intelligible to everyone; for the woman

κέθοιϲα   who far surpassed all mortals in

κ̣άλλο̣ϲ [ἀνθ]ρώπων Ἐλένα [τὸ]ν   beauty,

ἄνδρα   Helen, left her most brave husband

8   τ̣ὸ̣ν̣ [αρ]ιϲτον

[—]

κ̣αλλ[ίποι]ϲ̣᾽ ἔβα ᾽ϲ Τροΐαν   And sailed off to Troy, nor did she

πλέοι[ϲα   remember at all her child

κωὐδ[ὲ πα]ῖδοϲ οὐδὲ φίλων   or her dear parents; but [the Cyprian]

το[κ]ήων   led her away. . . .

πά[μπαν] ἐμνάϲθ⟨η⟩, ἀλλὰ παρ-

άγαγ᾽ αὔταν

12   `   ]ϲαν

[—]

]αμπτον γὰρ [

]. . .κούφωϲτ[   ]οη.[.]ν̣

..]μϵ νῦν Ἀνακτορί[ας ὀ]νϵμναι-
16   c᾽ οὐ] παρϵοίcας,
        [—]
      τᾶ]c ⟨κ⟩ϵ βολλοίμαν ἔρατόν τϵ
        βᾶμα
      κἀμάρυχμα λάμπρον ἴδην προcώπω
      ἢ τὰ Λύδων ἄρματα κἀν ὄπλοιcι
20   πϵcδομ]άχϵντας.
        [—]
          ].μϵν οὐ δύνατον γένϵcθαι
          ].ν ἀνθρωπ[. .(.) π]ϵδέχην
        δ᾽ ἄραcθαι
        [   ]
24   [   ]
        [   ]
        [   ]
        [   ]
28   προc[

        —

        ὢcδ[
        . .].[
        .].[.]ωλ.[
32   τ᾽ ἐξ ἀδοκή[τω.   ⊠
        —

[All of which] has now reminded me
of Anaktoria, who is not here.

Her lovely walk and the bright sparkle
        of her face
I would rather look upon than
all the Lydian chariots
and full-armed infantry.
        [This may be the end of the poem.]

---

17 (28)   METRUM: STROPHA SAPPHICA

⊠ Πλάcιον δη μ[
    πότνι᾽ ῞Ηρα cὰ χ[
    τὰν ἀράταν Ἀτ[ρϵίδαι   κλῆ-]
4   τοι βαcίληϵc·
        —

    ἐκτϵλέccαντϵc μ[
    πρῶτα μὲν πϵρι.[
    τυίδ᾽ ἀπορμάθϵν[τϵc
8   οὐκ ἐδύναντο
        —

    πρὶν cὲ καὶ Δί᾽ ἀντ[
    καὶ Θυώναc ἰμϵ[

Near to me, lady Hera,
[may your lovely form appear],
whom (famous) kings, the sons of
        Atreus,
entreated,

When they had accomplished [many
        labors],
first at Ilium [and then at sea]
setting out to here, they were not able
[to complete the journey];

Until they [called upon] you and Zeus
        Antiaios

νῦν δὲ κ[and the lovely [son] of Thuone.

12   κὰτ τὸ παλ̣[But now kindly [come to my aid]

—   according to the custom of old.

ἄγνα καὶ κα̣[Holy and beautiful . . .

π]αρθ[εν   maidens . . .

ἀ]μφι.[around . . .

16   [   ]

     [—]

[   ]   . . . to be . . .

.[.]. νιλ[to come to . . .

ἔμμενα̣[ι

20   [?]ρ̣⁽'⁾ ἀπίκε[σθαι.   ⊗

—

18 (29)

       ⊗   ⟨Π⟩άν κεδ[

          ⟨ἐ⟩ννέπην[

          γλῶcca μ[

4   μυθολογη[

         —

         κἀ̄νδρι .[

         μεcδον[

19 (30)   METRUM: STROPHA SAPPHICA

         ]

         ]μενοιca[

         ]θ' ἐν θύοιcι[

         ] ἔχοιcαν ἔcλ[

5   ]

         ]ει δὲ βαιcα[

         ]ὐ γὰρ ἴδμεν[

         ]ιν ἔργων

9   ]

         ]δ' ὑπίccω [

         κ]ἀπικυδ[

         ]τοδ' εἴπη[

20 (31)   METRUM: STROPHA SAPPHICA

]επι . ε̣ϲμα[
]ε, γάνοϲ δὲ και̣. . [
3   ]
τ]ύχαι ϲὺν ἔϲλαι
λί]μενοϲ κρέτηϲαι
γ]ᾶϲ μελαίναϲ
7   ]
]έλοιϲι ναῦται
] μεγάλαιϲ ἀήται[ϲ
]α κἀπὶ χέρϲω
11   ]
.̣]μοθεν πλέοι.[
]δε τὰ φόρτι᾽ εἰκ[
]νατιμ᾽ ἐπεὶ κ. [
15   ]
]ρέοντι πόλλ̣. . [
]αιδέκα̣[
]ει
19   ]
]ι̣ν ἔργα
] χέρϲω [
].α
23   ]
.̣]. .[

21 (32)   METRUM: STROPHA SAPPHICA

]
].επαβοληϲ[
]α̣νδ᾽ ὄλοφυν [. . . .]ε̣.
] τρομέροιϲ π.[. .]α̣λλα
5   ]
] χρόα γῆραϲ ἤδη
]ν ἀμφιβάϲκει
]ϲ πέταται διώκων
9   ]
]ταϲ ἀγαύαϲ
]ε̣α, λάβοιϲα]
]ι̣ἄειϲον ἄμμι

13 ⌊τὰν ἰόκολπον⌋]

       ]ρων μάλιϲτα
       ]αϲ π[λ]άναται

22 (33.36) METRUM: STROPHA SAPPHICA

]βλα.[
]εργον, . .λ΄α. .[
 ]ν ῥέθοϲ δοκιμ[
4]ηϲθαι
 ]ν̣ αὐάδην χ.[
δ]ὲ μή, χείμων[
].οιϲαναλγεα.[
8]δε
.].ε̣.[. . . .].[. . .κ]έλομαι ϲ.[. . . I bid you to sing
. .].γυλα.[. . .]αν̣θι λάβοιϲα.α.[of Gongula, Abanthis, taking up . . .
πᾶ]κτιν, ἆϲ ϲε δηὖτε πόθοϲ τ̣.[[your] harp, while once again desire
12 ἀμφιπόταται   flutters about you,
   ——

τὰν κάλαν· ἀ γὰρ κατάγωγιϲ αὔτα̣[
ἐπτόαιϲ᾽ ἴδοιϲαν, ἔγω δὲ χαίρω, [As you gaze upon?] the beautiful
           woman. For the
           drapery of her clothing set your heart
            aflutter as you
           looked, and I take delight.
καὶ γὰρ αὔτα δή πο[τ᾽] ἐμεμφ[For the holy Cyprus-born goddess
16 Κ]υπρογέν[ηα   herself
           once blamed me . . .

[—]
ὠϲ ἄραμα̣[ι   As I pray . . .
τοῦτο τῶ[this word . . .
β]όλλομα̣[ι   I wish. . . .

23 (35) METRUM: STROPHA SAPPHICA

]ἔρωτοϲ ἠλπ[. . . of *eros* (hoped?)
2   ]

αν]τιον εἰϲίδωϲ[For when I look upon you face to face,
  ] Ἑρμιόνα τεαυ[τα [not even] Hermione [seems] such as
 ] ξάνθαι δ᾽ Ἐλέναι ϲ᾽ ἐίϲ[κ]ην you,

6   ]κες

[nor is it unfitting] to liken you
to fair-haired Helen.

].ις θνάταις, τόδε δ' ἴσ[θι] τὰι cᾶι
]παίcαν κέ με τὰν μερίμναν
]λαις· ἀντιδ[. .]´[.]αθοις δὲ
10   ]

. . . for mortal women, but know this,
that by your . . . [you would free me]
of all my cares. . . .

]τας ὄχθοις
]ταιν
παν]νυχίς[δ]ην
14   ] [

. . . river banks . . .
. . . all night long. . . .

24 (34)   METRUM: STROPHA SAPPHICA

a = 24a + 29 (25a) LP

]ανάγα[
].[ ]εμνάcεcθ' ἀ[
κ]αὶ γὰρ ἄμμες ἐν νεό[τατι
4   ταῦτ' [ἐ]πόημμεν·

. . .
you will remember . . .
for we also in our youth
did these things.

———

πόλλα [μ]ὲν γὰρ καὶ κά[λα
. . .η.[ ]μεν, πολι[
.μμε[.]ο[.]είαις δ[
8   .]. .[.]. .[

For many lovely things . . .
. . . the city
we . . . with sharp . . .
. . .

b = 29 (25b) LP

.[
———
το.[
γα[.]. .[
ἀνδά[
5].αι.[

c = 24b LP

]νθα[
ζ]ώομ[εν
]ω· v. .[
]εναντ[
5]απάππ[
τ]όλμαν[

]ανθρω[
]ονεχ[

]παιcα[

d = 24c LP

].έδαφο[
]αικατε[
]ανέλο[
]
5].[ ].αι
λ]επτοφών[

].εα.[

25 METRUM: STROPHA SAPPHICA

]γμε.[
]προλιπ[
]νυᾶϲεπ[
ἄ]βρα·
ἐ]γλάθαν᾽ ἐϲ[
]ηϲμεθα̣[
]γυνθαλα[

26 (37) METRUM: STROPHA SAPPHICA

]θαμέω[
ὄˌττιναˌϲ γὰρ
εὖ θέω, κῆνοί με μάˌˌιϲτα πά[ντων
cίνονταˌι
] ἀλεμάτ[
].γονωμ̣[
].ιμ̣᾽ οὐ πρ[
]αι
] cέ, θέλω[
]το πάθη[
].αν, ἔγω δ᾽ ἔμ᾽ˌαὖται
τοῦτο cύˌνοιδα
].[.].τοιϲ[. . .].[
]εναμ[
].[.].[

27 (38) METRUM: STROPHA SAPPHICA

]κ̣αιπ̣[
].[.].[.]γοϲ[
]ϲι·
. . .]. καὶ γὰρ δὴ cὺ πάιϲ ποτ[
. . .]ι̣κ̣η̣ϲ μέλπεϲθ᾽ ἄγι ταῦτα[
. .] ζάλεξαι, κἄμμ᾽ ἀπὺ τωδεκ[
ἄ]δρα χάριϲϲαι·
[—]
c]τείχομεν γὰρ ἐϲ γάμον· εὖ δε[
κα]ὶ cὺ τοῦτ᾽, ἀλλ᾽ ὄττι τάχιϲτα[
πα]ρ̣[θ]ένοιϲ ἄπ[π]εμπε, θέοι[
]εν ἔχοιεν

For once you, too, (as) a child . . .

. . . come now, sing of these things . . .

. . . strive after . . . and from . . .

freely grant us *charis* [favor/grace].

For we are going to a wedding. And
you, too,

[know?] this well, but as quickly as possible

send away the girls, may the gods
have . . .

ὄδος μ[έ]γαν εἰς   [there is no] road to great Olympus
Ὀλ[υμπον   for mortals . . .
   ἀ]νθρω[π   ]αίκ.[

28

a	**b**	**c**
]γ[. .].[	]ζ[.].[	]. . .[
].ιτασαδ[	]τες χθό[	]πα[
].ανοεισαι[	]cθ᾿ ἐ[. .]cι[	]εξα[
]πο[	].ας[	]νε[
5	]κ[	].[

29

     a = 29 (2) LP   **b** = 29 (5) LP

]. ιων[   ]
]μέτριακα[
β]άθυ δου.[   ]ανταμε[
]αγ[   ].ι πότνια[
                      ]αψατ[
           5   ]ον

     c = 29 (6a) LP   **d** = 29 (8) LP

]πεπλ[   ]δέμαυ[
].ι[.]ορμοις[.]τε[   ]νίψοι[
3   ].[. . .].[.]ω   ]ντι. [

].α[. . .].[. .]απομ[   ]   [
].ω[. . . .]τ[
].ιγο[. . .].[. . . . . .].[**e** = 29 (9) LP
7   ].
                ]προςτετο[
].[.]λμ[   ].[.].[   ]τιςιν· κα[
]ντε Γόργοι .[.].[   ].γο[
]δε· [ ]. .[. .].[
11   ].μ.[

f = 29 (20) LP   **g** = 29 (22) LP

]   ] . . [
                                        ]ναιϲυ[
]˙εδόνη[   ]εγνωϲι.[
]απάμ[   ]ανδραϲβ[
]ρῆϲμε.[
5   ]

.˙]δαι ζαφ[
    ]μ[

h = 29 (24)LP   **i** = 29 (29) LP

] [   ]ρ]
                                        ]γδημεν.[
].οιϲα[.].   ].αβαϲκο.[
Γ]ύριννοι   ]κ[.]ναλ[
].αυταν   5   ].[.]. .[.
5   ]

]ϲ˙ ἔοιϲαν
]λοιϲα
    ].[

30 (39)   METRUM: STROPHA SAPPHICA

νύκτ[. . .].[the night . . .
—

πάρθενοι δ[The girls . . .
παννυχίϲδοι[ϲ]αι[all night long . . .
ϲὰν ἀείδοιϲ[ι]ν φ[ιλότατα καὶ νυμ-   singing of your love for the
5   φαϲ ἰοκόλπω.   violet-bosomed bride.
—

ἀλλ' ἐγέρθειϲ ἠϊθ[ε   But wake up and go [to find]
ϲτεῖχε ϲοὶϲ ὐμάλικ[αϲ   the unmarried youths of your own age.
ἤπερ ὄϲϲον ἀ λιγύφω[νοϲ   Let us see as much sleep as
9   ὔπνον [ἴ]δωμεν.   ⊗   the clear-voiced [nightingale?].
—

31 (2)   METRUM: STROPHA SAPPHICA

☒ Φαίνεταί μοι κῆνος ἴcoc θέοιcιν
　　 ἔμμεν' ὤνηρ, ὄττιc ἐνάντιόc τοι
　　 ἰcδάνει καὶ πλάcιον ἆδυ φωνεί-
4　　　 cαc ὑπακούει

He seems to me to be like the gods
—whatever man sits opposite you
and close by hears you talking sweetly.

　　 καὶ γελαίcαc ἰμέροεν, τό μ' ἦ μὰν
　　 καρδίαν ἐν cτήθεcιν ἐπτόαιcεν·
　　 ὡc γὰρ ⟨ἔc⟩ c' ἴδω βρόχε' ὤc με
　　　 φώνη-
8　　 c' οὐδὲν ἔτ' εἴκει,

And laughing charmingly; which
makes the heart within my breast take
　　 flight;
for the instant I look upon you, I can-
　　 not anymore
speak one word,

　　 ἀλλὰ †καμ† μὲν γλῶccα †ἔαγε†,
　　　 λέπτον
　　 δ' αὔτικα χρῶι πῦρ ὑπαδεδρό-
　　　 μακεν,
　　 ὀππάτεccι δ' οὐδὲν ὄρημμ', ἐπιβρό-
12　　 μειcι δ' ἄκουαι,

But in silence my tongue is broken, a
　　 fine
fire at once runs under my skin,
with my eyes I see not one thing, my
　　 ears
buzz,

　　 †ἔκαδε† μ' ἴδρωc κακχέεται,
　　　 τρόμοc δὲ
　　 παῖcαν ἄγρει, χλωροτιέρα δὲ
　　　 πι⌣οίαc
　　 ἔμμι, τεθι⌣νάκην δ' ὀ⌣λίγω 'πιδει⌣ύηc
16　　 φα⌣ίνομ' ἔμ' αὔτ[αι.

Cold sweat covers me, trembling
seizes my whole body, I am more
　　 moist than grass;
I seem to be little short of dying. . . .

　　 ἀλλὰ πὰν τόλματον, ἐπεὶ †καὶ
　　　 πένητα†

But all must be ventured. . . .

32 (10)   METRUM: STROPHA SAPPHICA

　　 αἴ με τιμίαν ἐπόηcαν ἔργα
　　 τὰ cφὰ δοῖcαι

33 (9)   METRUM: STROPHA SAPPHICA

αἴθ' ἔγω, χρυcοcτέφαν' Ἀφρόδιτα,
τόνδε τὸν πάλον ⟨. . . . . .⟩ λαχοίην

O golden-crowned Aphrodite,
would that I might obtain this lot . . .

34 (4) METRUM: STROPHA SAPPHICA

ἄϲτερεϲ μὲν ἀμφὶ κάλαν ϲελάνναν The stars around the beautiful moon
ἄψ ἀπυκρύπτοιϲι φάεννον εἶδοϲ keep hidden their glittering radiance,
ὄπποτα πλήθοιϲα μάλιϲτα λάμπῃ whenever in its fullness it shines
γᾶν. . . . [upon] the earth.

        *   *   *

ἀργυρία

35 (7) METRUM: STROPHA SAPPHICA

ἤ ϲε Κύπροϲ ἢ Πάφοϲ ἢ Πάνορμοϲ

36 (20) METRUM: STROPHA SAPPHICA?

καὶ ποθήω καὶ μάομαι

37 (14) METRUM: V. 2S. STROPHA SAPPHICA

καὶ ἔμον ϲτάλυγμον
    *   *   *
τὸν δ᾽ ἐπιπλάζοντ᾽ ἄνεμοι φέροιεν
καὶ μελέδωναι

38 (19) METRUM: STROPHA SAPPHICA, CF. TEST.

ὄπταιϲ ἄμμε

39 (17) METRUM: STROPHA SAPPHICA

πόδα⟨ϲ⟩ δὲ an embroidered sandal was hiding
ποίκιλοϲ μάϲληϲ ἐκάλυπτε, Λύδι- (her) feet,
ον κάλον ἔργον a beautiful piece of Lydian work

40 (8) = S. 40 + INC. AUCT. 13 LP METRUM: STROPHA SAPPHICA

ϲοὶ δ᾽ ἔγω λεύκαϲ †επιδωμον† αἶγοϲ
    *   *   *
κἀπιλείψω τοι. . . .

41 (12) METRUM: STROPHA SAPPHICA

ταὶϲ κάλαιϲ᾽ ὔμμιν ⟨τὸ⟩ νόημμα Toward you, beautiful women, my
τῶμον thoughts
οὐ διάμειπτον are not changeable . . .

42 (13)   METRUM: STROPHA SAPPHICA

ταῖσι ⟨—⟩ ψῦχρος μὲν ἔγεντο θῦμος
πὰρ δ' ἴεισι τὰ πτέρα

43 (54)   METRUM:]‑∪∪‑∪x, GL²ᵈ SUPPL. POSSIS

]αι·
]
]λεται
] ⟦κ⟧αλος   beautiful . . .
5   ]. ἄκαλα κλόνει   stirs up peaceful (waters) . . .
] κάματος φρένα   toil . . . the heart . . .
]ε κατισδάνε[ι]   sits down . . .
] ἀλλ' ἄγιτ', ὦ φίλαι,   But come, my dears,
], ἄγχι γὰρ ἀμέρα.   �   . . . for day is near.

44 (55)   METRUM: GL²ᵈ

Κυπρο.[−22−   ]ας·   Cyprus . . .
κᾶρυξ ἦλθε θε[‑10‑]ελε[. . .].θεις   The herald came,
Ἴδαος ταδεκα. . .φ[. .].ις τάχυς   Idaeus . . . swift messenger
ἄγγελος   [who said]:
3ᵃ   ⟨«   ⟩
τάς τ' ἄλλας Ἀσίας .[.]δε.αν κλέος   ". . . And of the rest of Asia . . . the
ἄφθιτον·   fame is undying.
5   Ἔκτωρ καὶ συνέταιρ[ο]ι ἄγοις·   Hektor and his companions are bring-
ἐλικώπιδα   ing a quick-glancing girl
Θήβας ἐξ ἰέρας Πλακίας τ' ἀπ'   from holy Thebes and the river
[ἀϊ]ν⟨ν⟩άω   Plakia—
ἄβραν Ἀνδρομάχαν ἐνὶ ναῦσιν ἐπ'   tender Andromache—in ships upon
ἄλμυρον   the salty
πόντον· πόλλα δ' [ἐλί]γματα   sea; many golden bracelets and purple
χρύσια κάμματα   garments
πορφύρ[α] καταΰτ[με]να, ποίκιλ'   . . . many-colored adornments,
ἀθύρματα,   countless silver cups and ivory."
10   ἀργύρα τ' ἀνάρ⌐ι⌐θμα ⌐ποτή⌐ρ⌐ια⌐
κἀλέφαις».
ὡς εἶπ'· ὀτραλέως δ' ἀνόρουσε   So he spoke. Quickly [Hektor's] dear
πάτ[η]ρ φίλος·   father leaped up;

φάμα δ᾽ ἦλθε κατὰ πτόλιν εὐρύ-
   χορον φίλοιc.
αὖτικ᾽ Ἰλίαδαι cατίναι[c] ὑπ᾽ ἐυ-
   τρόχοιc
ἆγον αἰμιόνοιc, ἐπ[έ]βαινε δὲ παῖc
   ὄχλοc

15 γυναίκων τ᾽ ἄμα παρθενίκα[ν]
   τ. .[. .].cφύρων,
χῶριc δ᾽ αὖ Περάμοιο θυγ[α]τρεc[
ἵππ[οιc] δ᾽ ἄνδρεc ὕπαγον ὐπ᾽
   ἄρ[ματα
π[   ]εc ἠίθεοι, μεγάλω[c]τι δ[
δ[   ]. ἀνίοχοι φ[. . . . .].[

20 π[᾽]ξα. ο[
    ⟨   desunt aliquot versus   ⟩
             ἴ]κελοι θέοι[c
             ] ἄγνον ἀολ[λε
ˌὄρˌματαιˌ[   ]νον ἐc Ἴλιο[ν
ˌαὖλοc δ᾽ ἀδυ[μ]έληcˌ[   ]τ᾽
   ὀνεμίγνυ[το

25 ˌκαὶ ψ[ό]φο[c κ]ροτάλˌ[ων   ]ωc
   δ᾽ ἄρα πάρ[θενοι
ˌἄειδον μέλοc ἄγνˌ[ον, ἴκα]νε δ᾽ ἐc
   αἴθ[ερα
ˌἄχω θεcπεcίαˌ γελˌ[
ˌπάνται δ᾽ ἦc κὰτ ὄδοˌ[ιc
ˌκράτηρεc| φίαλαί τ᾽ ὀˌ[. . .]υεδε
   [. .]. . εακ[.].[

30 ˌμύρρα καˌ|ˌὶ καcία λίβˌανόc τ᾽ ὀνε-
   μείχνυτο
ˌγύναικεc δ᾽ ἐλέλυcδοˌν ὄcαι προ-
   γενέcτερα[ι
ˌπάντεc δ᾽ ἄνδρεc ἐπˌήρατον ἴαχον
   ὄρθιον
ˌπάον᾽ ὀνκαλέοντεcˌ Ἐκάβολον
   εὐλύραν
ˌὔμνην δ᾽ Ἔκτορα κ᾽Αˌνδρομάχαν
   θεο⟨ε⟩ικέλο[ιc.   ⊗

the word went out over the broad-
   plained city to his friends.
At once the sons of Ilos yoked mules
to the well-wheeled chariots. The
   whole throng
of women and . . . of maidens . . .
But apart, the daughters of Priam . . .
and unmarried men yoked horses to
   the chariots,
and greatly . . .
   . . . charioteers . . .

. . . like to the gods . . .
. . . holy . . .
set forth . . . to Ilium
and the sweet-melodied aulos [and kith-
   aris] were mingled,
and the noise of castanets. . . . Then
   the maidens
sang a holy song; the divine echo
   reached the sky . . .
and everywhere along the road . . .
libation vessels . . . ,
myrrh and cassia and frankincense
   were mingled.

But the women, as many as were older,
   cried out,
and all the men shouted a high-pitched
   lovely song,
calling upon Paean, the far-shooting
   and well-lyred;
they sang of Hektor and Andromache,
   like to the gods.

44 A (= A. 304 LP)   METRUM: FR. A]–⏑⏑–⏑⏑–⏑x, GL²ᵈ SUPPL. POSSIS
FR. B xx–⏑⏑–[

a (COL. I)   a

]cανορες . .[[to golden-haired Phoibos], whom the
Φοίβωι χρυσοκό]μαι τὸν ἔτικτε   daughter of Koios (Leto) bore
Κόω .[after she had slept with the great-
μίγεισ(α)   Κρ]ονίδαι μεγαλω-   named son of Cronos.
νύμῳ⟨ι⟩.   [But Artemis] swore a great oath [of
Ἄρτεμις δὲ θέων] μέγαν ὅρκον   the gods]:
ἀπώμοσε   [By your] head, always I will be a
                                          virgin

5   κεφά]λαν· ἄϊ πάρθενος ἔσσομαι   . . . upon the tops of the moun-
    ].ων ὀρέων κορύφαις˙ ἔπι   tains . . .
    ]δε νεῦσον ἔμαν χάριν·   . . . grant me this favor.
    ἔνευ]σε θέων μακάρων πάτηρ·   The father of the blessed gods nodded
    ἐλαφάβ]ολον ἀγροτέραν θέοι   assent.
10   ].σιν ἐπωνύμιον μέγα·   The gods [called her] far-shooting
    ]ερος οὐδάμα πίλναται·   Huntress,
    ]. .[.] . . . μαφόβε[. .]έρω·   a great name.
                                           Eros never draws near to her. . . .

b (col. II)   b

ἔμμ[
και.[
ρ.ε.[
ω . . . [
5   Μοισαν ἀγλα[The splendid [gifts?] of the Muses . . .
    πόει καὶ Χαρίτων [makes . . . and of the Charites
    βραδίνοις ἐπεβ.[slender. . . .
    ὄργας μὴ ᾿πιλάθε.[not to forget the wrath . .
    θνάτοισιν· πεδ.χ[mortals . . .
10   ]δαλίω[

45 (44)   METRUM: GL²ᵈ, v. TEST

ἆς θέλετ᾿ ὔμμες

46 (42) METRUM: DEB. GL²ᵈ

ἔγω δ᾽ ἐπὶ μολθάκαν

τύλαν ⟨κα⟩cπολέω †μέλεα· κᾶν μὲν τετύλαγκαc ἀcπόλεα†

47 (50) METRUM: GL²ᵈ

Ἔροc δ᾽ ἐτίναξέ ⟨μοι⟩   Eros shook my heart, like the wind
φρέναc, ὼc ἄνεμοc κὰτ ὄροc δρύcιν   assailing the oaks on a mountain.
ἐμπέτων

48 (48) METRUM: GL²ᵈ

ἦλθεc, †καὶ† ἐπόηcαc, ἔγω δέ c᾽   You came, you did [well?], and I
ἐμαιόμαν,   wanted you;

ὄν δ᾽ ἔψυξαc ἔμαν φρένα καιο-   You made cool my heart, which was
μέναν πόθωι   burning with desire.

49 (40. 41) METRUM: GL²ᵈ

Ἠράμαν μὲν ἔγω cέθεν, Ἄτθι, πά-   I loved you, Atthis, once long
λαι ποτά   ago. . . .

    * * *

cμίκρα μοι πάιc ἔμμεν᾽ ἐφαίνεο   You seemed to me a small and grace-
κἄχαριc   less child.

50 (49) METRUM: GL²ᵈ

ὀ μὲν γὰρ κάλοc ὄccον ἴδην πέλε-   For one who is beautiful is such as far
ται ⟨κάλοc⟩,   as looks go,

ὀ δὲ κἄγαθοc αὔτικα καὶ κάλοc   but one who is good will then be beau-
ἔc⟨cε⟩ται.   tiful as well.

51 (46) METRUM: GL²ᵈ

οὐκ οἶδ᾽ ὄττι θέω· δύο μοι τὰ   I do not know what to do; my mind is
νοήματα   split.

52 (47) METRUM: GL²ᵈ?

ψαύην δ᾽ οὐ δοκίμωμ᾽ ὀράνω   I do not think that I will touch the sky
†δυcπαχέα†   with my two arms(?)

53 (57) METRUM: GL²ᶜ

Βροδοπάχεεc ἄγναι Χάριτεc, δεῦτε   Rosy-armed divine Graces, daughters
Δίοc κόραι   of Zeus, come hither. . . .

54 (56)   METRUM: GL²ᶜ

(Ἔρωτα)
ἔλθοντ᾽ ἐξ ὀράνω πορφυρίαν περ-
  θέμενον χλάμυν

. . . [Eros] coming from heaven wearing a purple cloak . . .

55 (58)   METRUM: GL²ᶜ

κατθάνοιςα δὲ κείςῃ οὐδέ ποτα
  μναμοςύνα ςέθεν
ἔςςετ᾽ οὐδὲ †ποκ᾽† ὕςτερον· οὐ γὰρ
  πεδέχῃς βρόδων
τῶν ἐκ Πιερίας, ἀλλ᾽ ἀφάνης κἀν
  Ἀίδα δόμωι
φοιτάςῃς πεδ᾽ ἀμαύρων νεκύων ἐκ-
  πεποταμένα.

You will lie dead, nor will there be
  anyone
remembering or desiring you later; for
  you have
no share in the roses of Pieria, but will
  roam unseen
in the house of Hades, having flown
  off among dim corpses.

56 (60)   METRUM: GL²ᶜ

οὐδ᾽ ἴαν δοκίμωμι προςίδοιςαν
  φάος ἀλίω
ἔςςεςθαι ςοφίαν πάρθενον εἰς
  οὐδένα πω χρόνον
τεαύταν

I do not think there will be at any time
  a woman who looks on the light of the
  sun
with wisdom such as yours

57 (61)   METRUM: VV. I−2 INC., V. 3 GL²ᶜ

τίς δ᾽ ἀγροΐωτις θέλγει νόον . . .
ἀγροΐωτιν ἐπεμμένα ςτόλαν . . .
οὐκ ἐπιςταμένα τὰ βράκε᾽ ἔλκην
  ἐπὶ τῶν ςφύρων;

What bumpkin girl charms [your]
  mind . . .
wearing her bumpkin dress . . .
not knowing how to draw her rags
  over her ankles?

58 (65A)   METRUM: ₍HIPP²ᶜ

```
              ].[
    2         ].δα[
              ]
    4         ].α
              ]ύγοιςα[   ]                    . . . fleeing(?)
    6
        ].[. .]. .[        ]ιδάχθην           . . . was bitten(?)
      ]χυ θ[.]οι[.]αλλ[. . . . . .]ύταν       . . .
    8   ].χθο.[.]ατί.[. . . . .]ειςα          . . .
      ]μένα ταν[. . . . ὤ]νυμόν ςε            name . . . you
```

10]νι θῆται cτ[ύ]μα[τι] πρόκοψιν

. . . places success upon the
mouth . . .

]πων κάλα δῶρα παῖδεc

beautiful gifts [of the deep-
bosomed Muses?] . . . youths

12]φιλάοιδον λιγύραν χελύνναν
πά]ντα χρόα γῆραc ἤδη

. . . the song-loving, clear-voiced
tortoise-lyre

14 λεῦκαί τ᾽ ἐγένο]ντο τρίχεc ἐκ μελ-
αίναν

. . . old age already [dried up?]
all (my? his?) skin
and (my?) hair has all turned from
black to white

]αι, γόνα δ᾽ [ο]ὐ φέροιcι

. . . and (my?) knees do not support (me?)

16]ηcθ᾽ ἴcα νεβρίοιcιν
ἀ]λλὰ τί κεν ποείην;

(to dance?) like fawns
. . . but what am I to do?

18] οὐ δύνατον γένεcθαι
] βροδόπαχυν Αὔων

. . . not possible to become
. . . rosy-armed Dawn [Eos]

20 ἔc]χατα γᾶc φέροιcα[
]ον ὔμωc ἔμαρψε[

. . . carrying [Tithonus?] to the
ends of the earth

22]άταν ἄκοιτιν
]ιμέναν νομίcδει

. . . but [old age?] seized (him?)
. . . immortal wife . . .

24]αιc ὀπάcδοι

. . . [he/she] thinks
. . . would give . . .

⌊ἔγω δὲ φίλημμ᾽ ἀβροcύναν,⌋
] τοῦτο καί μοι

But I love lushness. Eros has ob-
tained this(?) for me,

26 τὸ λά⌊μπρον ἔρωc ἀελίω καὶ τὸ
κά⌋λον λέ⌊λ⌋ογχε.   ⊗

and the brightness and beauty of
the sun.

—

59 (65B)

⊗ Ἐπιν[— 2 2 —   ].[. . .]γό.[
φίλει.[

—

καιν[

60 (84)   metrum:]-◡◡-◡-x, ^hipp[2c] suppl. possis

]τύχοιcα

] θέλ᾽ †ωνταπαίcαν

τέ]λεcον νόημμα

]έτων κάλημι

5   ] πεδὰ θῦμον αἶψα

ὄ]ϲϲα τύχην θελήϲη[ϲ

]ρ ἔμοι μάχεϲθα[ι

χ]λιδάνα⟨ι⟩ πίθειϲα[

]ι, ϲὺ δ᾽ εὖ γὰρ οἶϲθα

10   ]έτει τα[.].λε. .

]κλαϲ[

61

ἔγεντ.[

οὐ γάρ κ[ε   ⊠

62 (66) METRUM: x–⏑⏑––⏑⏑–[, ˍHIPP²ᶜ SUPPL. POSSIS

⊠ Ἐπτάξατε[

2 δάφναϲ ὄτα[

—

πὰν δ᾽ ἄδιον[

4 ἢ κῆνον ἐλο[

—

καὶ ταῖϲι μὲν ἀ[

6 ὀδοίποροϲ ἄν[. . . .].. .[

—

μύγιϲ δέ ποτ᾽ εἰϲάιον· ἐκλ[

8 ψύχα δ᾽ ἀγαπάταϲυ.[᾽

—

τέαυτα δὲ νῦν ἔμμ[

10 ἴκεϲθ᾽ ἀγανα[

—

ἔφθατε· κάλαν[

12 τά τ᾽ ἔμματα κα[⊠

—

63 (67) METRUM: x–⏑⏑––⏑⏑–[, ˍHIPP²ᶜ SUPPL. POSSIS

⊠ Ὄνοιρε μελαινα[

2 φ[ο]ίταιϲ, ὄτα τ᾽ ὔπνοϲ [

—

γλύκυϲ θ[έ]οϲ, ἦ δεῖν᾽ ὀνίαϲ

μ[

4 ζὰ χῶριϲ ἔχην τὰν δυναμ[

—

ἔλπιϲ δέ μ᾽ ἔχει μὴ πεδέχη[ν

6 μηδὲν μακάρων ἐλ̣[
[—]
οὐ̣ γάρ κ᾽ ἔον οὕτω[. ΄
8 ἀθύρματα κα.[

—

γένοιτο δέ μοι[
10 τοὶς πάντα[⊗

—

64   METRUM: V. S. 88 TEST

a

]λακ̣[
]
]νί.[
α]λίκεςςι[
5]
]παίδων[
]δηο̣ν
]
]
10   ]θεντ[
].θέοις[
]ν αἴςχρ[
]
]α μοῖ[
15]τετι[

b

].α[
]αίγα[
].δο.[
]   [

65 (68) METRUM: x–◡◡–[, ‸HIPP[2c] SUPPL. POSSIS, V. ETIAM S. 88 TEST

. . . . .] . . . α[
2 . . . . .]ρομε[[Andromeda?] . . .
. . . . .].ελας[
4 .ρο̣τήννεμε[
Ψάπφοι, ςεφίλ[Sappho, I love(?) you . . .
6 Κύπρωι β[α]cίλ[Cyprus . . . queen . . .
κ̣αίτοι μέγα δ.[yet great . . .
8 ὄ]ccοιc φαέθων̣ [to all for whom the shining [sun?] . . .
πάνται κλέοc [everywhere fame . . .

—

10 κ̣αί c᾽ ἐνν Ἀχέρ[οντ   even in the house of Acheron you. . . .
. .[. . . . . . .]ν̣π[

66

a	b

ζαταγ[

—

ἄμ᾽ ἐξα[

.]α[

]μο[

]οργι[

]ϲπίο[

].[

c

]μνα [

].κατεγ[

]κεκ[

67 (69)   METRUM: (A) ×–◡◡–[, ˰ HIPP²ᶜ SUPPL. POSSIS

a

. .]ων μα.[

[—]

κ]αὶ τοῦτ᾽ ἐπικε.[

3   δ]αίμων ὀλοφ.[

[—]

οὐ μὰν ἐφίληϲ[

5   νῦν δ᾽ ἔννεκα[

—

τὸ δ᾽ αἴτιον οὐτ[

7   οὐδὲν πόλυ[.].[

—

.]υδ᾽ [᾽ . ´

b

].ουδε[

]ταυτα.[

]λαιϲιμ[

]πλήονι[

5   ]᾽ ἀμφ[

].ϲθεο.[

]έρωϲ.[

68 (71AB)   METRUM: FR. A]∪∪−−∪∪−∪−x, ‿HIPP²ᶜ SUPPL. POSSIS

a

]ι̣ γάρ μ᾿ ἀπὺ τὰc ἐ.[
ὔ]μωc δ᾿ ἔγεν[το
] ἴcαν θέοιcιν
]αcαν ἀλίτρα[
5   Ἀν]δρομέδαν[.].αξ[
]αρ[. . .].α μάκα̣[ιρ]α
]ε̣ον δὲ τρόπον α[.].ύνη[
] κ̣όρο̣ν οὐ κατιcχε̣.[
]κ̣α[. . . . .]. Τυνδαρίδαι[c
10]αcυ[.]. . .κα[.] χαρίεντ᾿ ἀ.[

]κ᾿ ἄδολον [μ]ηκέτι cυν[
         .β..κη.
] Μεγάρα.[. .]γα[. . .]α[

b

].. . .φ[
].[.]᾿θύρα.[
]μ̣οι χάλε.[
  ]δεκύ[
5   ].οπάλην ὄλ̣[
     ]ε[

69

]ε. .[.]τ̣εγαμ[
]αc᾿ ἀλίτρα[
]έτ᾿ αὐ[

70 (76)   METRUM:]−−∪∪−[

]α̣μ.λ.[
]ναμ[
]γ δ᾿ εἶμ᾿ ε[
]ρcομέν[
5   ]λικ᾿ ὐπα[
]. . .[.]βα[
]c γὰρ ἐπαυ[
] μάν κ᾿ ἀπυθυc[
]αρμονίαc δ[

　　10　　　　　]αθην χόρον, ἄα[
　　　　　　　]δε λίγηα.[
　　　　　　　]ατόν cφι[
　　　　　　　] πάντεccι[
　　　　　　　]επ[.].[

71 (70) METRUM:]◡◡--◡◡-◡-x, �‸HIPP²ᶜ SUPPL. POSSIS

　　]μιccε Μίκα　　　　　　　Mika . . .

]ελα[. .ἀλ]λά c᾽ ἔγωὒκ ἐάcω　　. . . but I will not allow you . . .

]ν φιλότ[ατ᾽] ἤλεο Πενθιλήαγ[　. . . you preferred the friendship of

]δα κα[κό]τροπ᾽, ἄμμα[　　　　the Penthilidae

5　] μέλ[οc] τι γλύκερον .[　　　. . . o mischievous one . . . our . . .

]α μελλιχόφων[οc　　　　　　. . . some sweet song . . .

]δει, λίγυραι δ᾽ ἄη[　　　　　. . . gentle-voiced . . .

] δροc[ό]εccα[　　　　　　　. . . sweet-sounding [breezes?]

　　　　　　　　　　　　　　. . . covered with dew . . .

72

　　　　　　　]ανόρ[
　　　　　　　]αμμε[
　　　　　　　]νπε[
　　　　　　　]λην[
　　5　　　　]τεc· τ[
　　　　　　　].ωνω[
　　　　　　　]μώ[
　　　　　　　].[

73 (74) METRUM: -]◡◡-◡-x, ˸HIPP²ᶜ SUPPL. POSSIS, V. ETIAM
　　　　　　　S. 88 TEST

　　　　a

]γβ.[.].[.]υ
]α
]αν Ἀφροδι[τα　　　　　　. . . Aphrodite . . .
ἀ]δύλογοι δ᾽ ἐρ[　　　　　Loves(?) that speak sweet words . . .
5　]βαλλοι　　　　　　　. . . throws . . .
α]ιc ἔχοιcα　　　　　　. . . having . . .
].ένα θααc[c　　　　　　. . . blooms(?) . . .
]άλλει　　　　　　　. . . dew. . . .
]αc ἐέρcαc [

b

]ω.[
]αϲ[
]ιϲˑ ἐ[

74

a	**b**	**c**
]ων ἔκα[	]α[	].[
]αιπόλ[	]ποθο̣[	]αϲ ἴδρω[
]μ.[	].ώβα̣[	].υζαδ.[
]βροδο[		]ιν[
]ο̣νθ[	**d**	
]φαιμ[	].[.].ε[	
	]υπο.[	
	]μ̣[	

(a line 5:]ο̣νθ[)

75

a

]. .[.].[
]ηϲαδ.[

]λ̣α.[
]νίαν[
]δύ.[
]ιμεδα̣[
]μαϲτε̣[
].κ[

(line 5:]δύ.[)

b	**c**
]κα[	].[
].πιτα[	]δετα̣[
γέ]νεϲθα[ι	]δέ. . .[
]τῶ.[	]´μμι.[
]αν [	]ταμέ.[

(b line 5:]αν [; c line 5:]ταμέ.[)

76 (75)

]αυ πα̣[
τε]λέϲειε κ̣[
]ίη λελα[
]ε θέλω[

5   ]εχην[
       ]η· ἔφα.[
       ]αλίκ[

77 (79)

a

]α.[
]cετα[
]υμαι. .[
˙]τεχαρα̣[
5   ]ιδιδοῖc[
]δεν ἀμεc[
]οc cύγ᾽ ἀ[
].λονα[
].δαλ[

b

]. [
]μήτε̣[
]δίαιcα [
]εc· ἀλλ[
5   ]φρα[
].[

c

]α̣τω[
]ηαc
]
]τ̣αc·

78 (73)

].οναυ[
]ην οὐδε[
]ηc ἵμερ[
].αι δ᾽ ἄμα[
5   ].ανθοc·[
ἵ]μερον[
]ετερπ[

79

]υμ̣[
]ω[
]το.[
]τ᾽ αὖτον.[
5   ]ω πέλετ[
]να[

80 (77B)

].[
].τ̣οcεc.[

]παντα[
] ι δ᾿ ἀτέρα[
5   ]λοκα[
].[

81 (80)   METRUM: ‸HIPP²ᶜ

]απύθεс.[
]χιстαλ̣[
]ε̣μπ[

cὺ δὲ cτεφάνοιc, ὦ Δίκα, π‿έρ-
θεc‿θ᾿ ἐράτοιc φόβαιcιν
5 ὄρπακαc ἀνήτω cυν⟨α⟩‿έ‿ρρ‿αιc‿·
ἀπάλαιcι χέρcιν·
εὐάνθεα † γὰρ πέλεται † καὶ Χάριτεc μάκαιρα⟨ι⟩
μᾶλλον † προτερην †, ἀcτεφανώ-
τοιcι δ᾿ ἀπυcτρέφονται.

O Dika, put lovely garlands on your
tresses,
binding together shoots of dill in your
tender hands.
For the blessed Graces favor (?) more
the well-flowered,
but turn away the ungarlanded.

82 (63)   METRUM: ‸HIPP²ᶜ

⊗ **a** Εὐμορφοτέρα Μναcιδίκα τὰc
ἀπάλαc Γυρίννωc

Mnasidika of more beautiful shape than
tender Gurinno . . .

b καίτ᾿ ἐ[
μηδεν[
—
νῦν δ᾿ ἀ[
μή βόλλε̣[
[—]
5 εὐ]μορφο[τέρα

83 (81)

].αί.[
]λ᾿ αὖθι με[
]νώμεθ᾿ ὀ[
] δηῦτ᾿ ἐπιτ[
5]έντηδεμ[
].α γὰρ ἐκά[
].[.].[

84 (82)

].αις[
].ικιπ[
]ων κ[. .].[.?]ίνα[
]τονόνε.[.?].οϲε[
5]άβροιϲ ἐπιχ[?]ημ[
]αν Ἀρτεμι[
]ναβλ[

85 (83)

a

]..
᾿]λβον
]ακούην
]αύταν

b

]πάμενα[
]τ᾿ ὤϲτ᾿ ὀ πέλη[
]ακαν ϲό[

86 (64A DL. '44)   METRUM:]‑⏑⏑‑‑⏑⏑‑⏑‑x, ⏜HIPP²ᶜ SUPPL. POSSIS

].ακάλα.[
] αἰγιόχω λα[
]. Κυθέρη᾿ εὐχομ[
]ον ἔχοιϲα θῦμο[ν
5 κλ]ῦθί μ᾿ ἄραϲ αἴ π[οτα κἀτέρωτα
]αϲ προλίποιϲα κ[
]. πεδ᾿ ἔμαν ἰώ[
].ν χαλέπαι.[

. . . peaceful(?)
aegis-bearing [Zeus?]. . . .
Cytherea, I(?) pray [to you],
having a [willing?] heart:
Heed my prayer, if [ever before]
. . . leaving . . .
. . . to my . . .
. . . difficult. . . .

87

a = 87 (2) LP

]αμμ[
]ικα.[
]ποίϲαι[
]κλεηδον[
5].πλοκαμ[
]εϲδ᾿ ἀμα[
] ἀνθρώπ[
].υμαιν[
]τεκαιπ[
10

d = 87 (13) LP

]
]
]εϲθα
]ρπον ἄβαν
5]
]εϲθαι·
]
].
]
]

b = 87 (8) LP

μ]εριμνα[
]γῆν   [
]αικο[
]αι   [

e = 87 (16) LP

]εφι.[
β]ασιλη.[
]εγαδ.[
].oc.[

c = 87 (11) LP

[.]δω.[
τόλμ[
——

f = 87 (17) LP

.]δη[
.]κωcα[
]ν· coι[
].δηκ.[
]εcιππ[
].αλ.[
].εccα[
].[.].[

5

88   METRUM: –[   ]∪––∪∪–∪[–x‖
                        x–[   ]––∪∪–[∪–x‖   ͜HIPP^{x c}‖ ͜HIPP^{x c}‖ ͜HIPP^{x·1}
c‖‖
                        –[   ]∪∪–∪–x‖‖‖

a

].[

]ν προ. .[
]νωc πρὸc πότ[
].ατον χάλα[

4

].θέλοιc· οὐδυ[
].αcδοιc· ὀλιγα[
].ένα φέρεcθα[ι

7

b

].φια τις . . . [
].δ᾿ ἄδιον εἰcορ[
ο]ῖcθα καῦτα·

ἐμ[
10 τοῦ[
——

κ[
cε[
13 ἠ[
[—]

λέ]λαθ᾿ ἀλλονιά[
].αν· τιραδ[
]αί τις εἴποι

ἀ[　　　　　　　　　].cαν· ἔγω τε γαρ[

φιλη[　　　　　　　　]μ̣᾽ ἆc κεν ἔνη μ᾽ [

16 κᾶλ.[　　　　　　　　]αι μελήcην·

———

ἐcτ.[　　　　　　　　]φίλα φαῖμ᾽ ἐχύρα γέ[νεcθαι

.]χα̣[　　　　　　　　]ενα[.]αιc· ἀτ̣[

19　　　　　　　　]. .δ᾽ ὀνίαρ[ο]c̣ [

].̣ πίκροc ὔμ[

].[.]τα̣.θᾶδ[

22　　　　　　　　].α̣ τόδε δ᾽ ἴc[θ(ι)

].ὤττι c᾽ ἐ.[

]α φιλήcω[

25　　　　　　　]τ̣ω τι̣ λο[

]ccον γὰρ .[

]c̣θαι βελέω[ν

]. .[

90 (COMMENTARIUS)

a = 90 (1) LP

col. II

]χ̣·

———　　　　　　　].ντι

ν[　　　　　　　　　　].εcει

να[　　　　　　　　　].οντων

———

5 εν.[　　　　　　　　] Κυθερήαc τρό-

———

φοc[　　　　　　θ]ρέπτη ἐν ἄλλοιc

δὲ θυγ[ατέρα (τῆc) Ἀφρο]δίτηc εἴρηκε τὴ[ν

Πειθώ· .[　　　　　]ηcεφωνειημ[

———

τατcαλλη[　　　　　]. ἑαυτῆc πρ[οca-

10 γόρευε· ὔμ[　　]̣.[.]θ̣ελοιcα[. .].[

———

θικονετρ[ ]αcιν χ̈[ ]
—
ἄμμι̣ ἀγγ[ ]τινα[ ]
—
δαιμ[.]να̣θ̣[ ].ο̣cυν[.].
ἵνα η. .πε.[ ]
λεγ᾽ ⟦ο⟧ἄ̣ μμε[ ]
μεν[.].ϊε[ ]
δηε[.]π̣.c.[ ].
θελετ̣ε̣[ ]. .φι
—
οντεκ[ ]του
δυνατ[ ]ε̣ι̣μαι᾽
—
χερρεc[ ] καὶ κα-
τ᾽ ἰδίαν [ ].[ ]η̣c καὶ
πρὸc τὴ[ν μο]χ̣θ̣οῦν[-
—
τ̣[.]c̣ προ.[ ]τ̣ανυ[-
π̣τ̣ερυγ.[ ].ατο̣[
]ο̣φηc.[
].[

col. III

[
.[ἀγε-]
ρώχου[c ἄγαν ἐχού-]
cαc γέ̣ραc: .[
—
καὶ Γυριννι[
ταc τοιαύταc̣ .[.]. .[ἔ-]
—
γω τὸ κάλλοc ἐπετ.[
μέ⟨c⟩δον· τί γὰρ ἠνεμ[
εἶναι καὶ ἀρετῆc πο̣[ἀλ-]
λὰ μήποτε λέγει ὅτι ο[
καλλι̣ εὐφήμειcθα[
—○
μοι ζεφύρω π̣νευμα[

coì δ' ἀν[εμ]ọφόρητο[

]γονδεκα.[

25   ]c παϊτασμ[πρὸc]

Ἀνδρομέ]δην γέγρạ[πται

] ὑπὸ Ἀνδ[ρομέδηc

].ι οὐκευν[

]ϙαρρε.[

30   ]χητιc[

b = 90 (3) LP   **c** = 90 (4) LP

5   ]ọυτι.[   ]νομε[.].[

]ποιη. .τ.[   ].ταπυγ˙[

]ηθειαν.[   ]μενον˙ϊ[

]ειν˙φ[   ]γοημμαα[

]. .ηβ.[5   ]εφεροι.˙[

10   ]cλον [   ] . . . [

]δ̣.[.]ẹ[[μον]] [   ].γ[

]θῳcα.[

].ωμ[

]˙ cουαγ[

15   ]απαξ τουτ[

]ọυπαντα>[

] πρῶτον [

].[.]οιc προα[

]θανειν[

20   ]κρ̣έccον γὰ[ρ

d = 90(10^A) LP   **e** = 90 (10^B) LP

].c γαρ[   ].[

]ηκετ.[   ]θι γλυ[

]λατωc.[   ]ταεν[

].περιcα[   ]ç . . . [

5   ].ι θυμ̣[

].τοτη . . . [

]ọcφηcινα [

]νụποτου [

].[

10   ]υ[

].ι[

].αμενην [

]καὶ χαριε.[

ἐν ταύτηι] τῆι ὠ⟨ι⟩δῆ⟨ι⟩ λέ[γει ὅτι

15   ]Ἄτθιδος [

]αυτης[

].ηβαθυ[

   ].[

91 (64)   METRUM: ‸HIPP²ᶜ

ἀσαροτέρας οὐδάμα πω Εἴρανα,   . . . having never found anyone more

σέθεν τύχοισαν   annoying, Irana, than you . . .

92 (95)   METRUM: xx–ᴗ[

[

[

πε[

κρ[. . . . .]περ[

5   πέπλον[. . .]πυςχ[

καὶ κλε[. .]ςαω[

κροκοεντα[

πέπλον πορφυ[ρ. . . . . . .]δεξω[.]

χλαιναι περς[

10   στέφανοι περ[

καλ[.] οςςαμ[

φρυ[

πορφ[υρ

ταπα[

15   [

π[

93   METRUM:]ᴗᴗ–ᴗ–

     ]ις . . . εγ

  ]ω

  ]μοις

  ]αλίαν ἔχω

5   ] παρθένων

94 (96)   METRUM: GL‖ GL‖ GLᵈ‖‖

τεθνάκην δ᾽ ἀδόλως θέλω·
2 ἄ με ψιςδομένα κατελίμπανεν
   ⟨—⟩
   πόλλα καὶ τόδ᾽ ἔειπέ [μοι·
   ὤιμ᾽ ὡς δεῖνα πεπ[όνθ]αμεν,
5 Ψάπφ᾽, ἦ μάν ς᾽ ἀέκοις᾽
   ἀπυλιμπάνω.
   —
   τὰν δ᾽ ἔγω τάδ᾽ ἀμειβόμαν·
   χαίροις᾽ ἔρχεο κἄμεθεν
8 μέμναις᾽, οἶςθα γὰρ ὤς ⟨ς⟩ε πεδή-
   πομεν·
   —
   αἰ δὲ μή, ἀλλά ς᾽ ἔγω θέλω
   ὄμναιςαι [. . .(.)].[. .(.)].εαι
11 ὀ̣ς̣[– 10 –] καὶ κάλ᾽
   ἐπάςχομεν·
   —
   πό[λλοις γὰρ ςτεφάν]οις ἴων
   καὶ βρ[όδων . . .]κίων τ᾽ ὔμοι
14 κα. .[– 7 –] πὰρ ἔμοι π⟨ε⟩ρε-
   θήκα⟨ο⟩
   —
   καὶ πό̣ι̣λλαις ὑπα̣ι̣θύμιδας
   πλέκι̣ταις ἀμφ᾽ α̣ι̣πάλαι δέραι
17 ἀνθέων ἐ̣[– 6 –] πεποη-
   μέναις.
   ⟨—⟩
   καὶ π. . . . .[   ]. μύρωι
   βρενθείωι .[   ]ρυ[. .]ν
20 ἐξαλ⟨ε⟩ίψαο κα̣[ὶ ι̣βας]ι̣ληίωι
   ⟨—⟩
   καὶ ςτρώμν[αν ἐ]πὶ μολθάκαν
   ἀπάλαν παρ[   ]ο̣̣ͅγων
23 ἐξίης πόθο̣[ν   ].νίδων
   ⟨—⟩
   κωὔτε τις[οὔ]τε̣ τι
   ἶρον οὐδ᾽ ὐ[   ]

"Honestly, I wish I were dead!"
Weeping many tears she left me,

Saying this as well:
"Oh, what dreadful things have hap-
   pened to us,
Sappho! I don't want to leave you!"

I answered her:
"Go with my blessings, and remember
   me,
for you know how we cherished you.

"But if you have [forgotten], I want
to remind you . . .
of the beautiful things that happened
   to us:

"Close by my side you put around
   yourself
[many wreaths] of violets and roses
   and saffron. . . .

"And many woven garlands
made from flowers . . .
around your tender neck,

"And . . . with costly royal
myrrh . . .
you anointed . . . ,

"And on a soft bed
. . . tender . . .
you satisfied your desire. . . .

"Nor was there any . . .
nor any holy . . .

26 ἔπλετ᾽ ὄππ[οθεν ἄμ]μες ἀπέσκομεν,   from which we were away,
⟨—⟩
οὐκ ἄλcος .[   ].ρος   . . . nor grove. . . .”
                     ]ψοφος
                     ] . . . οιδιαι

95 (97)   METRUM: $-\cup-\text{xx}-[$ FORT. METRUM FR. 96
                        $\cup-6$
                        $\text{xx}-\cup\cup-[$
                        -9
                        $\text{xx}-\cup\cup-\cup[$

1 .ου[
   [—]
   ἦρ᾽ ἀ[
   δηρατ.[
4 Γογγυλα.[. . . Gongula . . .
   ⟨—⟩
   ἦ τι cᾶμ᾽ ἐθε.[Surely some sign . . .
   παιcι μάλιcτα.[. . . especially . . .
7 μαc γ᾽ εἴcηλθ᾽ ἐπ.[[Hermes?] came . . .
   ⟨—⟩
   εἶπον· ὦ δέcποτ᾽, ἐπ.[I said, “O Master . . .
   ο]ὐ μὰ γὰρ μάκαιραν [By the blessed [goddess],
10 ο]ὐδὲν ἄδομ᾽ ἔπαρθ᾽ ἀγα[I have no pleasure in taking up(?) . . .
   [—]
   κατθάνην δ᾽ ἴμερός τις [ἔχει με   But a desire to die [seizes me],
     καὶ   and to gaze upon the dewy
   λωτίνοιc δροcόεντας [ὄ-   lotus-covered banks of Acheron. . . .”
13 χ[θ]οιc ἴδην Ἀχερ[
   [—]
   .]. .δεcαιδ.[
   .].υδετου[
16 μητιcε[
   [—]

96 (98)   METRUM: CR 3GL BA ‖‖

   ] cαρδ.[. .]   . . . [Sardis?]
2 πόλ]λακι τυίδε [.]ων ἔχοιcα   Often turning her mind here . . .
   [—]
   ὠcπ.[. . .].ὠομεν, .[. . .]. .χ[. .]   [She honored you]

ϲε †θεαϲικελαν ἀρι-
5 γνωτα†, ϲᾶι δὲ μάλιϲτ᾽ ἔχαιρε
   μόλπαι·
   〈—〉
   νῦν δὲ Λύδαιϲιν ἐμπρέπεται γυναί-
   κεϲϲιν ὥϲ ποτ᾽ ἀελίω
8]δύντοϲ ἀ βροδοδάκτυλοϲ
   〈ϲελάννα〉
   〈—〉
   πάντα περ〈ρ〉έχοιϲ᾽ ἄϲτρα· φάοϲ
   δ᾽ ἐπί-
   ϲχει θάλαϲϲαν ἐπ᾽ ἀλμύραν
11 ἴϲωϲ καὶ πολυανθέμοιϲ
   ἀρούραιϲ·
   —
   ἀ δ᾽ 〈ἐ〉έρϲα κάλα κέχυται, τεθά-
   λαιϲι δὲ βρόδα κἄπαλ᾽ ἄν-
14 θρυϲκα καὶ μελίλωτοϲ
   ἀνθεμώδηϲ·
   〈—〉
   πόλλα δὲ ζαφοίταιϲ᾽ ἀγάναϲ ἐπι-
   μνάϲθειϲ᾽ Ἄτθιδοϲ ἰμέρωι
17 λέπταν ποι φρένα κ[.]ρ . . .
   βόρηται·
   〈—〉
   κῆθι δ᾽ ἔλθην ἀμμ.[. .]. .ιϲα τόδ᾽ οὐ
   νωντα[. .]υϲτο̣νυμ̣[. .(.)] πόλυϲ
20 γαρύε̣ι [. .(.)]αλον[. . . . .(.)]τ̣ο̣
   μέϲϲον·
   —
   ε]ῦ̣μαρ[εϲ μ]ὲ̣ν οὐ.α.μι θέαιϲι μόρφαν ἐπή[ρατ]ον ἐξίϲω
23 ϲθαί ϲυ[. .]ρο̣ϲ ἔχη〈ι〉ϲθα[. . .].
   νίδηον
   —
   [   ]τ̣ο[. . .(.)]ρατι-
   μαλ[   ].ερο̣ϲ
26 καὶ δ[.]μ̣[   ]οϲ Ἀφροδίτα
   —

like an easily recognized goddess,
she rejoiced especially in your song.

But now she stands out among the Lydian women
as after sunset
the rosy-fingered moon

Surpasses all the stars; the light
spreads over the salty sea
equally as over the many-flowered
fields.

And the dew grows beautifully liquid
and roses and tender chervil
flourish, and flowery honey-lotus.

But she, roaming about far and wide,
remembers gentle Atthis with desire;
her tender heart is surely heavy [be-
cause of your fate].

. . . to come . . .

It is not easy [for us] to equal
goddesses in loveliness of form . . .

. . . eros . . .
. . . Aphrodite . . .

καμ[   ] νέκταρ ἔχευ᾽ ἀπὺ   . . . pouring nectar from
χρυcίαc [   ]γαν   golden . . .
29 . . .(.)]απουρ[   ] χέρcι Πείθω   . . . with her hands . . . Persuasion . . .
[   ]θ[. .]ηcενη
[   ]ακιc
32 [   ]. . . . . .αι

[   ]εc τὸ Γεραίcτιον   . . . into the Geraistion . . .
[   ]γ φίλαι   . . . dear . . .
35 [   ]υcτον οὐδενο[
[   ]ερον ἰξο[μ

97 METRUM INCERTUM

1–12 legi non possunt

13 ἀερ[
    περα[
    κυ[
    cιν[
    cὺ δ᾽ . .[
    τ̣ο̣υ. .[   ].υπνου

19–23 legi non possunt

24 κ̣αλλε α̣υ[
    περιπτερα[
    .]νιαν ἐλεφαν[
    . .]ρ̣παcκ̣α̣.[

98 (98AB DL., SUPPL.)   METRUM: GL ‖ GL ‖ CR GL ⦀

a   **a**

1 . .].θοc· ἀ γάρ μ᾽ ἐγέννα̣[τ   . . . for my mother [said that]
   [—]   in her youth it was indeed a great orna-
   c]φᾶc ἐπ᾽ ἀλικίαc μέγ[αν   ment if someone had tresses
   κ]όcμον αἴ τιc ἔχη φόβα⟨ι⟩c̣[wrapped in a purple [band].
4 πορφύρωι κατελιξαμέ[να
   ⟨—⟩
   ἔμμεναι μάλα τοῦτο .[
   ἀλλα ξανθοτέρα⟨ι⟩c ἔχη[But the girl who has hair
7 τα⟨ὶ⟩c κόμα⟨ι⟩c δάϊδοc προφ[brighter than a fiery torch
   [—]

c]τεφάνοιϲιν ἐπαρτία[ιϲ
ἀνθέων ἐριθαλέων· [

10 μ]ιτράναν δ᾽ ἀρτίωϲ κλ[
[—]
ποικίλαν ἀπὺ Ϲαρδίω[ν
. . .].αονίαϲ πόλ{ε}ιϲ [

should wear [?] wreaths
of blooming flowers.
Just now a many-colored
headband from Sardis . . .

b

—ϲοὶ δ᾽ ἔγω Κλέι ποικίλαν [
—οὐκ ἔχω—πόθεν ἔϲϲεται;—[

3 —μιτράν⟨αν⟩· ἀλλὰ τὼι Μυτιλη-
νάωι [

        * * *

          ].[

παι.α.ειον ἔχην πο.[

6 αἰκε.η ποικιλαϲκ . . . (.) [
—

ταῦτα τὰϲ Κλεανακτιδα[
φυγαϲ †. .ιϲαπολιϲεχει†

9 μνάματ᾽· .ἴδε γὰρ αἶνα διέρρυε[ν
—

b

For you, Kleis, I have no
many-colored headband, nor
do I know where one will come from.
But for the Mytilenean . . .

. . . grows many-colored (?) . . .
. . . these memories of the exile
of the sons of Kleanax . . .
. . . for they wasted away terribly . . .

99 LP = A. 303A

ALKAIOS FR. 303A V. (= SAPPHO FR. 99 L.-P.)

a

METRUM: ˏGL‖ ˏGL IA ‖‖

.].γα. .εδα βαῑο̣[ν   ].α
[—]
δ[.]οῖ Πωλυαγακτ[ιδ]α. .[
. . .αιϲϲαμιαϲι.ιε.[.]τọιϲ. . . .[.]
—

χορδαιϲιδιακρεκην

5 ọλιϲβ.δόκọιϲ⟨ι⟩ περκαθ. . . .ενοϲ
—

.ου.[. .]ϲι φιλοφ[ρό]νωϲ
]. . . . δ᾽ ἐλελίϲδ[ε]ται πρ.τανέωϲ
]ọγοϲ δὲ διο[. .]ω.
].ναλωδ᾽.[.]. .ενητε[. .].χ. . ⊠

a

After a little . . .

. . . the son(s) of Polyanax
. . .

to strum on the strings. . . .
receiving the dildo (?) . . .

. . . kindly
it quivers. . . .

. . .
. . . [possibly the end of this poem]

b

METRUM: 2 IA‖ ?‖ 2 IA‖‖

⊗ Λάτωc] τε καὶ Δί[οc] πάϊ[.]
    ]. .ε. . . .[.]επ⁂[ ]-
  βοργιαν[
  Γρύνηαν] ὐλώδη⟨ν⟩ λίπων
    ].ε̣ν χρη[c]τ̣ήριον
5   ].[   ].ε̣υμε̣c[. .].[.]ων
    ]. . . .[. . . . .]
    ]. . . . . .α[. .]ε̣ραιc
    ]ρ̣cανον[.]. .ρ̣γιαν
    ]υ̣cομεν [ ]
10   ]ν ὐ̣μνε[   ]
  κ̣α̣[   ]ε̣να[.]φο.[. . .]ν.
  ἀδελφέαν
  ὠ̣cπαι[   ].ι̣ο.[. . .].[ ]

  ——

  .υτιcδε[. . .]κε̣ι.θε̣λη[   ]
  δειχ̣γυc . . .]ε δηῦτε Πω̣λ̣υα̣νακ-
  τίδαν
15 τὸν μάργον ὄνδ̣ειξ̣αι θέλω.

  ——

b

[possibly the beginning of a new poem]

O child of (Leto) and Zeus,
come . . .

leaving wooded [Gryneia?]
  . . . to the oracle
  . . .

sing . . .

. . . sister

show (?) . . . again . . . the sons of
  Polyanax . . .
I want to expose the greedy
  [man?] . . .

100 (85)   METRUM INCERTUM

ἀμφι δ᾽ ἄβροιc ⟨ ⟩ λαcίοιc· εὐ
⟨F⟩ ἐπύκαccεν

(She?) covered her well with delicate
  shag

101 (99)   METRUM FORT.: GL‖ GL‖ GLᵈ‖‖, CF. S. 94

(πρὸc τὴν Ἀφροδίτην)
χερρόμακτρα δὲ †καγγόνων†
πορφύραι †καταυταμενά-
τατιμάcειc† ἔπεμψ᾽ ἀπὺ Φωκάαc
δῶρα τίμια †καγγόνων†

101 A (89) = A. 347B LP   METRUM INCERTUM, FORT. GL‖ HIPP‖

πτερύγων δ᾽ ὔπα
κακχέει λιγύραν ἀοίδαν,
ὄπποτα φλόγιον †καθέ-
ταν† ἐπιπτάμενον †καταυδείη†

102 (114)   METRUM: IA GL BA

⊗ Γλύκηα μᾶτερ, οὔ τοι δύναμαι
    κρέκην τὸν ἴϲτον
    πόθωι δάμειϲα παῖδοϲ βραδίναν δι᾽
    Ἀφροδίταν

Sweet mother, I am not able to weave
at my loom,
overwhelmed with desire for a youth
because of tender Aphrodite.

103   METRUM:]–◡◡–◡◡–◡[
                  (x)x–]◡◡––◡◡––[◡◡–◡–(–)   GL²ᶜ VEL ˏHIPP²ᶜ
                  ◡]◡––◡◡––◡◡–◡[–(–)
                  ◡]◡––◡◡––◡◡–◡[–(–)
    5   –◡]◡––◡◡––◡◡–◡–[–   3 CHO BA
                  ]–◡◡––◡[
                  ]⟨◡◡⟩––◡◡–◡––   3 CHO BA VEL ˏHIPP²ᶜ
                  xx–◡◡–]–◡◡––◡◡–◡[–   GL²ᶜ
                  xx–◡◡––]◡◡––◡◡–◡–[GL²ᶜ
    10   ]––◡◡–◡––[UT V. 7

                  ].εν τὸ γὰρ ἐννεπε[.]η προβ[
                  ].ατε τὰν εὔποδα νύμφαν [
                  ]τα παῖδα Κρονίδα τὰν ἰόκ[ολπ]ον [
                  ].ϲ ὄργαν θεμένα τὰν ἰόκ[ολ]ποϲ α [
    5   ]. . ἄγναι Χάριτεϲ Πιέριδέ[ϲ τε] Μοῖ[ϲαι
                  ].[. ὄ]ππ̣οτ᾽ ἀοιδαι φρέν[. . .]αν.[
                  ]ϲαιοιϲα λιγύραν [ἀοί]δαν
                  γά]μβρον, ἄϲαροι γὰρ ὐμαλικ[
                  ]ϲε φόβαιϲι⟨ν⟩ θεμέγα λύρα.[
    10   ]. .η χρυϲοπέδιλ̣[ο]ϲ Αὔωϲ [

103 A (149AB DL., SUPPL.)   DE METRO V. TEST
                            a

    col. I   col. II

    ]   ϲμικρ[
    ]θην   τὰν ϲφ[
    ]οιϲ   πολλα[
    ]   πρὶγ γα̣[
                                    ———
    5   ]οι   πόλλαιϲ[
    ]   τὼν ϲφῶ[ν

]   ὠδαμελ[

]   χει[◻

]

                                     Γόργ[

b

εἰς Κυπ[

ι — — .[

— — — τ[

— — — ωγ[

—

103 B (= INC. AUCT. 26 LP)   METRUM:]--◡◡--[, INCERTUM

]ρηον θαλάμω τωδες[

]ις εὔποδα νύμφαν ἀβ[

].νυνδ[

]ν μοι·[

]ας γε. [

103 C

a

]προλ[

]φερην[

]. ιδεθελ[

Ἀρ]χεάνασσα[

5   ]δήποτ᾽ ὀνα[

]νασαμέν[

]εν ἐπηρατ[

]ν[

b

]α.[

ἔ]κλυον ε[

]ρανγ . . δες δ[

πα]ρθενικαις. [

5   ]. μ[

].[

104 (1 2 0. 1 3 3)   METRUM: (A) V. 1: 6 DA $_\wedge$, V. 2: IA $|$ PHER^{2d} ? (CF. S. 1 3 6)
(B) INCERTUM

a

Ἔϲπερε πάντα φέρηιϲ ὄϲα φαίνολιϲ   Hesperus, you bring all that the shining
   ἐϲκέδαϲ᾽ Αὔωϲ,   Dawn scattered,
φέρηιϲ ὄιν, φέρηιϲ αἶγα, φέρηιϲ   you bring the sheep, you bring the
   ἄπυ μάτερι παῖδα   goat, you bring the child back to its
                       mother.

b

ἀϲτέρων πάντων ὁ κάλλιϲτοϲ   . . . the most beautiful of all the
                       stars . . .

105 (1 1 6. 1 1 7)   METRUM: 6 DA $_\wedge$

a

οἶον τὸ γλυκύμαλον ἐρεύθεται ἄκ-   [the bride]
   ρωι ἐπ᾽ ὔϲδωι,   just like a sweet apple which ripens on
ἄκρον ἐπ᾽ ἀκροτάτωι, λελάθοντο δὲ   the uppermost bough,
   μαλοδρόπηεϲ·   on the top of the topmost; but the
οὐ μὰν ἐκλελάθοντ᾽, ἀλλ᾽ οὐκ ἐδύ-   apple-gatherers have forgotten it,
   ναντ᾽ ἐπίκεϲθαι   or rather, they haven't altogether
                       forgotten it, but they could not
                       reach it.

105 B LP: V. 105A TEST (ET S. 2 1 8)

b = 105C LP

οἶαν τὰν ὐάκινθον ἐν ὤρεϲι   [the bride?]
   ποίμενεϲ ἄνδρεϲ   like a hyacinth in the mountains which
πόϲϲι καταϲτείβοιϲι, χάμαι δὲ τε   the shepherd men
   πόρφυρον ἄνθοϲ . . .   trample with their feet, but the purple
                       flower [lying] on the ground. . . .

106 (1 1 5)   METRUM: 6 DA $_\wedge$

πέρροχοϲ, ὠϲ ὄτ᾽ ἄοιδοϲ ὁ Λέϲβιοϲ   . . . superior, just as when a Lesbian
   ἀλλοδάποιϲιν   singer [outdoes] foreign ones . . .

107 (5 3)   METRUM INCERTUM

ἦρ᾽ ἔτι παρθενίαϲ ἐπιβάλλομαι;

108 (116A)

ὦ κάλα, ὦ χαρίεccα κόρα

O beautiful woman, O one full of grace . . .

109 (122)

δώcομεν, ἦcι πάτηρ

110 (124) = 110A LP   METRUM: PHER^d

⊠ Θυρώρωι πόδεс ἐπτορόγυιοι,
   τὰ δὲ cάμβαλα πεμπεβόεια,
   πίccυγγοι δὲ δέκ᾽ ἐξεπόνηcαν

[At the wedding]
the door-keeper's feet are seven fath-
   oms long,
and his sandals are made of five ox-
   hides,
and ten shoemakers worked away to
   make them.

111 (123)   METRUM INC., FORT. PHER ‖ IA ‖ ˰PHER^d‖ IA ‖‖

⊠ Ἴψοι δὴ τὸ μέλαθρον,
   ὑμήναον,
   ἀέρρετε, τέκτονεс ἄνδρεс·
   ὑμήναον.
5 γάμβροс †(εἰс)έρχεται ἶcoc
      Ἄρευι†,
   ⟨ὑμήναον,⟩
   ἄνδροс μεγάλω πόλυ μέcδων.
   ⟨ὑμήναον.⟩

Rise high the roof-beams!
Sing the Hymeneal!
Raise it high, O carpenter men!
Sing the Hymeneal!
The bridegroom enters, like to Ares,
by far bigger than a big man.

112 (128)   METRUM: CHO BA (‖) CHO BA ‖

⊠ Ὄλβιε γάμβρε, coὶ μὲν δὴ γάμοс
      ὡс ἄραο
   ἐκτετέλεcτ᾽, ἔχηιс δὲ πάρθενον, ἂν
      ἄραο.
   coὶ χάριεν μὲν εἶδοс, ὄππατα
      ⟨δ᾽ . . . .⟩
   μέλλιχ᾽, ἔροс δ᾽ ἐπ᾽ ἰμέρτωι κέχυ-
      ται προcώπωι
5 ⟨. . . . .⟩ τετίμακ᾽
   ἔξοχά c᾽ Ἀφροδίτα

Fortunate bridegroom, your marriage
   that you prayed for
has been brought to pass, and you have
   the girl for whom you prayed.
And you—your appearance is full of
   grace, your eyes . . .
gentle, and *eros* flows from your lovely
   face . . .
Aphrodite has given you extraordinary
   honor.

113 (130)   METRUM: 3 IO ?

οὐ γὰρ
ἀτέρα νῦν πάις, ὦ γάμβρε, τεαύτα

114 (131)   METRUM: V.1 3 CHO BA, V.2 INC.

(νύμφη).	παρθενία, παρθενία, ποῖ με λίποισ᾽ ἀ⟨π⟩οίχηι;	Bride: Maidenhood, maidenhood, where have you gone and left me?
(παρθενία).	†οὐκέτι ἤξω πρὸς σέ, οὐκέτι ἤξω†	Maidenhood: No more will I come back to you, no more will I come back.

115 (127)   METRUM: PHER²ᵈ

⊠ Τίωι σ᾽, ὦ φίλε γάμβρε, κάλωσ   To what, dear bridegroom, may I suit-
  εἰκάσδω;   ably liken you?
ὄρπακι βραδίνωι σε μάλιστ᾽   I liken you most to a slender
  εἰκάσδω   sapling. . . .

116 (128,6)   METRUM INCERTUM (HIPP‖ HIPP‖ ?)

χαῖρε, νύμφα, χαῖρε, τίμιε γάμβρε,   Farewell, bride, farewell, honored
  πόλλα   bridegroom, many . . .

117 (129)   METRUM: 3 IA ˏ ? (CF. TEST)

⊠ †χαίροισ ἀ νύμφα†, χαιρέτω δ᾽ ὀ   May you fare well, bride, and may the
  γάμβροσ   bridegroom fare well, too.

117 A

ξοάνων προθύρων

117 B (132) = INC. AUCT. 24 LP

  a   Ἔσπερ᾽ ὐμήναον
  b   ὦ τὸν Ἀδώνιον

118 (103)   METRUM INCERTUM

ἄγι δὴ χέλυ δῖα †μοι λέγε†   Come now, divine lyre, speak to me,
φωνάεσσα †δὲ γίνεο†   and sounding forth be [my compan-
                                        ion?] . . .

119 (153)   METRUM INCERTUM

αἰμιτύβιον στάλασσον

120 (108)   METRUM: GL$^{1 \,(vel\,2)\,c}$

ἀλλά τις οὐκ ἔμμι παλιγ-
κότων
ὄργαν, ἀλλ᾽ ἀβάκην τὰν φρέν᾽
ἔχω . . .

But I am not someone resentful in my
feelings; I have a gentle heart.

121 (100)   METRUM INCERTUM

ἀλλ᾽ ἔων φίλος ἄμμιν λέχος ἄρνυσο
νεώτερον·
οὐ γὰρ τλάσομ᾽ ἔγω σύν ⟨τ᾽⟩ οἴκην
ἔσσα γεραιτέρα

But since you are our friend, seek a
younger bed.
For I would not dare to live with you,
since I am older.

122 (111)   METRUM INCERTUM

(*S. dicit se vidisse*)
ἄνθε᾽ ἀμέργοισαν παῖδ᾽ ἄγαν
ἀπάλαν

[I saw] an exceedingly tender girl pluck-
ing flowers

123 (15)   METRUM: CR HIPP ?

ἀρτίως μὲν ἁ χρυσοπέδιλος Αὔως

Just now golden-sandalled Dawn . . .

124 (155)   METRUM: --◡◡-◡◡-⟨x-◡-◡--⟩ = ERASM ITH, V. TEST

αὖτα δὲ σὺ Καλλιόπα

. . . but you yourself, Kalliope . . .

125 (101)   METRUM INCERTUM

†αυταόρα† ἐστεφαναπλόκην

126 (134)   METRUM INCERTUM

δαύοις(᾽) ἀπάλας ἐτα⟨ί⟩ρας ἐν
στήθεσιν

. . . [a woman]
sleeping on the bosom of a tender companion [*hetaira*] . . .

127 (154)   METRUM: ITH |ITH‖

✠ Δεῦρο δηὖτε Μοῖσαι χρύσιον
λίποισαι . . .

Hither again, O Muses, leaving your
golden [house] . . .

128 (90)   METRUM: 3CHO BA

✠ Δεῦτέ νυν ἄβραι Χάριτες καλλίκο-
μοί τε Μοῖσαι

Come hither now, tender Graces and
beautiful-haired Muses

129 (146 ET 18)   METRUM INCERTUM

a   ἔμεθεν δ᾽ ἔχηιϲθα λάθαν

b   ἤ τιν᾽ ἄλλον ἀνθρώπων ἔμεθεν φίληϲθα

130 (137) = 130. 131 LP   METRUM: GL[d]

⊠ Ἔροϲ δηὖτέ μ᾽ ὀ λυϲιμέληϲ δόνει,
   γλυκύπικρον ἀμάχανον ὄρπετον

       * * *

 Ἄτθι, ϲοὶ δ᾽ ἔμεθεν μὲν ἀπήχθετο
φροντίϲδην, ἐπὶ δ᾽ Ἀνδρομέδαν
   πότη⟨ι⟩

Eros the loosener of limbs shakes me
   again—
Bittersweet, untamable, crawling
   creature.

       * * *

Atthis, it has become hateful to you to
   think
of me; but you fly instead to Andromeda.

132 (152)   METRUM INCERTUM

⊠ Ἔϲτι μοι κάλα πάιϲ χρυϲίοιϲιν ἀν-
   θέμοιϲιν
ἐμφέρη⟨ν⟩ ἔχοιϲα μόρφαν Κλέιϲ
  ⟨ ⟩ ἀγαπάτα,
ἀντὶ τᾶϲ ἔγωὐδὲ Λυδίαν παῖϲαν
οὐδ᾽ ἐράνναν . . .

I have a child whose beauty
resembles golden flowers: beloved
   Kleis,
whom [I would not exchange]
either for all of Lydia or a lovely . . .

133 (144A. B)   METRUM: IA 2IO ANACL

⊠ Ἔχει μὲν Ἀνδρομέδα κάλαν
   ἀμοίβαν

     * * *

Ψάπφοι, τί τὰν πολύολβον
Ἀφροδίταν. . . . ;

Andromeda has a beautiful gift in
   exchange . . .

Sappho, why do you [call upon?]
Aphrodite who is rich in happiness?

134 (87)   METRUM: 3 IO ANACL

⊠ Ζὰ ⟨.⟩ ἐλεξάμαν ὄναρ Κυπρογενηα

I addressed [you] in a dream, Cyprus-
   born

135 (86)   METRUM: 3 IO

⊠ Τί με Πανδίονιϲ, ὦἘϊρανα,
   χελίδων. . . . ;

Why, Irana, does the swallow, daughter of Pandion, [awaken?] me?

1 3 6 (1 2 1)   METRUM: PHER^{2d}

ἦρος ἄγγελος ἱμερόφωνος ἀήδων

. . . the nightingale, lovely-voiced messenger of spring . . .

1 3 7 (1 4 9)   METRUM:STROPHA ALCAICA (SED V. CRIT)

θέλω τί τ᾽ εἴπην, ἀλλά με κωλύει
αἴδωσ . . .

. . . .

I wish to say something to you,
but shame prevents me.

1 3 8 (1 5 1)   METRUM: IA ˏGL VEL IA ˏGL IA ?

cτᾶθι †κᾰντα† φίλοσ
καὶ τὰν ἐπ᾽ ὄccοιc᾽ ὀμπέταcον
χάριν

. . . stand firm if you are a friend(?)
and spread around the grace that is on
your eyes

1 3 9 (1 5 6 B)

θέοι δ[. . .]. νεcω.[. . .]. τικαδακ[. . .
θε̣[.].[.]ηλ̣[.] . . . [   ]ηλα[

1 4 0 (1 0 7) = 1 4 0 A LP   METRUM: PHER^{2c}

⊠ Κατθνάcκει, Κυθέρη᾽, ἄβροc
Ἄδωνιc· τί κε θεῖμεν;
καττύπτεcθε, κόραι, καὶ κατερ-
είκεcθε χίτωναc

"Tender Adonis is dying, Cytherea.
What are we to do?"
"Beat your breasts, maidens, and rend
your chitons."

1 4 1 (1 3 5) METRUM: VV. I ET 4 ˏPHER ?
VV. 2 .3 ET 5 .6 INC.

κῆ δ᾽ ἀμβροcίαc μὲν
κράτηρ ἐκέκρατ᾽
    Ἔρμαιc δ᾽ ἔλων ὄλπιν θέοιc᾽
ἐοινοχόηcε.
κῆνοι δ᾽ ἄρα πάντεc
5 καρχάcι᾽ ἦχον
    κᾰλειβον· ἀράcαντο δὲ πάμ-
παν ἔcλα γάμβρωι

There a mixing bowl of ambrosia had
    been mixed,
while Hermes, taking up the jug,
poured wine for the gods.
These all held their cups and made liba-
tions.
They prayed for all good things for the
bridegroom.

1 4 2 (1 1 9)   METRUM: 6 DAˏ (PHER^{3d})

Λάτω καὶ Νιόβα μάλα μὲν φίλαι
ἦcαν ἔταιραι

Leto and Niobe were very dear
friends . . .

143 (118) METRUM: 6 DA$_{\wedge}$ (PHER^{3d})

χρύσειοι ⟨δ'⟩ ἐρέβινθοι ἐπ' ἀϊόνων ἐφύοντο

Golden chickpeas grew upon the banks . . .

144 (143) METRUM: GL^{xd}

μάλα δὴ κεκορημένοις
Γόργωϲ

. . . quite fed up indeed with Gorgo . . .

145 (113)

μὴ κίνη χέραδοϲ

146 (52) METRUM: PHER^{d}, SED ALIA POSSIS

μήτε μοι μέλι μήτε μέλιϲϲα

Neither the honey nor the bee for me

147 (59) METRUM INCERTUM

μνάϲεϲθαί τινα φα⟨ῖ⟩μι †καὶ ἕτερον† ἀμμέων

I say that even later someone will remember us . . .

148 (92) METRUM INCERTUM

ὁ πλοῦτοϲ ἄνευ ἀρέταϲ οὐκ ἀϲίνηϲ πάροικοϲ
(ἀ δ' ἀμφοτέρων κρᾶϲιϲ †εὐδαιμονίαϲ ἔχει τὸ ἄκρον†)

149 (125) METRUM: PHER^{xd} ?

ὄτα πάννυχοϲ ἄϲφι κατάγρει

150 (109) METRUM: GL^{2c} ?

οὐ γὰρ θέμιϲ ἐν μοιϲοπόλων ⟨δόμωι⟩
θρῆνον ἔμμεν' ⟨. . . . . . .⟩ οὔ κ' ἄμμι πρέποι τάδε

For it is not right for there to be lamentation
in the house of those who serve the Muses.
That would not be suitable for us.

151 (106) METRUM: PHER^{c}

ὀφθάλμοιϲ δὲ μέλαιϲ νύκτοϲ ἄωροϲ

The black sleep of night [covers] the eyes . . .

152 (142) METRUM: GL^{xd} ?

παντοδάπαιϲ⟨ι⟩ μεμ⟨ε⟩ιχμένα χροίαιϲιν

153 (91) METRUM INCERTUM

πάρθενον ἀδύφωνον   . . . sweet-voiced maiden . . .

154 (88) METRUM: ˬGL BA ‖

⊠ Πλήρης μὲν ἐφαίνετ᾽ ἀ cελάν⟨ν⟩α,   The moon gleamed in its fullness,
αἰ δ᾽ ὠc περὶ βῶμον ἐcτάθηcαν   and as the women stood around the
               altar . . .

155 (150) METRUM: CR │ ˬHIPP^d VEL CR ˬGL

πόλλα μοι τὰν Πωλυανάκτιδα   I'm overjoyed to say farewell to you,
παῖδα χαίρην   Miss Overlord.

156 (138) METRUM INCERTUM, GL^{2d} POSSIS

πόλυ πάκτιδοc ἀδυμελεc-   [a woman] by far more sweet-
τέρα . . .   melodied than a harp,
χρύcω χρυcοτέρα. . . .   more golden than gold . . .

157 (16) METRUM: STROPHA SAPPHICA ?

πότνια Αὔωc   Lady Dawn . . .

158 (126) METRUM: 2 AD?

(Cαπφὼ παραινεῖ)
cκιδναμέναc ἐν cτήθεcιν ὄργαc
μαψυλάκαν γλῶccαν πεφύλαχθαι

159 (110) METRUM INCERTUM

(Venus loquitur)   . . . you and my servant Eros . . .
cύ τε κἆμοc θεράπων Ἔροc

160 (11) METRUM: STROPHA SAPPHICA ?

τάδε νῦν ἐταίραιc   Now I will sing beautifully
ταὶc ἔμαιc †τέρπνα† κάλωc ἀείcω   to delight (?) my women
               companions . . .

161 (130A)

τανδεφυλάccετε ἐννε[. .]οι γάμβροι [. . . . .]υ πολίων βαcίλη εc

162 (156A)

τίοισιν ὀφθάλμοισι[ν];

163 (147)

τὸ μέλημα τὦμον   My darling . . .

164 (112)

τὸν Ϝὸν παῖδα κάλει

165 (3)

φαίνεταί Ϝοι κῆνος

166 (105)   METRUM: GLᶜ?

φαῖϲι δή ποτα Λήδαν ὑακίνθινον   Indeed, they say that once Leda found
⟨. . .⟩ ὤϊον εὔρην πεπυκάδμενον   an egg, colored like a hyacinth,
                                                        covered with . . .

167 (139)   METRUM: GLˣᵈ

ὠίω πόλυ λευκότερον   whiter by far than an egg . . .

168 (21)   METRUM: STROPHA SAPPHICA ?

ὦ τὸν Ἄδωνιν

168 A (104) = 178 LP   METRUM: GL ?

Γέλλωϲ παιδοφιλωτέρα   . . . more fond of children than Gello
                                                        [a bogy-woman who was said to de-
                                                        vour bad children]

168 B (94)   METRUM: ⌃HIPP‖

⊗ Δέδυκε μὲν ἀ ϲελάννα   The moon has set,
καὶ Πληΐαδεϲ· μέϲαι δὲ   and the Pleiades. The night
νύκτεϲ, παρὰ δ᾽ ἔρχετ᾽ ὤρα,   is at its midpoint, the moment passes,
ἔγω δὲ μόνα κατεύδω.   and I sleep alone.

168 C   METRUM: STROPHA ALCAICA ? (VEL ‑‑˘‑‑| HEM)

ποικίλλεται μέν   . . . it is many-colored—
γαῖα πολυϲτέφανοϲ   the earth, much-garlanded . . .

169

ἀγαγοίην

I would lead

169 A

ἀθρήματα

[wedding] presents

170

Αἶγα

Goat

171

ἄκακος

innocent

172

ἀλγεcίδωρος

giver of pain

173

ἀμαμάξυδ(-ος, -ες)

vine

174

[ἀμάρα]

trench

175

αὐα

Dawn

176

βάρβιτος. βάρωμος. βάρμος

barbitos, baromos, barmos [variant forms of the name for a long-armed type of lyre]

177

βεῦδος

a dress

179

γρύτα

cosmetic bag

180

Ἕκτωρ

[Zeus] the Holder

181

ζάβατον   fordable

182

ἰοίην   I would go

183

κατώρης *sive* κατάρης   [wind] slanting downward

184

κίνδυν   danger

185

μελίφωνος   honey-voiced

186

μήδεϊα   Medea

187

Μοισάων   of the Muses

188

μυθόπλοκος   [Eros] weaver of stories

189

νίτρον   soda

190

πολυίδριδι   very knowledgeable

191

cέλιν⟨ν⟩α   celery

192 (133A)

χρυςαςτράγαλοι φίαλαι   saucers with golden knobs

NOTES

Introduction: A Woman-Centered Perspective on Sappho

1. For an excellent discussion of what is known about women's lives during the period in which Sappho lived, see "Women in Archaic Greece: Talk in Praise and Blame," in *Women in the Classical World: Image and Text,* ed. Elaine Fantham, Helene Peet Foley, Natalie Boymel Kampen, Sarah B. Pomeroy, and H. A. Shapiro, pp. 10–55 (Oxford: Oxford University Press, 1994). As these authors point out (p. 11), "reconstructing the social life of this period is highly problematic." The most successful recent attempt to place Sappho's poetry within the context of Archaic Lesbos may be found in Margaret Williamson, *Sappho's Immortal Daughters* (Cambridge, Massachusetts: Harvard University Press, 1995). I have not yet seen the study by Lyn Hatherly Wilson, *Sappho's Sweetbitter Songs,* forthcoming from Routledge. For a thought-provoking analysis that focuses not on the reconstructed social context of Sappho's time but rather on the poet as a disruptive figure in the history of Greek literature, see Page duBois, *Sappho Is Burning* (Chicago: University of Chicago Press, 1995).

2. See, for example, Holt Parker, "Sappho Schoolmistress," *Transactions of the American Philological Association* 123 (1993): 309–51, who argues that interpretations of her poetry have been unduly colored by the assumption that she was an older woman in a position of authority whose audience consisted of young, unmarried girls. André Lardinois, "Subject and Circumstance in Sappho's Poetry," *Transactions of the American Philological Association* 124 (1994): 57–84, agrees with Parker that the "schoolmistress" paradigm is inappropriate but argues that her poetry was nevertheless addressed primarily to girls and young women. For other stud-

ies that address questions of the social context of Sappho's poetry, see, for example, Claude Calame, *Les Choeurs de jeunes filles en Grèce archaïque* (Rome: Edizioni dell'Ateneo and Bizzarri, 1977); Judith P. Hallett, "Sappho and Her Social Context: Sense and Sensuality," *Signs* 4 (1979): 447–64; Anne Pippin Burnett, *Three Archaic Poets: Archilochus, Alcaeus, Sappho* (Cambridge, Massachusetts: Harvard University Press, 1983); and Bruno Gentili, *Poetry and Its Public in Ancient Greece,* trans. A. Thomas Cole (Baltimore: Johns Hopkins University Press, 1988).

3. For the most recent archaeological report on the reputed place of Sappho's birth, the town of Eresos (modern Skala Eresou) on the southwest coast of Lesbos, see Gerald P. Schaus and Nigel Spencer, "Notes on the Topography of Eresos," *American Journal of Archaeology* 98 (1994): 411–30. As they point out, little excavation has been undertaken in the area. On the ancient acropolis, towering over the little modern beach village below, one does still find a few traces of walls built of polygonal masonry, dated by archaeologists to the general period in which Sappho lived. For a recent report on other archaeological work on the island, see Hector Williams, "Secret Rites of Lesbos," *Archaeology* 47 (1994): 34–40, which deals with a sanctuary of Demeter and Kore.

4. Adrienne Rich, "Compulsory Heterosexuality and Lesbian Existence," *Signs* 5 (1980): 631–60, coined the expression "compulsory heterosexuality." For a more recent discussion of the similar notion of "presumptive heterosexuality," see Judith Butler, *Gender Trouble: Feminism and the Subversion of Identity* (New York: Routledge, 1990).

5. On the notion of overlapping patterns in relationships between women that define what Adrienne Rich referred to as a "lesbian continuum," see Claudia Card, *Lesbian Choices* (New York: Columbia University Press, 1995), pp. 28–35. Card goes even further to suggest that the term *lesbian* should be understood to cover multiple, interconnected continua. For an opposing point of view, see Susan Stanford Friedman, *Psyche Reborn: The Emergence of H.D.* (Bloomington: Indiana University Press, 1981), p. 46, who, noting the ambiguities of the labels *lesbian, bisexual,* and *heterosexual,* suggests, "Perhaps we need to invent more words to distinguish among the physical, psychological, and political phenomena coexisting under the umbrella of 'lesbianism.'" Despite the increasing attention in contemporary scholarship to issues of gender and sexuality, a certain nervousness and defensiveness continues to affect modern approaches to Sappho; see, for example, Rae Dalven, ed. and trans., *Daughters of Sappho: Contemporary Greek Women Poets,* p. 19 (Rutherford: Fairleigh Dickinson University Press, 1994): "As for Sappho's reputed homosexuality, about which so much has been written through the centuries, one must keep in mind that modern social and sexual habits differ considerably from those of Sappho's time. . . . There is no evidence that Sappho herself took part in homosexual practices."

6. For a helpful discussion of desire as a social construct, see Martha Nussbaum, "Therapeutic Arguments and Structures of Desire," *differences* 2 (1990): 46–66.

7. See, for example, Judy Grahn, *The Highest Apple: Sappho and the Lesbian Poetic Tra-*

dition (San Francisco: Spinsters, Ink, 1985), and Dolores Klaich, *Woman + Woman: Attitudes Toward Lesbianism* (New York: Morrow, 1974).

8. For a detailed study of this concept in connection with the tradition of French literature inspired by Sappho, see Joan DeJean, *Fictions of Sappho, 1546–1937* (Chicago: University of Chicago Press, 1989). For the imaginary conversation with Sappho, see Amy Lowell, "The Sisters," in *The Complete Poetical Works* (Boston: Houghton Mifflin, 1955), p. 459 (discussed below in chapter 7).

9. Eva-Maria Voigt, ed., *Sappho et Alcaeus: Fragmenta* (Amsterdam: Athenaeum-Polak and Van Gennep, 1971). The *V.* following the fragment numbers in the present volume refers to her numbering system, which is essentially the same as that used in an earlier edition by Edgar Lobel and Denys Page, eds., *Poetarum Lesbiorum Fragmenta* (Oxford: Clarendon Press, 1955), usually abbreviated as L.-P. These two editions are the ones generally used by scholars today. Older editions use completely different numbering systems. As for my translations, many of them appeared originally in Jane McIntosh Snyder, *The Woman and the Lyre: Women Writers in Classical Greece and Rome* (Carbondale: Southern Illinois University Press, 1989).

10. For a helpful discussion of the problems of translating Sappho, see Diane J. Rayor, "Translating Fragments," *Translation Review* 32–33 (1990): 15–18.

11. David A. Campbell, ed. and trans., *Greek Lyric* (Cambridge, Massachusetts: Harvard University Press, 1982), vol. 1.

12. See Wilhelm Schubart and Ulrich von Wilamowitz-Moellendorff, eds., *Griechische Dichter-fragmente,* Berliner Klassikertexte vol. 5.2 (Berlin: Weidmann, 1907).

13. Medea Norsa, "Dai papiri della Società Italiana: Versi di Saffo in un ostrakon del sec. II a.C.," *Annali della Scuola Normale Superiore di Pisa* 6 (1937): 8–15.

14. Fr. 103 V. (P. Oxy. 2294).

15. For a somewhat higher estimate, see Paul Friedrich, *The Meaning of Aphrodite* (Chicago: University of Chicago Press, 1978), p. 127, who estimates that the collection might have included as many as 500 poems.

1. Sappho and Aphrodite

1. On notions of Sappho as priestess, see Jane McIntosh Snyder, *The Woman and the Lyre: Women Writers in Classical Greece and Rome* (Carbondale: Southern Illinois University Press, 1989), pp. 12–13. Until recently, the modern approach to Sappho was largely derived from the influential (if excessively Victorian) analysis of her work by Ulrich von Wilamowitz-Moellendorff, *Sappho und Simonides: Untersuchungen über griechische Lyriker* (Berlin: Weidmann, 1913), pp. 17–78. Among more recent attempts to place Sappho in some sort of role within a social context: Reinhold Merkelbach, "Sappho und ihr Kreis," *Philologus* 101 (1957) 1–29; Claude Calame, *Les Choeurs de jeunes filles en Grèce archaïque* (Rome: Edizioni dell'Ateneo and Bizzarri, 1977); and the influential article by Judith Hallett "Sappho and Her Social Context: Sense and Sensuality," *Signs* 4 (1979): 447–64.

2. Sappho's text is cited throughout this book according to the numbering system

in the edition by Eva-Maria Voigt, abbreviated as V. (for the Greek text, see appendix 2).

3. See the helpful discussion in Bernard Knox, "The Lost Lesbian," *New Republic* 210, no. 21 (1994): 35–42, which provides general background information about Sappho's lyrics and favorable reviews of *Sappho: A Garland: The Poems and Fragments of Sappho*, trans. Jim Powell (New York: Farrar, Straus, Giroux, 1993), and Peter Green, *The Laughter of Aphrodite: A Novel About Sappho of Lesbos* (Berkeley: University of California Press, 1993), a fictional account of Sappho's life originally published in 1965.

4. Regarding the standard features of Greek prayers, see Mabel Lang, "Reason and Purpose in Homeric Prayers," *Classical World* 68 (1975): 309–14, and James V. Morrison, "The Function and Context of Homeric Prayers: A Narrative Perspective," *Hermes* 119 (1991): 145–57.

5. The text of the opening of this hymn is not absolutely certain. On *poikilothron'*, see Denys Page, *Sappho and Alcaeus* (Oxford: Clarendon Press, 1955), pp. 4–5, who discusses the evidence for preferring this reading to the variant reading *poikilophron*. See, however, Ruth Neuberger-Donath, "Sappho Fr. 1.1: ΠΟΙΚΙΛΟΘΡΟΝ᾽ oder ΠΟΙΚΙΛΟΦΡΟΝ᾽," *Wiener Studien* 82 (1969): 15–17, who points out that the adjective "of the many-colored throne" does not occur elsewhere, whereas the adjective "of many-colored wiles" is found in both Alkaios and Euripides, and is therefore, she thinks, the more likely reading. See also John J. Winkler, "Double Consciousness in Sappho's Lyrics," in *The Constraints of Desire* (New York: Routledge, 1990), pp. 172–75, who explores the overtones of the possible derivation of *poikilothron'* as from not *thronos* ("chair") but *throna* ("drugs"); he connects the idea of Aphrodite as having magical drugs with the incantatory qualities of the hymn.

6. See the major study by Barbara Hughes Fowler, "The Archaic Aesthetic," *American Journal of Philology* 105 (1984): 119–49.

7. See Jane McIntosh Snyder, "The Web of Song: Weaving Imagery in Homer and the Lyric Poets," *Classical Journal* 76 (1981): 193–96.

8. For a thorough study of the incantatory qualities of Sappho's poems and the notion of spellbinding verse, see Charles Segal, "Eros and Incantation: Sappho and Oral Poetry," *Arethusa* 7 (1974): 139–60.

9. S. R. Slings, "Sappho Fr. 1.8 V.: Golden House or Golden Chariot?" *Mnemosyne* 44 (1991): 404–10, argues against the majority view (that the position of *chrusion* is ambiguous) and presents a case for taking the adjective only with *domon*, "house."

10. For the Greek sources on sparrows, see Page, *Sappho and Alcaeus*, pp. 7–8.

11. For details see David A. Campbell, ed., *Greek Lyric Poetry* (New York: St. Martin's Press, 1967), p. 266. Maryline Parca, "Sappho 1.18–19," *Zeitschrift für Papyrologie und Epigraphik* 46 (1982): 47–50, argues for a reading of the problematic line in the Greek that she translates as "Whom should I persuade this time, setting out to bring her to your love?"

12. An example of the erotic use of *philotas* may be found in Homer, *Odyssey* 10.335, where Circe issues a sexual invitation to Odysseus.

13. K. J. Dover, *Greek Homosexuality* (Cambridge, Massachusetts: Harvard University Press, 1978), p. 178. The male-oriented frame of reference in connection with the approaches generally taken to Sappho is revealed in his subsequent comment: "This obliteration of the usual distinction between a dominant and a subordinate partner is contrary to what the evidence for Greek male homosexuality would have led us to expect."

14. On the similarity between Aphrodite's speech and the formulae found in ancient magical spells, see A. Cameron, "Sappho's Prayer to Aphrodite," *Harvard Theological Review* 32 (1939): 1–17, esp. pp. 8–13. For an interesting interpretation of the "Hymn to Aphrodite" as a request not for reversal but rather for revenge and justice (in the sense that the woman who is now the object of unrequited love will one day herself be in the position of feeling unrequited love for someone else), see Anne Giacomelli, "The Justice of Aphrodite in Sappho Fr. 1," *Transactions of the American Philological Association* 110 (1980): 135–42. While this article has many good points, it seems to me to underestimate the importance of the (admittedly problematic) line 19, where Aphrodite seems to be asking whom she should bring back into the relationship of *philotas* ("friendship" or "erotic love") with Sappho.

15. John D. Marry, "Sappho and the Heroic Ideal," *Arethusa* 12 (1979): 71–92, argues that Sappho is deliberately exposing "the code of Homeric chivalry to a certain inevitable irony" (p. 71). For an interpretation in which irony is seen as dominating the entire poem, see Keith Stanley, "The Rôle of Aphrodite in Sappho Fr. 1," *Greek, Roman, and Byzantine Studies* 17 (1976): 305–21. For a reading that emphasizes the Archaic view of *eros* as domination, see Page duBois, *Sappho Is Burning* (Chicago: University of Chicago Press, 1995), pp. 7–9, who argues that Sappho shares her male contemporaries' conception of love as a battlefield; in her view, the "Hymn to Aphrodite" cannot therefore be interpreted as representing "reciprocal feminine sexuality" (p. 9).

16. See Snyder, *The Woman and the Lyre*, p. 11.

17. As Marilyn Skinner puts it, in "Aphrodite Garlanded: Erôs and Poetic Creativity in Sappho and Nossis," in *Rose di Pieria,* ed. Francesco de Martino, pp. 79–96 (Bari: Levante Editori, 1991), esp. p. 80: "in Aphrodite's presence, the kinetic urgency of sexual tension is channeled into a driving creative force."

18. See Jesper Svenbro, "La stratégie de l'amour: Modèle de la guerre et théorie de l'amour dans la poésie de Sappho," *Quaderni di Storia* 10 (1984): 57–79, who sees echoes of the bellicose events of *Iliad* 5 throughout the "Hymn to Aphrodite."

19. Medea Norsa, "Dai papiri della Società Italiana: Versi di Saffo in un ostrakon del sec. II a.C.," *Annali della Scuola Normale Superiore di Pisa* 6 (1937): 8–15.

20. Anne Pippin Burnett, *Three Archaic Poets: Archilochus, Alcaeus, Sappho* (Cambridge, Massachusetts: Harvard University Press, 1983), p. 263, points out the oddity of the topographical emphasis in the poem. On Sappho's use elsewhere of imagi-

nary landscapes (as metaphors for the soul), see Deborah Boedeker, "Sappho and Acheron," in *Arktouros: Hellenic Studies Presented to Bernard M. W. Knox,* ed. G. W. Bowersock, Walter Burkert, and Michael C. J. Putnam, pp. 40–52 (Berlin: de Gruyter, 1979).

21. Richard Jenkyns, *Three Classical Poets: Sappho, Catullus, and Juvenal* (Cambridge, Massachusetts: Harvard University Press, 1982), pp. 23–26.

22. Robert Bagg, "Love, Ceremony, and Daydream in Sappho's Lyrics," *Arion* 3 (1964): 44–82, esp. p. 52.

23. Burnett, *Three Archaic Poets,* p. 269, gives several examples of the sexual connotations of apples, roses, etc., and attributes a social function to the poem: to celebrate the "coming of age" of the girls in Sappho's "circle."

24. See, for example, Kathryn Bond Stockton, "Bodies and God: Poststructuralist Feminists Return to the Fold of Spiritual Materialism," *boundary 2* 19 (1992): 113–49.

25. For a detailed analysis of the eroticism suggested in Sappho's description of the landscape here, see Kai Heikkilä, "Sappho Fragment 2 L.-P.: Some Homeric Readings," *Arctos* 26 (1992): 39–53.

26. Voigt prints these two sets of lines as possibly belonging together, whereas other editors print them as two separate fragments that happen to be in the same meter.

27. Bonnie MacLachlan, "What's Crawling in Sappho Fr. 130," *Phoenix* 43 (1989): 95–99, makes a conjectural case for the "crawling creature" as being a bee. While this proposal fits nicely with the idea of pleasure and pain (the honey and the sting), too little of the fragment remains for us to be sure what specific creature Sappho had in mind; indeed, we might equally well speculate that she left the particular beast to the hearer's imagination. On the concept of Eros as "bittersweet," see Renate Schlesier, "Der Bittersüsse Eros," *Archiv für Begriffsgeschichte* 30 (1986–1987): 70–83.

28. Virginia Woolf, "On Not Knowing Greek," in *The Common Reader* (New York: Harcourt, Brace, and World, 1925), pp. 36–37.

2. The Construction of Desire

1. Joan DeJean, "Sex and Philology: Sappho and the Rise of German Nationalism," *Representations* 27 (1989): 148–71, esp. p. 157. See also Jane McIntosh Snyder, *The Woman and the Lyre: Women Writers in Classical Greece and Rome* (Carbondale: Southern Illinois University Press, 1989), pp. 7–13.

2. I have followed Page's suggestion (*Sappho and Alcaeus* [Oxford: Clarendon Press, 1955], p. 25) of keeping the reading *epirrombeisi* instead of accepting (as Voigt does) Bergk's conjecture *epibromeisi* (my ears "roar").

3. [Longinus], *De Sublimitate* 10, ed. D. A. Russell (Oxford: Clarendon Press), 1968.

4. Judith Roof, *A Lure of Knowledge: Lesbian Sexuality and Theory* (New York: Columbia University Press, 1991), pp. 239–40.

5. See William M. Calder III, "F. G. Welcker's *Sapphobild* and Its Reception in Wilamowitz," *Hermes Einzelschriften* 49 (Stuttgart: Steiner, 1986): 131–56.

6.   Ulrich von Wilamowitz-Moellendorff, *Sappho und Simonides: Untersuchungen über griechische Lyriker* (Berlin: Weidmann, 1913), pp. 56–59; cf. Snyder, *The Woman and the Lyre,* pp. 19–21.

7.   See Mary R. Lefkowitz, "Critical Stereotypes and the Poetry of Sappho," *Greek, Roman, and Byzantine Studies* 14 (1973): 113–23. For arguments against the earlier interpretations of Wilamowitz and Page, see George L. Koniaris, "On Sappho, Fr. 31 (L.-P.)," *Philologus* 112 (1968): 173–86.

8.   However, see Joel B. Lidov, "The Second Stanza of Sappho 31: Another Look," *American Journal of Philology* 114 (1993): 503–35, who rightly points out that the text of lines 7–8 bears reconsideration. He proposes a reading that would translate something like "For when I saw you, it was not possible for me to speak even one thing in a small voice."

9.   See the important article by Eva Stehle, "Sappho's Gaze: Fantasies of a Goddess and Young Man," *differences* 2 (1990): 88–125.

10. Koniaris, "On Sappho, Fr. 31 (L.-P.)," 179.

11. A useful commentary on the fluttering heart may be found in Enzo Degani and Gabriele Burzacchini, eds., *Lirici Greci* (Florence: La Nuova Italia, 1977), pp. 142–43.

12. Ruth Padel, *In and out of the Mind: Greek Images of the Tragic Self* (Princeton: Princeton University Press, 1993), esp. chapter 2 on "Innards," pp. 12–48.

13. For a detailed discussion of the metrical and textual problems, see Page, *Sappho and Alcaeus,* p. 24. For later allusions to Sappho's broken tongue in Theocritus (2.108–9) and Lucretius (3.155, *infringi linguam*), see Maria Grazia Bonanno, "Saffo 31,9 V.: γλῶσσα ἔαγε," *Quaderni Urbinati di Cultura Classica* 43 (1993): 61–68.

14. Eleanor Irwin, *Colour Terms in Greek Poetry* (Toronto: Hakkert, 1974), pp. 31–78. Cf. Robert J. Edgeworth, "Sappho Fr. 31.14 L.-P.: ΧΛΩΡΟΤΕΡΑ ΠΟΙΑΣ," *Acta Classica* 27 (1984): 121–24; Brent Berlin and Paul Kay, *Basic Color Terms: Their Universality and Evolution* (Berkeley: University of California Press, 1969), pp. 70–71; Birch Moonwomon, "Color Categorization in Early Greek," *Journal of Indo-European Studies* 22 (1994): 37–65, esp. pp. 46 and 51.

15. On the associations among sleep, death, and love, see Emily Vermeule, *Aspects of Death in Early Greek Art and Poetry* (Berkeley: University of California Press, 1979), pp. 145–77.

16. Irwin, *Colour Terms in Greek Poetry,* p. 67.

17. See the useful discussion by Dolores O'Higgins, "Sappho's Splintered Tongue: Silence in Sappho 31 and Catullus 51," *American Journal of Philology* 111 (1990): 156–67.

18. On Sappho's consciousness as a female poet reading Homer, see John J. Winkler, "Double Consciousness in Sappho's Lyrics," in *The Constraints of Desire* (New York: Routledge, 1990), p. 169.

19. Winkler, *Constraints of Desire,* pp. 178–80.

20. Winkler, *Constraints of Desire,* p. 179.

21. For a modern example, Gertrude Stein, see Catharine R. Stimpson, "The Soma-

grams of Gertrude Stein," in *The Female Body in Western Culture,* ed. Susan Rubin Suleiman, pp. 30–43 (Cambridge, Massachusetts: Harvard University Press, 1986).

22. See Lorraine Gamman and Margaret Marshment, eds., *The Female Gaze: Women as Viewers of Popular Culture* (Seattle: Real Comet Press, 1989); E. Ann Kaplan, "Is the Gaze Male?" in *Powers of Desire: The Politics of Sexuality,* ed. Ann Snitow, Christina Stansell, and Sharon Thompson, pp. 309–27 (New York: Monthly Review Press, 1983); and Mary Ann Doane, *The Desire to Desire: The Woman's Film of the 1940's* (Bloomington: Indiana University Press, 1987).

23. Jeanette Winterson, *Written on the Body* (New York: Knopf, 1993), p. 89.

24. The classic discussion comparing the two poems is that of Richmond Lattimore, "Sappho 2 and Catullus 51," *Classical Philology* 39 (1944): 184–87. For a recent analysis influenced by Bakhtin, see Paul Allen Miller, "Sappho 31 and Catullus 51: The Dialogism of Lyric," *Arethusa* 26 (1993): 183–99; although I disagree with his premise that Sappho's poem must have been written as a wedding song, I find his discussion of the intertextual qualities of Catullus's version instructive.

25. On Catullus's transformation of the Sappho narrator into an object, see Willis Barnstone, *The Poetics of Translation: History, Theory, Practice* (New Haven: Yale University Press, 1993), p. 100.

26. Roy Arthur Swanson, review of Joan DeJean, *Fictions of Sappho,* in *Journal of the History of Sexuality* 2 (1991): 111.

27. Barnstone, *The Poetics of Translation,* p. 100.

28. For a detailed discussion of the textual problems, see Jane McIntosh Snyder, "The Configuration of Desire in Sappho Fr. 22 L.-P.," *Helios* 21 (1994): 3–8, where the ideas expressed in this section appear in somewhat different form.

29. See Skinner, "Aphrodite Garlanded: Erôs and Poetic Creativity in Sappho and Nossis," in *Rose di Pieria,* ed. Francesco de Martino, p. 85 (Bari: Levante Editori, 1991).

30. Barbara Hughes Fowler, "The Archaic Aesthetic," *American Journal of Philology* 105 (1984): 148–49.

31. Fowler, "The Archaic Aesthetic," 137.

32. M. L. West, "Burning Sappho," *Maia* 22 (1970): 319.

33. On the importance of *kinesis* ("movement") as a recurring theme in Sappho's poetry, see Frederic Will, "Sappho and Poetic Motion," *Classical Journal* 61 (1966): 259–62.

34. The name Gongula also appears in an ancient commentary on lyric poetry (Sappho fr. 213A V.) and is also associated with Sappho in the mediaeval encyclopedia known as the *Suda.*

35. For a helpful discussion of Sappho's use of epic motifs here that avoids the biographical method of interpretation, see Deborah Boedeker, "Sappho and Acheron," in *Arktouros: Hellenic Studies Presented to Bernard M. W. Knox,* ed. G. W. Bowersock, Walter Burkert, and Michael C. J. Putnam, pp. 40–52 (Berlin: de Gruyter, 1979). On Ezra Pound's mistranslation of Sappho fr. 95 V. in his poem

"Papyrus," see Wilhelm Seelbach, "Ezra Pound und Sappho fr. 95 L.-P." *Antike und Abendland* 16 (1970): 83–84.

36. Page, *Sappho and Alcaeus,* p. 86.

3. Eros *and Reminiscence*

1. P. Berol. 9722. See Wilhelm Schubart and Ulrich von Wilamowitz-Moellendorff, eds., *Griechische Dichter-fragmente,* Berliner Klassikertexte vol. 5.2 (Berlin: Weidmann, 1907). Included together with the two substantial fragments discussed in the present chapter were two that are virtually unreadable (fr. 92 V. and fr. 93 V.) and also fr. 95 V. (discussed in chapter 2).

2. See Hesiod, *Theogony* 53–80, who explains how Mnemosyne bore nine daughters to Zeus (Kleio, Euterpe, Thaleia, Melpomene, Terpsichore, Erato, Polumnia, Ouranie, and Kalliope). He describes their birthplace near the topmost peak of Mount Olympus as also being the home of the Graces (*Charites*) and of Desire (*Himeros*).

3. Denys Page, *Sappho and Alcaeus* (Oxford: Clarendon Press, 1955), p. 95.

4. Despite his useful observations about the moon simile, I must disagree with the argument of C. Carey, "Sappho Fr. 96 LP," *Classical Quarterly* 28 (1978): 366–71, on the point that "while the poetess and her addressee concentrate on this hypnotic, purely pictorial description, all emotion is drained from the poem" (p. 368).

5. E.g., Thomas McEvilley, "Sapphic Imagery and Fragment 96," *Hermes* 101 (1972): 257–78, esp. p. 262. He translates *gunaikes* as "wives." Contrast Holt Parker, "Sappho Schoolmistress," *Transactions of the American Philological Society* 123 (1993): 309–51, esp. p. 337; he points out that assumptions that frr. 94 and 96 involve young girls who leave Sappho's "circle" to be married are quite possibly completely erroneous.

6. The Greek word for "moon" that appears in the parchment (*mena*) is metrically incorrect and should no doubt be emended to the word that Sappho uses elsewhere, *selanna.* See Richard Janko, "Sappho Fr. 96,8 L-P: A Textual Note," *Mnemosyne* 35 (1982): 222–23.

7. I am indebted to my student Rod Boyer for calling my attention to the possible double level of meanings here (M.A. thesis, Department of Classics, Ohio State University, 1995).

8. Cf. *Homeric Hymn to Selene.*

9. See Louise Weld and William Nethercut, "Sappho's Rose-Fingered Moon: A Note," *Arion* 5 (1966): 28–31, on the "extraordinary description of delicate flowers at full bloom under the light of the moon" (p. 31).

10. *Anthologia Palatina* 5.170. See Jane McIntosh Snyder, *The Woman and the Lyre: Woman Writers in Classical Greece and Rome* (Carbondale: Southern Illinois University Press, 1989), p. 72, and cf. Marilyn Skinner, "Sapphic Nossis," *Arethusa* 22 (1989): 5–18, esp. p. 9.

11. Deborah Boedeker, "Sappho and Acheron," in *Arktouros: Hellenic Studies Presented to Bernard M. W. Knox,* edited by G. W. Bowersock, Walter Burkert, and Michael

C. J. Putnam, pp. 48–49. (Berlin: de Gruyter, 1979), discusses the erotic over-tones of dew and flowers in the "Deception of Zeus" scene and in Sappho frr. 95 V. and 96 V.

12.   See Rebecca Hague, "Sappho's Consolation for Atthis, Fr. 96 LP," *American Journal of Philology* 105 (1984): 29–36, esp. p. 31.

13.   Others have tried to make the simile relevant to the rest of the lines by assuming that Sappho means to describe the "actual" night on which the woman in Lydia is roaming about and thinking of Atthis. See, among many others, Alexander Turyn, *Studia Sapphica, Eos* suppl. 6 (Paris: Les Belles Lettres, 1929), p. 59.

14.   A helpful discussion of erotic vocabulary in Sappho may be found in Giuliana Lanata, "Sul linguaggio amoroso di Saffo," *Quaderni Urbinati di Cultura Classica* 1 (1966): 63–79, esp. p. 73.

15.   See, for example, J. M. Edmonds, "Some New Fragments of Sappho, Alcaeus, and Anacreon," *Proceedings of the Cambridge Philological Society* 136/138 (1927): 13–30.

16.   See Hague, "Sappho's Consolation for Atthis," who assumes that the poem falls into the genre of *consolatio*.

17.   Thomas McEvilley, "Sapphic Imagery and Fragment 96."

18.   Anne Pippin Burnett, "Desire and Memory (Sappho Frag. 94)," *Classical Philology* 74 (1979): 16–27. Contrast Emmet Robbins, "Who's Dying in Sappho Fr. 94?," *Phoenix* 44 (1990): 111–21, who persists in assigning the death-wish line to the Sappho figure, citing Helen's death wishes in the *Iliad* as models.

19.   For an analysis of the complex relationships among singer, speaker, and audience in Greek poetry, see Eva Stehle, *Performance and Gender in Ancient Greece,* forthcoming from Princeton University Press. My own thinking about performance owes much to her insightful interpretations.

20.   See Ellen Greene, "Apostrophe and Women's Erotics in the Poetry of Sappho," *Transactions of the American Philological Association* 124 (1994): 41–56, esp. p. 49: "The repetition of θέλω [*thelo,* "I wish"] in the parallel contexts of death and memory suggests the active transformative power of the poetic voice as it re-places the will to die with the will to create."

21.   Page, *Sappho and Alcaeus,* p. 83.

22.   For a similar allusion (without context) to soft bedding, see fr. 46 V.

23.   Eva S. Stigers [Stehle], "Sappho's Private World," *Women's Studies* 8 (1981): 47–63.

24.   See, for example, John Rauk, "Erinna's *Distaff* and Sappho Fr. 94," *Greek, Roman, and Byzantine Studies* 30 (1989): 101–16, who assigns the first extant line to the Sappho figure and interprets the song as a lament on the occasion of the address-ee's departure to be married.

25.   Burnett, "Desire and Memory (Sappho Frag. 94)," 26, n. 37.

4. Sappho's Challenge to the Homeric Inheritance

1.   Jesper Svenbro, "Sappho and Diomedes: Some Notes on Sappho 1 LP and the Epic," *Museum Philologum Londieniense* 1 (1975) 37–49, esp. p. 46. The question

of the exact relationship between epic and lyric has been a matter of considerable scholarly debate; see, for example, J. T. Hooker, *The Language and Text of the Lesbian Poets* (Innsbruck: Institut für Sprachwissenschaft, 1977), who argues that Sappho's poetry draws independently from the same source as epic.

2. Deborah Boedeker, "Sappho and Acheron," in *Arktouros: Hellenic Studies Presented to Bernard M. W. Knox,* edited by G. W. Bowersock, Walter Burkert, and Michael C. J. Putnam, p. 52 (Berlin: de Gruyter, 1979).

3. For an opposing view, see George L. Koniaris, "On Sappho, Fr. 16 (L.P.)," *Hermes* 95 (1967): 257–68, esp. p. 263: "That this ἔγω [*ego*, "I"] is physically speaking a woman we all understand, but I think that it is absolutely unwarranted to claim that Sappho, when she writes ἔγω, means to say 'I being a woman.'" Garry Wills, "The Sapphic 'Umwertung aller Werte,'" *American Journal of Philology* 88 (1967): 434–42, argues along similar lines: "She does not contrast woman's world with man's, as many think" (p. 442).

4. See William H. Race, *The Classical Priamel from Homer to Boethius, Mnemosyne* suppl. 74 (Leiden: Brill, 1982).

5. For a recent modification of the approach to the poem through logical principles, see the application of semiotic narrative theory offered by Claude Calame, "Sappho et Helene: Le Mythe comme argumentation narrative et parabolique" in *Parole, Figure, Parabole,* ed. Jean Delorme, pp. 209–29 (Lyon: Presses Universitaires de Lyon, 1987).

6. See, for example, Richmond Lattimore, trans., *Greek Lyrics* (Chicago: University of Chicago Press, 1971), p. 40; he renders line 4 as "but I say / she whom one loves best / is the loveliest." The most recent translations aim for a more literal rendering of the neutrality of the Greek text; compare Diane J. Rayor, trans., *Sappho's Lyre* (Berkeley: University of California Press, 1991), p. 55 ("I say it is whatever one loves"), and Jim Powell, trans., *Sappho: A Garland: The Poems and Fragments of Sappho* (New York: Farrar, Straus, Giroux, 1993), p. 28 ("but I say it's what- / ever you love best").

7. Page duBois, "Sappho and Helen," *Arethusa* 11 (1978): 89–99. See also her chapter on Helen in *Sappho Is Burning* (Chicago: University of Chicago Press, 1995), pp. 98–126. As Joseph A. Dane, "Sappho Fr. 16: An Analysis," *Eos* 69 (1981): 185–92, observes, Helen's status as lover *and* beloved renders her a complex, multivocal figure whom Sappho uses to good advantage.

8. Might Sappho's choice of Helen as an illustrative example in this song be colored by the Homeric description of what she left behind as a *omelikien erateinen* (*Iliad* 3.175), that is, a "lovely" (the adjective deriving from the same root as *eros*) group of age-mates? Evidently, despite their loveliness, the *eros* that they inspired in Helen was not as great as that inspired by Paris. I am indebted to Judith Hallett for calling the details of this description to my attention.

9. But see John Winkler, The *Contraints of Desire* (New York: Routledge, 1990), p. 178, who proposes that the missing subject of the verb "led" might have been Helen herself.

10. See Denys Page, *Sappho and Alcaeus* (Oxford: Clarendon Press, 1955), p. 53. The

comment of Synnøve des Bouvrie Thorsen, "The Interpretation of Sappho's Fragment 16 L.-P.," *Symbolae Osloenses* 53 (1978): 5–23, regarding the opening stanza of fr. 16, would seem to apply to the whole poem: "It cannot be judged by logical reasoning" (p. 9). John Winkler, "Gardens of Nymphs: Public and Private in Sappho's Lyrics," *Women's Studies* 8 (1981): 65–91, esp. p. 74, goes so far as to view the poem as a parody of logical argumentation. For an opposing point of view, see Glen W. Most, "Sappho Fr. 16.6–7 L-P," *Classical Quarterly* 31 (1981): 11–17, who applies a passage from Aristotle's *Rhetoric* to his analysis of the poem.

11. On the aristocratic name, see Enzo Degani and Gabriele Burzacchini, eds., *Lirici Greci* (Florence: La Nuova Italia, 1977), p. 136.

12. See Christopher Brown, "Anactoria and the Χαρίτων ἀμαρύγματα: Sappho fr. 16,18 Voigt," *Quaderni Urbinati di Cultura Classica* 32 (1989): 7–15, who points out (p. 8) that *amaruchma* refers to a "flashing" or "sparkling," particularly with reference to the eyes. See also Eleanor Irwin, *Colour Terms in Greek Poetry* (Toronto: Hakkert, 1974), p. 216, for this and other Greek terms that suggest both brightness and movement.

13. Gregson Davis, *Polyhymnia: The Rhetoric of Horatian Lyric Discourse* (Berkeley: University of California Press, 1991), pp. 34–35, cites Sappho fr. 16 V. as an "elegant example of figurative assimilation," whereby Sappho incorporates the language of martial spectacles into her description of Anaktoria.

14. The most recent version of this theory may be found in Brown, "Anactoria," 14; see also Carl Theander, "Studia Sapphica," *Eranos* 32 (1934): 57–85.

15. Denys Page, "The Authorship of Sappho β2 (Lobel)," *Classical Quarterly* 30 (1936): 10–15, disputes Wilamowitz's 1914 attempt to deny Sappho's authorship.

16. See Hermann Fränkel, *Early Greek Poetry and Philosophy,* trans. Moses Hadas and James Willis (New York: Harcourt Brace Jovanovich, 1973), p. 174: "The song of Hector and Andromache ends with an account of a song on Hector and Andromache; it leads into itself in a circle."

17. See, for example, Hermann Fränkel, *Wege und Formen frühgriechischen Denkens* (Munich: Beck, 1960), 41.

18. See Johannes T. Kakridis, "Zu Sappho 44 LP," *Wiener Studien* 79 (1966): 21–26, esp. p. 26.

19. Page, *Sappho and Alcaeus,* p. 71.

20. On the whole, modern critics have devoted relatively little attention to fr. 44, which is generally viewed as an aberrant poem within the corpus of Sappho's fragments. Here, for example, is the opinion of Richard Jenkyns, *Three Classical Poets: Sappho, Catullus, and Juvenal* (Cambridge, Massachusetts: Harvard University Press, 1982), p. 61: "So under the guise of mythological narrative she is really giving her audience a vivid picture of contemporary life. In any case, it cannot be said that this fragment adds to her reputation. Quaint, lively and fluent, it is the work of an able poet; but there is no subtlety in it, and no inspiration." For a counterargument to Jenkyns, see Lawrence P. Schrenk, "Sappho Frag. 44 and the 'Iliad'," *Hermes* 122 (1994): 144–50; he argues that allusions to *Iliad* 22.466–72 (Andromache's wedding to Hektor) and to *Iliad* 24.699–804 (Hek-

tor's funeral) render the poem another example of Sappho's portrayal of love as *glukupikron,* "bittersweet."

21.   For arguments against the view of Hermann Fränkel regarding what he saw as choral feaures of Sappho fr. 16 V., see E. M. Stern, "Sappho Fr. 16 L.P.: Zur Strukturellen Einheit ihrer Lyrik," *Mnemosyne* 23 (1970): 348–61.

22.   See William H. Race, "Sappho, Fr. 16 L.-P. and Alkaios, Fr. 42 L.-P.: Romantic and Classical Strains in Lesbian Lyric," *Classical Journal* 85 (1989): 16–33; he views Sappho's concern as being with individuals, while Alkaios focuses more on the fate of a whole people and their city.

5. The Aesthetics of Sapphic Eros

1.   Claude Calame, *Les Choeurs de jeunes filles en Grèce archaïque* (Rome: Edizioni dell'Ateneo and Bizzarri, 1977), vol. 1, p. 367, is a case in point. He posits the existence of Sappho's *thiasos* ("company," "troop") on the basis of analogies from the later Hellenistic period, and then in that light interprets Sappho fr. 150 V. as using *moisopolon* ("servants of the Muses") in a "sens institutionnel."

2.   Mangus Enquist and Anthony Arak, "Symmetry, Beauty, and Evolution," *Nature* 372 (1994): 169–72.

3.   The earliest account of the birth of the three Graces is in Hesiod, *Theogony* 907–11.

4.   On the threatening aspects of the *Charites* as they are depicted in Hesiod's *Theogony,* see Page duBois, "Eros and the Woman," *Ramus* 21 (1992): 97–116, esp. p. 110.

5.   See David M. Halperin, *One Hundred Years of Homosexuality* (New York: Routledge, 1990), pp. 30–32.

6.   Bonnie MacLachlan, *The Age of Grace: Charis in Early Greek Poetry* (Princeton: Princeton University Press, 1993).

7.   See *American Heritage Dictionary* (Boston: Houghton Mifflin, 1981), p. 1518, *gher-*[6]; Hjalmar Frisk, *Griechisches etymologisches Wörterbuch* (Heidelberg: Winter, 1954–1970), 1062–65, s.v. χαίρω.

8.   In the *Homeric Hymn to Demeter* (214–15), *charis* itself is said to be visible in Demeter's eyes.

9.   See Alkman fr. 1.21 *Poetae Melici Graeci.*

10.   The same epithet, rosy-armed, is applied to the Dawn (Eos) in fr. 58 V. (line 19).

11.   Himerius, *Orationes* 28.2. See Voigt fr. 221 (among the testimonia) for the Greek text. David A. Campbell, *Greek Lyric,* vol. 1 (Cambridge, Massachusetts: Harvard University Press, 1982), p. 43, interprets the passage somewhat differently as follows, adding a cautionary note as to the uncertainty of both text and translation: "Sappho alone among women loved beauty along with the lyre and therefore dedicated all her poetry to Aphrodite and the Loves, making a girl's beauty and graces the pretext for her songs." The translation "loved beauty" is based on a supplement added to the text by Wilamowitz (καλῶν), which I suggest be omitted.

12.   Elsewhere in the *Iliad* (18.382), *Charis* is fully personified as the wife of Heph-

aistos, the smith god; the description there seems to be an obscure variant of the usual account according to which Hephaistos is married to Aphrodite.

13.   MacLachlan, *The Age of Grace,* p. 7.

14.   For an apparently sarcastic use of *chairo* in Sappho (in the sense of "farewell and good riddance!"), see fr. 155 V: *polla moi tan Poluanaktida paida chairen* ("I'm overjoyed to say farewell to you, Miss Overlord").

15.   See MacLachlan, *The Age of Grace,* p. 64. It should be noted, however, that if the fifth-century Theban poet Pindar is representative in speaking about male homoerotic desire, youthfulness is no barrier to the presence of *charis* in that context. See Pindar fr. 123.10–15 (Snell), where the poet is praising Theoxenos, son of Hagesilas: "But because of [Aphrodite] I melt like the wax / of sacred bees, stung by the sun's heat, / whenever I look upon the fresh-limbed bloom of young men. / So even in Tenedos / Persuasion and *Charis* dwell / in the son of Hagesilas." Note the striking resemblance to Sappho fr. 31.7: "For the instant I look upon you."

16.   On Nossis see Marilyn B. Skinner, "Sapphic Nossis," *Arethusa* 22 (1989): 5–18; also her "Nossis *Thelyglossos:* The Private Text and the Public Book," in *Women's History and Ancient History,* ed. Sarah B. Pomeroy, pp. 20–47 (Chapel Hill: University of North Carolina Press, 1991). The erotic associations of the *Charites* continue down to as late as the first century B.C., when the Roman poet Lucretius uses the term *Chariton mia* (a transliteration from the Greek for "one of the Graces") as an example of a lover's term of endearment (*De Rerum Natura* 4.1162).

17.   On the absence of *habros* in Homer and on various linguistic innovations in Greek lyric, see Elena Walter-Karydi, "ΧΡΩΣ—Die Entstehung des griechischen Farbwortes," *Gymnasium* 98 (1991): 517–33, esp. p. 531. Warren D. Anderson, *Music and Musicians in Ancient Greece* (Ithaca: Cornell University Press, 1994), p. 76, points out the positive connotations of *habros* in the poetry of the sixth-century B.C. poet Stesichorus of Himera (Sicily).

18.   See Leslie Kurke, "The Politics of ἁβροσύνη in Archaic Greece," *Classical Antiquity* 11 (1992): 91–120. She takes Sappho's statement regarding her fondness for *habrosune* in fr. 58 V. (see discussion below) as being *politically* programmatic.

19.   See MacLachlan, *The Age of Grace,* pp. 59–61.

20.   On the programmatic nature of this assertion, see Eleonora Cavallini, "Presenza di Saffo e Alceo nella poesia greca fino ad Aristofane," *Quaderni del Giornale Filologico Ferrarese* 7 (1986): 61 and 75.

21.   Ferdinand Stiebitz, "Mitteilungen zu Sappho 65 Diehl," *Philologische Wochenschrift* 46 (1926): 1259–62.

22.   Eva Stehle, "Sappho's Gaze: Fantasies of a Goddess and Young Man," *differences* 2 (1990): 88–125.

23.   Page, *Sappho and Alcaeus,* pp. 129–30.

24.   *Anthologia Palatina* 6.47 (Antip. Sid.)

25.   On the the connections among the words *charis, poikilos,* and *daidalos* ("curiously

wrought"), see Françoise Frontisi-Ducroux, *Dédale: Mythologie de l'artisan en Grèce ancienne* (Paris: Maspero, 1975), pp. 68–73, who points out the the idea of brightness conveyed by the last two words is composite, fleeting, and unstable, suggesting the animation of living beings. For some intriguing modern analogues in connection with nineteenth-century taxonomies of addiction and homosexuality, see Eve Kosofsky Sedgwick, *Epistemology of the Closet* (Berkeley: University of California Press, 1990), pp. 174–75; she discusses the "commodity-based orientalism" of Oscar Wilde's *The Picture of Dorian Gray,* noting the frequent occurrence of the "drug-tinged" adjectives "curious" and "subtle," which "record, on the one hand, the hungrily inventive raptness of the curious or subtle perceiving eye or brain; and, on the other, the more than answering intricacy of the curious or subtle objects perceived."

26. See Winkler, *Constraints of Desire,* pp. 162–87, esp. p. 172.

27. A similar description appears in the poetry of the sixth-century B.C. lyric poet Anakreon of Teos, who refers to a girl who is *poikilosambalos,* "wearing an embroidered sandal" (fr. 358 *Poetae Melici Graeci*).

28. Page, *Sappho and Alcaeus,* p. 98.

29. Demetrius, *De Elocutione* 164 (*peri hermeneias*).

6. Sappho's Other Lyric Themes

1. For an intriguing (if sometimes baffling) discussion of the preeminence of the fragment over the whole in modern aesthetic theory in the light of the work of Walter Benjamin, see Christine Buci-Glucksmann, *Baroque Reason: The Aesthetics of Modernity,* trans. Patrick Camiller (London: Sage, 1994), pp. 69–73. See also Page duBois, *Sappho Is Burning* (Chicago: University of Chicago Press, 1995), pp. 31–54 ("The Aesthetics of the Fragment"); as she points out (p. 39), "We can accept the fragmentary for what it is, appreciate the few words of Sappho that we have inherited, rather than setting them, for example, against the fuller, more adequate corpus of Pindar, and naming him the greater poet."

2. The fragment in which Apollo and Artemis are addressed is assigned by some scholars to Alkaios (as Alkaios fr. 303A by Voigt) and by others to Sappho (as Sappho fr. 99 by Lobel-Page); see discussion of this so-called *olisbos* fragment at the end of the present chapter.

3. Some scholars also attempt to connect fr. 3 V. with Charaxos, but it is so fragmentary that little sense can be made of it. In addition, fr. 7 V. appears to contain mention of the name Doricha.

4. See G. S. Kirk, "A Fragment of Sappho Reinterpreted," *Classical Quarterly* 13 (1963): 51–52, who was the first to propose that the hyperbole involves the notion that the bridegroom is "fantastically ithyphallic" (p. 51).

5. See Anne Carson, *Eros the Bittersweet: An Essay* (Princeton: Princeton University Press, 1986), p. 26.

6. Judy Grahn, *The Highest Apple: Sappho and the Lesbian Poetic Tradition* (San Franciso: Spinsters, Ink, 1985), p. 11. Despite some minor factual errors (e.g., regarding

the mode of preservation of Sappho's one complete song, p. 10), this is a useful study of nine modern poets in the Sapphic tradition: Emily Dickinson, Amy Lowell, H.D., Gertrude Stein, Adrienne Rich, Audre Lorde, Olga Broumas, Paula Gunn Allen, and Judy Grahn.

7. See Kenneth Quinn, ed., *Catullus: The Poems* (London: MacMillan, 1970), p. 280: "There is almost certainly an allusion to a poem attributed to Sappho of which a fragment survives."

8. A similar treatment may have occurred in fr. 107 V., *er' eti parthenias epiballomai?* ("Indeed, do I still desire virginity?"), but the fragment is too short to be sure.

9. Carl Theander, "Atthis et Andromeda," *Eranos* 44 (1946): 62–67. He reads *es choron* ("to the dance") in place of *es gamon* ("to a wedding").

10. Denys Page, *Sappho and Alcaeus* (Oxford: Clarendon Press), p. 126.

11. On the importance of weaving as a female occupation in Greek society, see Robert James Forbes, "Fabrics and Weavers," in *Studies in Ancient Technology* (Leiden: Brill, 1955—), vol. 4, pp. 220–51; Jane McIntosh Snyder, "The Web of Song: Weaving Imagery in Homer and the Lyric Poets," *Classical Journal* 76 (1981): 193–96; and Elizabeth Wayland Barber, *Women's Work, the First 20,000 Years: Women, Cloth, and Society in Early Times* (New York: Norton, 1994).

12. The phrase is quoted by Aristotle, *Poetics* 1454b.36–37.

13. Patricia Klindienst Joplin, "Epilogue: Philomela's Loom," in *Coming to Light: American Women Poets in the Twentieth Century,* ed. Diane Wood Middlebrook and Marilyn Yalom, p. 254 (Ann Arbor: University of Michigan Press, 1985).

14. Max Treu, ed., *Sappho* (Munich: Heimeran, 1954), p. 162. The fragment was first published by E. Lobel and D. Page, "A New Fragment of Aeolic Verse," *Classical Quarterly* 2 (1952): 1–3, who assign the fragment either to Sappho or to Alkaios.

15. Bruno Snell, "Der Anfang eines äolischen Gedichts," *Hermes* 81 (1953): 118–19, points out that the sentiment expressed at the very end of part (b) sounds more characteristic of Alkaios than of Sappho.

16. Another example may occur in fr. 144 V., *mala de kekoremenois / Gorgos,* where the reference seems to be to people who are "quite fed up with Gorgo."

17. Giuseppe Giangrande, "Sappho and the ὄλισβος," *Emerita* 48 (1980): 250.

18. See also the references to perfume and expensive gifts in fr. 101 V., to "adornments" (*athurmata,* as in Sappho fr. 44.9 V.) in fr. 63.8 V., and to soft cushions in fr. 46 V. as possible further examples of *habrosune.*

19. Judith P. Hallett, "Beloved Cleïs," *Quaderni Urbinati di Cultura Classica* 10 (1982): 21–31, argues that the adjective (*agapetos,* "beloved," "highly valued") that Sappho uses to describe Kleis rules out any erotic connotation, and points out that its use in the *Iliad* and the *Odyssey* is always with reference to biological offspring.

20. See Eva-Maria Voigt, ed., *Sappho et Alcaeus: Fragmenta* (Amsterdam: Athenaeum-Polak and Van Gennep), p. 239 (regarding line 17).

21. The question of the literary exchange of differing views between the two fellow Lesbian poets is raised by Sappho fr. 137 V. (preserved in Aristotle's *Rhetoric*);

interpretation of the fragment is fraught with difficulties, but Aristotle seems to be implying that Sappho wrote a poem in answer to a poem written by Alkaios.

22. Cf. also Sappho fr. 185 V., *meliphonos* ("honey-voiced").

23. On the question of authorship, see Treu, *Sappho,* pp. 211–12; Diskin Clay, "Fragmentum Adespotum 976," *Transactions of the American Philological Association* 101 (1970): 119–29, who favors the attribution to Sappho.

24. Despite the apparent simplicity of the poetry, the interpretation of this fragment is the subject of much controversy. The word that I have translated as "night" is actually plural in the Greek, but such usage is attested elsewhere (e.g., Plato *Republic* 621b). The word that I have translated as "moment" (*ora*) is variously interpreted as "hour" or "time" or "right moment." For a summary of the arguments, see Enzo Degani and Gabriele Burzacchini, eds., *Lirici Greci* (Florence: La Nouva Italia), pp. 188–90. David Sider, "Sappho 168B Voigt: Δέδυκε μὲν ἀ Σελάννα," *Eranos* 84 (1986): 57–59, argues that all three senses of *ora* are felt.

Epilogue: Sappho and Modern American Women Poets

1. Giovanna Bemporad, *Esercizi: Poesie e traduzioni* (Milan: Garzanti, 1980), p. 103. I am indebted to Professors Gabriele Burzacchini and Sotera Fornaro for information on twentieth-century Italian poets influenced by Sappho, including Amalia Guglielminetti (1881–1961) and Ada Negri (1870–1945). For an example of lyrics from Victorian England that were inspired by Sappho, see Michael Field, *Long Ago* (London: Bell, 1889), and Yopie Prins, "Sappho Doubled: Michael Field," *Yale Journal of Criticism* 8 (1995): 165–86; "Michael Field" was the pen name of Katherine Bradley and Edith Cooper. See also Chris White, "'Poets and lovers evermore': The Poetry and Journals of Michael Field," in *Sexual Sameness: Textual Differences in Lesbian and Gay Writing,* ed. Joseph Bristow, pp. 26–43 (New York: Routledge, 1992).

2. Ned Rorem, *Four Madrigals* (New York: Music Press, 1948), with texts based on translations from Sappho by C. M. Bowra.

3. For a brief overview of Sappho's influence on American women poets in general, see Emily Stipes Watts, *The Poetry of American Women from 1632 to 1945* (Austin: University of Texas Press, 1977), pp. 75–78.

4. See Lillian Faderman, "Lowell, Amy Lawrence," in *Encyclopedia of Homosexuality,* ed. Wayne R. Dynes, 1:750–51 (New York: Garland, 1990).

5. For a recent reappraisal of the contributions of Lowell (and H.D.) to the Imagist aesthetic, see Andrew Thacker, "Amy Lowell and H.D.: The Other Imagists," *Women: A Cultural Review* 4 (1993): 49–59. See also Cheryl Walker, *Masks Outrageous and Austere: Culture, Psyche, and Persona in Modern Women Poets* (Bloomington: Indiana University Press, 1991), pp. 16–43 ("Amy Lowell and the Androgynous Persona") and pp. 105–34 ("Women and Time: H.D. and the Greek Persona").

6. All the quotations from Lowell are taken from *The Complete Poetical Works of Amy Lowell* (Boston: Houghton Mifflin, 1955).

7. On the so-called Ada Dwyer poems, see Richard Benvenuto, *Amy Lowell* (Boston:

Twayne, 1985), pp. 126–31, and Faderman, "Lowell, Amy Lawrence," in *Encyclo-pedia of Homosexuality.* See also Lillian Faderman, "Warding Off the Watch and Ward Society: Amy Lowell's Treatment of the Lesbian Theme," *Gay Books Bulletin* 1 (1979): 23–27, who discusses Lowell's association of the "Ada" figure with flowers, gardens, moonlight, and other imagery suggestive of female sexuality.

8. Amy Lowell, *Tendencies in Modern American Poetry* (New York: Macmillan, 1917), p. 251. See also Barbara Guest, *Herself Defined: The Poet H.D. and Her World* (New York: Doubleday, 1984), pp. 69–71.

9. See Janice S. Robinson, *H.D.: The Life and Work of an American Poet* (Boston: Houghton Mifflin, 1982); Guest, *Herself Defined;* Rachel Blau DuPlessis, *H.D.: The Career of That Struggle* (Brighton: Harvester Wheatsheaf, 1986).

10. Alicia Ostriker, "The Poet as Heroine: Learning to Read H.D.," in *Writing Like a Woman* (Ann Arbor: University of Michigan Press, 1983); Gary Burnett, *H.D. Between Image and Epic: The Mysteries of Her Poetics* (Ann Arbor: UMI Research Press, 1990); Susan Stanford Friedman, *Psyche Reborn: The Emergence of H.D.* (Bloomington: Indiana University Press, 1981) and *Penelope's Web: Gender, Moder-nity, H.D.'s Fiction* (Cambridge: Cambridge University Press, 1990). On the difficulties in defining H.D.'s sexuality, see Friedman, *Psyche Reborn,* p. 45.

11. Barbara Guest, *Herself Defined,* p. 33.

12. See esp. Susan Gubar, "Sapphistries," *Signs* 10 (1984): 43–62, esp. pp. 47 and 55.

13. See Robinson, *H.D.: The Life and Work,* p. 76. In this connection, I look forward to reading the ideas of Erika Rohrbach, "H.D. and Sappho: A Precious Inch of Palimpsest," in the second of two volumes of essays (both previously unpublished and already published) compiled by Ellen Greene, forthcoming from the Univer-sity of California Press.

14. Susan Gubar, "Sapphistries," 47.

15. From *Notes on Thought and Vision* & *The Wise Sappho* (San Francisco: City Lights Books, 1982), pp. 57–58.

16. All of H.D.'s poems cited in the present chapter are available in *H.D.: Collected Poems, 1912–1944,* ed. Louis L. Martz (New York: New Directions, 1983). For a somewhat literalist interpretation of the relationship between original and take-off in the case of the six poems with Sapphic epigraphs, see Thomas Burnett Swann, *The Classical World of H.D.* (Lincoln: University of Nebraska Press, 1962), pp. 109–21. He seems to subscribe to the lascivious Sappho school: "Among her readers there are those who underrate H.D. because of her renunciations and withdrawals. But to many others her very exclusiveness is more attractive than Sappho's promiscuity. In their eyes, the inviolate spirit is at least as much to be honored as the reckless heart" (p. 121).

17. *Collected Poems,* pp. 181–84. This poem also appears under the title "Amaranth" in a longer form, with additional material at the end, in *Collected Poems,* pp. 310–15.

18. Eileen Gregory, "Rose Cut in Rock: Sappho and H.D.'s Sea Garden," *Contemporary Literature* 27 (1986): 525–52, esp. p. 528. She presents a detailed and convincing argument in favor of a deliberate arrangement of the poems in this volume.

19. See Robert Babcock, "H.D.'s 'Pursuit' and Sappho," *H.D. Newsletter* 3 (1990): 43–47.

20. Gregory, "Rose Cut in Rock," 536.

21. Friedman, *Penelope's Web,* p. 58.

22. On the expression of resistance to Freud in this poem, see Friedman, *Penelope's Web,* pp. 304–6.

23. Broumas has yet to receive the critical attention that she merits. For an appreciation of her early achievement in winning the Yale Younger Poets Award, see Erika Duncan, *Unless Soul Clap Its Hands: Portraits and Passages* (New York: Schocken Books, 1984), pp. 139–49. See also Liz Yorke, "Constructing a Lesbian Poetic for Survival: Broumas, Rukeyser, H.D., Rich, Lorde," in *Sexual Sameness,* ed. Bristow, pp. 187–209; the present chapter obviously takes issue with her claim that "modern and contemporary poets have built on [Sappho's] surviving fragments to invent a classical inheritance where none truly exists" (p. 193). On Broumas's early work, see also Ellen Cronan Rose, "Through the Looking Glass: When Women Tell Fairy Tales," in *The Voyage In: Fictions of Female Development,* ed. Elizabeth Abel, Marianne Hirsch, and Elizabeth Langland, pp. 209–27 (Hanover: University Press of New England, 1983).

24. Mary J. Carruthers, "The Re-Vision of the Muse: Adrienne Rich, Audre Lorde, Judy Grahn, Olga Broumas," *Hudson Review* 36 (1983): 293–322, esp. p. 306.

25. Olga Broumas, *Beginning with O* (New Haven: Yale University Press, 1977), p. 74.

26. Judy Grahn, *The Highest Apple: Sappho and the Lesbian Poetic Tradition* (San Francisco: Spinsters, Ink, 1985), pp. 34–35.

BIBLIOGRAPHY

Alkaios. In *Sappho et Alcaeus: Fragmenta*, edited by Eva-Maria Voigt, pp. 177–355. Amsterdam: Athenaeum-Polak and Van Gennep, 1971.

Alkman. In *Poetae Melici Graeci*, edited by Denys Page, pp. 2–91. Oxford: Clarendon Press, 1967.

American Heritage Dictionary, edited by William Morris. Boston: Houghton Mifflin, 1981.

Anakreon. In *Poetae Melici Graeci*, edited by Denys Page, pp. 172–235. Oxford: Clarendon Press, 1967.

Anderson, Warren D. *Music and Musicians in Ancient Greece*. Ithaca: Cornell University Press, 1994.

Anthologia Palatina. In *The Greek Anthology: Hellenistic Epigrams*, edited by A. S. F. Gow and D. L. Page. 2 vols. Cambridge: Cambridge University Press, 1965.

Aristotle. *Poetics* [*De Arte Poetica*], edited by I. Bywater. Oxford: Clarendon Press, 1958.

Babcock, Robert. "H.D.'s 'Pursuit' and Sappho." *H.D. Newsletter* 3 (1990): 43–47.

Bagg, Robert. "Love, Ceremony, and Daydream in Sappho's Lyrics." *Arion* 3 (1964): 44–82.

Barber, Elizabeth Wayland. *Women's Work: The First 20,000 Years: Women, Cloth, and Society in Early Times*. New York: Norton, 1994.

Barnstone, Willis. *The Poetics of Translation: History, Theory, Practice*. New Haven: Yale University Press, 1993.

Bemporad, Giovanna. *Esercizi: Poesie e traduzioni*. Milan: Garzanti, 1980.

Benvenuto, Richard. *Amy Lowell*. Boston: Twayne, 1985.

Bergren, Ann L. T. "Language and the Female in Early Greek Thought." *Arethusa* 16 (1983): 69–95.

Berlin, Brent and Paul Kay. *Basic Color Terms: Their Universality and Evolution.* Berkeley: University of California Press, 1969.

Boedeker, Deborah. "Sappho and Acheron." In *Arktouros: Hellenic Studies Presented to Bernard M. W. Knox,* edited by G. W. Bowersock, Walter Burkert, and Michael C. J. Putnam, pp. 40–52. Berlin: de Gruyter, 1979.

Bonanno, Maria Grazia. "Saffo 31,9 V.: γλῶσσα ἔαγε." *Quaderni Urbinati de Cultura Classica* 43 (1993): 61–68.

Broumas, Olga. *Beginning with O.* New Haven: Yale University Press, 1977.

Brown, Christopher. "Anactoria and the Χαρίτων ἀμαρύγματα: Sappho fr. 16,18 Voigt." *Quaderni Urbinati di Cultura Classica* 32 (1989): 7–15.

Buci-Glucksmann, Christine. *Baroque Reason: The Aesthetics of Modernity,* translated by Patrick Camiller. London: Sage, 1994.

Burnett, Anne Pippin. "Desire and Memory (Sappho Frag. 94)." *Classical Philology* 74 (1979): 16–27.

———. *Three Archaic Poets: Archilochus, Alcaeus, Sappho.* Cambridge, Massachusetts: Harvard University Press, 1983.

Burnett, Gary. *H.D. Between Image and Epic: The Mysteries of Her Poetics.* Ann Arbor: UMI Research Press, 1990.

Butler, Judith. *Gender Trouble: Feminism and the Subversion of Identity.* New York: Routledge, 1990.

Calame, Claude. *Les Choeurs de jeunes filles en Grèce archaïque.* Rome: Edizioni dell'Ateneo and Bizzarri, 1977.

———. "Sappho et Helene: Le Mythe comme argumentation narrative et parabolique." In *Parole, Figure, Parabole,* edited by Jean Delorme, pp. 209–29. Lyon: Presses Universitaires de Lyon, 1987.

Calder, William M., III. *F. G. Welcker's Sapphobild and Its Reception in Wilamowitz. Hermes* Einzelschriften 49:131–56. Stuttgart: Steiner, 1986.

Cameron, A. "Sappho's Prayer to Aphrodite." *Harvard Theological Review* 32 (1939): 1–17.

Campbell, David A., ed. *Greek Lyric Poetry.* New York: St. Martin's Press, 1967.

Campbell, David A., ed. and trans. *Greek Lyric.* Vol. 1, *Sappho and Alcaeus.* Cambridge, Massachusetts: Harvard University Press, 1982.

Card, Claudia. *Lesbian Choices.* New York: Columbia University Press, 1995.

Carey, C. "Sappho Fr. 96 LP." *Classical Quarterly* 28 (1978): 366–71.

Carruthers, Mary J. "The Re-Vision of the Muse: Adrienne Rich, Audre Lorde, Judy Grahn, Olga Broumas." *Hudson Review* 36 (1983): 293–322.

Carson, Anne. *Eros the Bittersweet: An Essay.* Princeton: Princeton University Press, 1986.

Cavallini, Eleonora. "Presenza di Saffo e Alceo nella poesia greca fino ad Aristofane." *Quaderni del Giornale Filologico Ferrarese* 7 (1986).

Clay, Diskin. "Fragmentum Adespotum 976." *Transactions of the American Philological Association* 101 (1970): 119–29.

Collecott, Diana. "H.D.'s 'Gift of Greek,' Bryher's 'Eros of the Sea.'" *H.D. Newsletter* 3 (1990): 11–14.

Dalven, Rae, ed. *Daughters of Sappho: Contemporary Greek Women Poets.* Rutherford: Fairleigh Dickinson University Press, 1994.

Dane, Joseph A. "Sappho Fr. 16: An Analysis." *Eos* 69 (1981): 185–92.

Davis, Gregson. *Polyhymnia: The Rhetoric of Horatian Lyric Discourse.* Berkeley: University of California Press, 1991.

Degani, Enzo and Gabriele Burzacchini, eds. *Lirici Greci.* Florence: La Nuova Italia, 1977.

DeJean, Joan. *Fictions of Sappho, 1546–1937.* Chicago: University of Chicago Press, 1989.

———. "Looking Like a Woman: The Female Gaze in Sappho and Lafayette." *L'Esprit Créateur* 28 (1988): 34–45.

———. "Sex and Philology: Sappho and the Rise of German Nationalism." *Representations* 27 (1989): 148–71.

Demetrius. *De Elocutione* [*On Style*], edited by W. Rhys Roberts. Cambridge: Cambridge University Press, 1902.

Doane, Mary Ann. *The Desire to Desire: The Woman's Film of the 1940's.* Bloomington: Indiana University Press, 1987.

Doolittle, Hilda [H.D.]. *H.D.: Collected Poems, 1912–1944*, edited by Louis L. Martz. New York: New Directions, 1983.

———. *Notes on Thought and Vision & The Wise Sappho.* San Francisco: City Lights Books, 1982.

Dover, K. J. *Greek Homosexuality.* Cambridge, Massachusetts: Harvard University Press, 1978.

Duban, Jeffrey M. *Ancient and Modern Images of Sappho: Translations and Studies in Archaic Greek Love Lyric.* Washington, D.C.: University Press of America, 1983.

duBois, Page. "Eros and the Woman." *Ramus* 21 (1992): 97–116.

———. "Sappho and Helen." *Arethusa* 11 (1978): 89–99.

———. *Sappho Is Burning.* Chicago: University of Chicago Press, 1995.

Duncan, Erika. *Unless Soul Clap Its Hands: Portraits and Passages.* New York: Schocken Books, 1984.

DuPlessis, Rachel Blau. *H.D.: The Career of That Struggle.* Brighton: Harvester Wheatsheaf, 1986.

Edgeworth, Robert J. "Sappho Fr. 31.14 L.-P.: ΧΛΩΡΟΤΕΡΑ ΠΟΙΑΣ." *Acta Classica* 27 (1984): 121–24.

Edmonds, J. M. "Some New Fragments of Sappho, Alcaeus, and Anacreon." *Proceedings of the Cambridge Philological Society* 136/138 (1927): 13–30.

Edwards, M. J. "A Quotation of Sappho in Juvenal *Satire 6*." *Phoenix* 45 (1991): 255–57.

Enquist, Mangus and Anthony Arak. "Symmetry, Beauty, and Evolution." *Nature* 372 (1994): 169–72.

Fadermann, Lillian. "Lowell, Amy Lawrence." In *Encyclopedia of Homosexuality*, edited by Wayne R. Dynes, 1:750–51. New York: Garland, 1990.

———. "Warding Off the Watch and Ward Society: Amy Lowell's Treatment of the Lesbian Theme." *Gay Books Bulletin* 1 (1979): 23–27.

Fantham, Elaine, Helene Peet Foley, Natalie Boymel Kampen, Sarah B. Pomeroy, and

H. A. Shapiro, eds. *Women in the Classical World: Image and Text*. Oxford: Oxford University Press, 1994.

Field, Michael. *Long Ago*. London: Bell, 1889.

Forbes, Robert James. *Studies in Ancient Technology*. 9 vols. Leiden: Brill, 1955—.

Fowler, Barbara Hughes. "The Archaic Aesthetic." *American Journal of Philology* 105 (1984): 119–49.

Fränkel, Hermann. *Early Greek Poetry and Philosophy*, translated by Moses Hadas and James Willis. New York: Harcourt Brace Jovanovich, 1973.

———. *Wege und Formen frühgriechischen Denkens*. Munich: Beck, 1960.

Friedman, Susan Stanford. " 'I go where I love': An Intertextual Study of H.D. and Adrienne Rich." *Signs* 9 (1983): 228–45.

———. *Penelope's Web: Gender, Modernity, H.D.'s Fiction*. Cambridge: Cambridge University Press, 1990.

———. *Psyche Reborn: The Emergence of H.D.* Bloomington: Indiana University Press, 1981.

Friedrich, Paul. *The Meaning of Aphrodite*. Chicago: University of Chicago Press, 1978.

Frisk, Hjalmar. *Griechisches etymologisches Wörterbuch*. Heidelberg: Winter, 1954–1970.

Frontisi-Ducroux, Françoise. *Dédale: Mythologie de l'artisan en Grèce ancienne*. Paris: Maspero, 1975.

Gamman, Lorraine and Margaret Marshment, eds. *The Female Gaze: Women as Viewers of Popular Culture*. Seattle: Real Comet Press, 1989.

Gans, Eric. "The Birth of the Lyric Self: From Feminine to Masculine." *Helios* 8 (1981): 33–47.

Garzya, Antonio. "Per la fortuna di Saffo a bisanzio." *Jahrbuch der Österreichischen Byzantinistik* 20 (1971): 1–5.

Gentili, Bruno. *Poetry and Its Public in Ancient Greece*, translated by A. Thomas Cole. Baltimore: Johns Hopkins University Press, 1988.

Giacomelli, Anne. "The Justice of Aphrodite in Sappho Fr. 1." *Transactions of the American Philological Association* 110 (1980): 135–42.

Giangrande, Giuseppe. "Sappho and the ὄλισβος." *Emerita* 48 (1980): 249–50.

Grahn, Judy. *The Highest Apple: Sappho and the Lesbian Poetic Tradition*. San Francisco: Spinsters, Ink, 1985.

Green, Peter. *The Laughter of Aphrodite: A Novel About Sappho of Lesbos*. Berkeley: University of California Press, 1993. Originally published 1965.

Greene, Ellen. "Apostrophe and Women's Erotics in the Poetry of Sappho." *Transactions of the American Philological Association* 124 (1994): 41–56.

Gregory, Eileen. "Rose Cut in Rock: Sappho and H.D.'s *Sea Garden*." *Contemporary Literature* 27 (1986): 525–52.

Griffith, R. Drew. "In Praise of the Bride: Sappho Fr. 105(A) L-P, Voigt." *Transactions of the American Philological Association* 119 (1989): 55–61.

Gubar, Susan. "Sapphistries." *Signs* 10 (1984): 43–62.

Guest, Barbara. *Herself Defined: The Poet H.D. and Her World*. New York: Doubleday, 1984.

Hague, Rebecca. "Ancient Greek Wedding Songs: The Tradition of Praise." *Journal of Folklore Research* 20 (1983): 131–43.

———. "Sappho's Consolation for Atthis, Fr. 96 LP." *American Journal of Philology* 105 (1984): 29–36.

Hallett, Judith P. "Beloved Cleïs." *Quaderni Urbinati di Cultura Classica* 10 (1982): 21–31.

———. "Female Homoeroticism and the Denial of Roman Reality in Latin Literature." *Yale Journal of Criticism* 3 (1989): 209–27.

———. "Sappho and Her Social Context: Sense and Sensuality." *Signs* 4 (1979): 447–64.

Halperin, David M. *One Hundred Years of Homosexuality*. New York: Routledge, 1990.

Harvey, Elizabeth D. "Ventriloquizing Sappho: Ovid, Donne, and the Erotics of the Feminine Voice." *Criticism* 31 (1989): 115–38.

Heikkilä, Kai. "Sappho Fragment 2 L.-P.: Some Homeric Readings." *Arctos* 26 (1992): 39–53.

Heitsch, Ernst. "Zum Sappho-Text." *Hermes* 95 (1967): 385–92.

Herodotus. *Historiae*, edited by C. Hude. 2 vols. Oxford: Clarendon Press, 1963.

Herschberg, I. S. and J. E. Mebius. "ΔΕΔΥΚΕ ΜΕΝ Α ΣΕΛΑΝΝΑ." *Mnemosyne* 43 (1990): 150–51.

Hesiod. *Theogony*, edited by M. L. West. Oxford: Clarendon Press, 1966.

Himerius. *Himerii Declamationes et Orationes*, edited by A. Colonna. Rome: Typis Publicae Officinae Polygraphicae, 1951.

Höllein, Harmut. "Wer, Sappho, fügt dir ein Leid zu? Affekt und Distanz in frühgriechischer Dichtung." *Gymnasium* 98 (1991): 255–63.

Homer. *Homeri Opera*, edited by David B. Monro and Thomas W. Allen. 5 vols. Oxford: Clarendon Press, 1962.

Homeric Hymn to Demeter, edited by N. J. Richardson. Oxford: Clarendon Press, 1974.

Hooker, J. T. *The Language and Text of the Lesbian Poets*. Innsbruck: Institut für Sprachwissenschaft, 1977.

Irwin, Eleanor. *Colour Terms in Greek Poetry*. Toronto: Hakkert, 1974.

Janko, Richard. "Sappho Fr. 96,8 L-P: A Textual Note." *Mnemosyne* 35 (1982): 222–23.

Jenkyns, Richard. *Three Classical Poets: Sappho, Catullus, and Juvenal*. Cambridge, Massachusetts: Harvard University Press, 1982.

Joplin, Patricia Klindienst. "Epilogue: Philomela's Loom." In *Coming to Light: American Women Poets in the Twentieth Century*, edited by Diane Wood Middlebrook and Marilyn Yalom, pp. 254–67. Ann Arbor: University of Michigan Press, 1985.

Kakridis, Johannes T. "Zu Sappho 44 LP." *Wiener Studien* 79 (1966): 21–26.

Kaplan, E. Ann. "Is the Gaze Male?" In *Powers of Desire: The Politics of Sexuality*, edited by Ann Snitow, Christina Stansell, and Sharon Thompson, pp. 309–27. New York: Monthly Review Press, 1983.

Kirk, G. S. "A Fragment of Sappho Reinterpreted." *Classical Quarterly* 13 (1963): 51–52.

Klaich, Dolores. *Woman + Woman: Attitudes Toward Lesbianism*. New York: Morrow, 1974.

Knox, Bernard. "The Lost Lesbian." *New Republic* 210, no. 21 (1994): 35–42.

Koniaris, George L. "On Sappho, Fr. 1 (Lobel-Page)." *Philologus* 109 (1965): 30–38.

———. "On Sappho, Fr. 16 (L.P.)." *Hermes* 95 (1967): 257–68.

———. "On Sappho, Fr. 31 (L.-P.)." *Philologus* 112 (1968): 173–86.

Kurke, Leslie. "The Politics of ἀβροσύνη in Archaic Greece." *Classical Antiquity* 11 (1992): 91–120.

Lanata, Giuliana. "Sul linguaggio amoroso di Saffo." *Quaderni Urbinati di Cultura Classica* 1 (1966): 63–79.

Lang, Mabel. "Reason and Purpose in Homeric Prayers." *Classical World* 68 (1975): 309–14.

Lardinois, André. "Lesbian Sappho and Sappho of Lesbos." In *From Sappho to de Sade: Moments in the History of Sexuality*, edited by Jan Bremmer, pp. 15–35. London: Routledge, 1989.

———. "Subject and Circumstance in Sappho's Poetry." *Transactions of the American Philological Association* 124 (1994): 57–84.

Latacz, Joachim. "Realität und Imagination: Eine neue Lyrik-Theorie und Sapphos φαίνεταί μοι κῆνος-Leid." *Museum Helveticum* 42 (1985): 67–94.

Lattimore, Richmond. "Sappho 2 and Catullus 51." *Classical Philology* 39 (1944): 184–87.

Lattimore, Richmond, trans. *Greek Lyrics*. Chicago: University of Chicago Press, 1971.

Lefkowitz, Mary R. "Critical Stereotypes and the Poetry of Sappho." *Greek, Roman, and Byzantine Studies* 14 (1973): 113–23.

Liberman, Gauthier. "À propos de Sappho." *Revue de Philologie* 63 (1989): 229–337.

———. "Lire Sappho dans Démétrios, *Sur le style*." *Quaderni Urbinati di Cultura Classica* 40 (1992): 45–48.

Lidov, Joel B. "The Second Stanza of Sappho 31: Another Look." *American Journal of Philology* 114 (1993): 503–35.

Lobel, Edgar and Denys Page. "A New Fragment of Aeolic Verse." *Classical Quarterly* 2 (1952): 1–3.

Lobel, Edgar and Denys Page, eds. *Poetarum Lesbiorum Fragmenta*. Oxford: Clarendon Press, 1955.

[Longinus]. *De Sublimitate*, edited by D. A. Russell. Oxford: Clarendon Press, 1968.

Lowell, Amy. *The Complete Poetical Works of Amy Lowell*. Boston: Houghton Mifflin, 1955.

———. *Tendencies in Modern American Poetry*. New York: Macmillan, 1917.

Lucretius. *De Rerum Natura*, edited by Cyril Bailey. Oxford: Clarendon Press, 1959.

McEvilley, Thomas. "Sapphic Imagery and Fragment 96." *Hermes* 101 (1972): 257–78.

MacLachlan, Bonnie. *The Age of Grace: Charis in Early Greek Poetry*. Princeton: Princeton University Press, 1993.

———. "What's Crawling in Sappho Fr. 130." *Phoenix* 43 (1989): 95–99.

Marry, John D. "Sappho and the Heroic Ideal." *Arethusa* 12 (1979): 71–92.

Merkelbach, Reinhold. "Sappho und ihr Kreis." *Philologus* 101 (1957): 1–29.

Miller, Paul Allen. "Sappho 31 and Catullus 51: The Dialogism of Lyric." *Arethusa* 26 (1993): 183–99.

Milne, H. J. M. "Sappho's Ode to Gongyla (Fr. 36D.)." *Hermes* 68 (1933): 475–76.

Moonwomon, Birch. "Color Categorization in Early Greek." *Journal of Indo-European Studies* 22 (1994): 37–65.

Mora, Édith. *Sappho: Histoire d'un poète.* Paris: Flammarion, 1966.

Moravcsik, G. "Sapphos Fortleben in Byzanz." *Acta Antiqua* 12 (1964): 473–79.

Morrison, James V. "The Function and Context of Homeric Prayers: A Narrative Perspective." *Hermes* 119 (1991): 145–57.

Most, Glen W. "Sappho Fr. 16.6–7 L-P." *Classical Quarterly* 31 (1981): 11–17.

Mulroy, David. *Early Greek Lyric Poetry.* Ann Arbor: University of Michigan Press, 1992.

Murgatroyd, Paul. "Sappho 31.7–16 V." *Hermes* 116 (1988): 477–78.

Neuberger-Donath, Ruth. "Sappho Fr. 1.1: ΠΟΙΚΙΛΟΘΡΟΝ˙ oder ΠΟΙΚΙΛΟΦΡΟΝ˙." *Wiener Studien* 82 (1969): 15–17.

Norsa, Medea. "Dai papiri della Società Italiana: Versi di Saffo in un ostrakon del sec. II a.C." *Annali della Scuola Normale Superiore di Pisa* 6 (1937): 8–15.

Nussbaum, Martha. "Therapeutic Arguments and Structures of Desire." *differences* 2 (1990): 46–66.

O'Higgins, Dolores. "Sappho's Splintered Tongue: Silence in Sappho 31 and Catullus 51." *American Journal of Philology* 111 (1990): 156–67.

Ostriker, Alicia. *Writing Like a Woman.* Ann Arbor: University of Michigan Press, 1983.

Padel, Ruth. *In and out of the Mind: Greek Images of the Tragic Self.* Princeton: Princeton University Press, 1993.

Page, Denys. "The Authorship of Sappho β2 (Lobel)." *Classical Quarterly* 30 (1936): 10–15.

———. *Sappho and Alcaeus.* Oxford: Clarendon Press, 1955.

Parca, Maryline. "Sappho 1.18–19." *Zeitschrift für Papyrologie und Epigraphik* 46 (1982): 47–50.

Parker, Holt. "Sappho Schoolmistress." *Transactions of the American Philological Association* 123 (1993): 309–51.

Pelliccia, Hayden. "Sappho 16, Gorgias' *Helen*, and the Preface to Herodotus' *Histories*." *Yale Classical Studies* 29 (1992): 63–84.

Petropoulos, J. B. "Sappho the Sorceress—Another Look at Fr. 1 (LP)." *Zeitschrift für Papyrologie und Epigraphik* 97 (1993): 43–56.

Pindar. [*Pindarus*], edited by Bruno Snell. Leipzig: Teubner, 1955.

Plato. *Republic* [*Res Publica*], edited by I. Burnet. Oxford: Clarendon Press, 1958.

Powell, Jim, trans. *Sappho: A Garland: The Poems and Fragments of Sappho.* New York: Farrar, Straus, Giroux, 1993.

Prins, Yopie. "Sappho Doubled: Michael Field." *Yale Journal of Criticism* 8 (1995): 165–86.

Putnam, Michael C. J. "*Throna* and Sappho I.1." *Classical Journal* 61 (1960): 79–83.

Quinn, Kenneth, ed. *Catullus: The Poems.* London: MacMillan, 1970.

Race, William H. *The Classical Priamel from Homer to Boethius.* Mnemosyne suppl. 74. Leiden: Brill, 1982.

———. "Sappho, Fr. 16 L.-P. and Alkaios, Fr. 42 L.-P.: Romantic and Classical Strains in Lesbian Lyric." *Classical Journal* 85 (1989): 16–33.

Radt, S. L. "Sapphica." *Mnemosyne* 23 (1970): 337–47.

Rauk, John. "Erinna's *Distaff* and Sappho Fr. 94." *Greek, Roman, and Byzantine Studies* 30 (1989): 101–16.

Rayor, Diane. "Translating Fragments." *Translation Review* 32–33 (1990): 15–18.

Rayor, Diane, trans. *Sappho's Lyre.* Berkeley: University of California Press, 1991.

Rich, Adrienne. "Compulsory Heterosexuality and Lesbian Existence." *Signs* 5 (1980): 631–60.

Rissman, Leah. *Love as War: Homeric Allusion in the Poetry of Sappho.* Königstein: Hain, 1983.

Robbins, Emmet. "Who's Dying in Sappho Fr. 94?" *Phoenix* 44 (1990): 111–21.

———. "Sappho Fr. 94: A Further Note." *Phoenix* 44 (1990): 381.

Robinson, Janice S. *H.D.: The Life and Work of an American Poet.* Boston: Houghton Mifflin, 1982.

Rohrbach, Erika. "H.D. and Sappho: A Precious Inch of Palimpsest." In volume edited by Ellen Greene. Berkeley: University of California Press, forthcoming.

Roof, Judith. *A Lure of Knowledge: Lesbian Sexuality and Theory.* New York: Columbia University Press, 1991.

Rorem, Ned. *Four Madrigals.* New York: Music Press, 1948.

Rose, Ellen Cronan. "Through the Looking Glass: When Women Tell Fairy Tales." In *The Voyage In: Fictions of Female Development*, edited by Elizabeth Abel, Marianne Hirsch, and Elizabeth Langland, pp. 209–27. Hanover: University Press of New England, 1983.

Schaus, Gerald P. and Nigel Spencer. "Notes on the Topography of Eresos." *American Journal of Archaeology* 98 (1984): 411–30.

Schlesier, Renate. "Der bittersüsse Eros." *Archiv für Begriffsgeschichte* 30 (1986–1987): 70–83.

Schrenk, Lawrence P. "Sappho Fr. 44 and the 'Iliad.'" *Hermes* 122 (1994): 144–50.

Schubart, Wilhelm and Ulrich von Wilamowitz-Moellendorff, eds. *Griechische Dichterfragmente.* Berliner Klassikertexte vol. 5.2. Berlin: Weidmann, 1907.

Sedgwick, Eve Kosofsky. *Epistemology of the Closet.* Berkeley: University of California Press, 1990.

Seelbach, Wilhelm. "Ezra Pound und Sappho fr. 95 L.-P." *Antike und Abendland* 16 (1970): 83–84.

Segal, Charles. "Eros and Incantation: Sappho and Oral Poetry." *Arethusa* 7 (1974): 139–60.

Sider, David. "Sappho 168B Voigt: Δέδυκε μὲν ἀ Σελάννα." *Eranos* 84 (1986): 57–59.

Sinos, Dale S. "Sappho, Fr. 31 LP: Structure and Context." *Aevum* 56 (1982): 25–32.

Skinner, Marilyn. "Aphrodite Garlanded: Erôs and Poetic Creativity in Sappho and Nossis." In *Rose di Pieria*, edited by Francesco de Martino, pp. 79–96. Bari: Levante Editori, 1991.

———. "Nossis *Thelyglossos*: The Private Text and the Public Book." In *Women's History and Ancient History*, edited by Sarah B. Pomeroy, pp. 20–47. Chapel Hill: University of North Carolina Press, 1991.

———. "Sapphic Nossis." *Arethusa* 22 (1989): 5–18.

Slings, S. R. "Sappho Fr. 1.8 V.: Golden House or Golden Chariot?" *Mnemosyne* 44 (1991): 404–10.

Snell, Bruno. "Der Anfang eines äolischen Gedichts." *Hermes* 81 (1953): 118–19.

Snyder, Jane McIntosh. "The Configuration of Desire in Sappho Fr. 22 L.-P." *Helios* 21 (1994): 3–8.

———. *Sappho*. New York: Chelsea House, 1995.

———. "The Web of Song: Weaving Imagery in Homer and the Lyric Poets." *Classical Journal* 76 (1981): 193–96.

———. *The Woman and the Lyre: Women Writers in Classical Greece and Rome*. Carbondale: Southern Illinois University Press, 1989.

Stanley, Keith. "The Rôle of Aphrodite in Sappho Fr. 1." *Greek, Roman, and Byzantine Studies* 17 (1976): 305–21.

Stehle, Eva. *Performance and Gender in Ancient Greece*. Princeton: Princeton University Press, forthcoming.

———. "Sappho's Gaze: Fantasies of a Goddess and Young Man." *differences* 2 (1990): 88–125.

Stehle [Stigers], Eva. "Retreat from the Male: Catullus 62 and Sappho's Erotic Flowers." *Ramus* 6 (1977): 83–102.

Stern, E. M. "Sappho Fr. 16 L.-P.: Zur Strukturellen Einheit ihrer Lyrik." *Mnemosyne* 23 (1970): 348–61.

Stiebitz, Ferdinand. "Mitteilungen zu Sappho 65 Diehl." *Philologische Wochenschrift* 46 (1926): 1259–62.

Stigers [Stehle], Eva S. "Sappho's Private World." *Women's Studies* 8 (1981): 47–63.

Stimpson, Catharine R. "The Somagrams of Gertrude Stein." In *The Female Body in Western Culture*, edited by Susan Rubin Suleiman, pp. 30–43. Cambridge, Massachusetts: Harvard University Press, 1986.

Stockton, Kathryn Bond. "Bodies and God: Poststructuralist Feminists Return to the Fold of Spiritual Materialism." *boundary 2* 19 (1992): 113–49.

Svenbro, Jesper. "Sappho and Diomedes: Some Notes on Sappho 1 LP and the Epic." *Museum Philologum Londieniense* 1 (1975): 37–49.

———. "La stratégie de l'amour: Modèle de la guerre et théorie de l'amour dans la poésie de Sappho." *Quaderni di Storia* 10 (1984): 57–79.

Swann, Thomas Burnett. *The Classical World of H.D.* Lincoln: University of Nebraska Press, 1962.

Swanson, Roy Arthur. Review of *Fictions of Sappho*, by Joan DeJean. *Journal of the History of Sexuality* 2 (1991): 110–13.

Thacker, Andrew. "Amy Lowell and H.D.: The Other Imagists." *Women: A Cultural Review* 4 (1993): 49–59.

Theander, Carl. "Atthis et Andromeda." *Eranos* 44 (1946): 62–67.

———. "Lesbiaca." *Eranos* 41 (1943): 139–68.

———. "Studia Sapphica." *Eranos* 32 (1934): 57–85.

Theocritus. In *Bucolici Graeci*, edited by A. S. F. Gow. Oxford: Clarendon Press, 1969.

Thorsen, Synnøve des Bouvrie. "The Interpretation of Sappho's Fragment 16 L.-P." *Symbolae Osloenses* 53 (1978): 5–23.

Treu, Max, ed. *Sappho*. Munich: Heimeran, 1954.

Tsagarakis, Odysseus. "Broken Hearts and the Social Circumstances in Sappho's Poetry." *Rheinisches Museum* 129 (1986): 1–17.

Turyn, Alexander. *Studia Sapphica*. Eos suppl. 6. Paris: Les Belles Lettres, 1929.

Vermeule, Emily. *Aspects of Death in Early Greek Art and Poetry*. Berkeley: University of California Press, 1979.

Voigt, Eva-Maria, ed. *Sappho et Alcaeus: Fragmenta*. Amsterdam: Athenaeum-Polak and Van Gennep, 1971.

Walker, Cheryl. *Masks Outrageous and Austere: Culture, Psyche, and Persona in Modern Women Poets*. Bloomington: Indiana University Press, 1991.

Walter-Karydi, Elena. "ΧΡΩΣ—Die Entstehung des griechischen Farbwortes." *Gymnasium* 98 (1991): 517–33.

Watts, Emily Stipes. *The Poetry of American Women from 1632 to 1945*. Austin: University of Texas Press, 1977.

Weissenberger, Michael. "Liebeserfahrung in den Gedichten Sapphos und das Problem des Archaischen." *Rheinisches Museum* 134 (1991): 209–37.

Weld, Louise and William Nethercut. "Sappho's Rose-Fingered Moon: A Note." *Arion* 5 (1966): 28–31.

West, M. L. "Burning Sappho." *Maia* 22 (1970): 307–30.

White, Chris. " 'Poets and lovers evermore': The Poetry and Journals of Michael Field." In *Sexual Sameness: Textual Differences in Lesbian and Gay Writing*, edited by Joseph Bristow, pp. 26–43. New York: Routledge, 1992.

Wilamowitz-Moellendorff, Ulrich von. *Sappho und Simonides: Untersuchungen über griechische Lyriker*. Berlin: Weidmann, 1913.

Will, Frederic. "Sappho and Poetic Motion." *Classical Journal* 61 (1966): 259–62.

Williams, Hector. "Secret Rites of Lesbos." *Archaeology* 47 (1994): 34–40.

Williamson, Margaret. *Sappho's Immortal Daughters*. Cambridge: Harvard University Press, 1995.

Wills, Garry. "The Sapphic 'Umwertung aller Werte.'" *American Journal of Philology* 88 (1967): 434–42.

Wilson, Lyn Hatherly. *Sappho's Sweetbitter Songs*. London: Routledge, forthcoming.

Winkler, John J. *The Constraints of Desire*. New York: Routledge, 1990.

———. "Gardens of Nymphs: Public and Private in Sappho's Lyrics." *Women's Studies* 8 (1981): 65–91.

Winterson, Jeanette. *Art & Lies: A Piece for Three Voices and a Bawd*. New York: Knopf, 1995.

———. *Written on the Body*. New York: Knopf, 1993.

Woolf, Virginia. "On Not Knowing Greek." In *The Common Reader*, pp. 39–59. New York: Harcourt, Brace, and World, 1925.

Yorke, Liz. "Constructing a Lesbian Poetic for Survival: Broumas, Rukeyser, H.D., Rich, Lorde." In *Sexual Sameness: Textual Differences in Lesbian and Gay Writing*, edited by Joseph Bristow, pp. 187–209. New York: Routledge, 1992.

INDEX